AMERICAN HEGEMONY

AMERICAN HEGEMONY

POLITICAL MORALITY

IN A ONE-SUPERPOWER

WORLD

LEA BRILMAYER

YALE UNIVERSITY PRESS

NEW HAVEN & LONDON

Designed by Deborah Dutton

Set in Joanna text by Keystone Typesetting, Inc.,

Orwigsburg, Pennsylvania.

Printed in the United States of America by Vail-Ballou Press,

Binghamton, New York.

Brilmayer, Lea.

American hegemony : political morality in a one-superpower

world / Lea Brilmayer.

p.   cm.

Includes bibliographical references and index.

ISBN 0–300–06033–5

1. Political ethics—United States.   I. Title.

JK468.E7B75   1994

327.1′01—dc20

94–11807

CIP

A catalogue record for this book is available from the

British Library.

The paper in this book meets the guidelines for permanence

and durability of the Committee on Production Guidelines

for Book Longevity of the Council on Library Resources.

10 9 8 7 6 5 4 3 2 1

To W. C. H.

CONTENTS

PREFACE

This book is in many respects a continuation of my earlier work on international ethics, *Justifying International Acts* (Cornell University Press, 1989). Some of my colleagues who have read this book in manuscript have found the parallels obvious, for both deal with the relevance of political morality to international relations. In that book and this one I have tried to refocus international ethics, which tends to rely on the analogy between interstate and interpersonal relations, on the analogy between interstate relations and questions of domestic governance. In both cases this is an argument for a "vertical" as opposed to a "horizontal" perspective on world politics.

The characterization as vertical reflects my claim that some of the most interesting and important but hitherto neglected features of world politics arise from systematic power asymmetries. These asymmetries create vertical structures of dominance that are comparable, from a normative point of view, to vertical structures of domestic governance; and existing normative theories of domestic governance are therefore applicable, by analogy, to world politics. I developed arguments for this claim in my earlier work, and the present book builds on those arguments without attempting to repeat them.

There are two important differences between the two books. First, *American Hegemony* focuses specifically on the applicability to world politics of democratic liberalism and on the application of liberalism to a particular problem, hegemony. *Justifying International Acts* dealt with the general claim that international political ethics must be treated consistently with domestic political ethics, whatever domestic political commitments one happens to have. This high level of generality frustrated many readers, who thought that a book on international ethics should have a clearer concrete payoff. Some also claimed, I think unfairly, that my unwillingness to commit to a particular political theory was tantamount to a belief that all theories are equally good, a claim that I addressed then and address again briefly in the following pages. These readers will be heartened to see that the present work takes on a single theory (liberalism) and that while my recommendations are still hedged about with qualifications and reservations, they are considerably more concrete than those of the previous book.

A second difference is less obvious but more important. In the prior book, I addressed the relations between states and individuals with ties to other nations. The present book deals with relations between states. Focusing on the relations between states and individuals has the advantage of making the vertical dimensions of the analysis clear, because in both the domestic and the international settings, the object of attention is a relationship between a human being and a governmental entity. It has a disadvantage, however, in that world politics is not customarily conceived in terms of the effect that a state has on foreign individuals. Instead, the usual paradigm is the relations of one state to another. The present book is, in this sense, more consistent with the usual way of envisioning international relations. I nonetheless treat international politics as involving vertical relations, on the ground that when formally equal but empirically unequal states interact, political relations result. Hegemony is an institution of persistent dominance of weak states by a stronger one; and although weak and strong states are formally equal in the legal sense, normative analysis of the actual empirical power asymmetry is nonetheless required. Some of my doubts about leaving behind the analysis of state/individual relations come out in the final two chapters of this book, where I argue that liberalism cannot satisfactorily explain the "state actor" model traditional to international ethics.

Because of the connection between these two projects, I continue to feel a great debt to colleagues who encouraged and assisted my work on the earlier book. Ian Shapiro, in particular, provided a model of collegial encouragement that I have not forgotten. Harold Koh invited me to speak at the Yale Law School workshop on international law and politics, despite the fact that he is apparently dismayed by most of my conclusions. Larry Kramer's friendly suggestions were always very welcome, as is his presence at the New York University Law School, and Hal Maier's reactions to the earlier book remain in my mind. Two colleagues from the Yale Political Science Department, Alex Wendt and David Lumsdaine, gave me splendid critical reactions to the current manuscript; Alex, in particular, knows very well how many lunches it takes to root out even the smallest errors. Among the other colleagues who helped the project along are Anne-Marie Slaughter Burley, Andy Moravcsik, David Wippman, and several anonymous reviewers, all of whom devoted a great deal of high-quality attention that, I feel sure, they would rather have devoted to their own projects. Jack Donnelly was generous enough to read and comment on an early version of chapter 2.

Since coming to the NYU Law School I have found a whole new set of wonderful readers and critics; in particular, Chris Eisgruber, Francis Kamm, Lewis Kornhauser, Ted Meron, Thomas Nagel, David Richards, and Frank Upham, as well as other participants at the many faculty workshops around the school. My dean, John Sexton, not only found me the sabbatical time to finish this manuscript (for which I cannot say thank you often enough) but also provides an exceptional environment full of emotional support and intellectual excitement. My research there has been supported by the Filomen D'Agostino and Max E. Greenberg Faculty Research Fund. The Law School has been a wonderful community to live and work in. NYU has given me the blessing of marvelously competent and enjoyable people to work with, especially Doreen Ryan, Adam Lichtstein, Josh Davis and (God bless her!) Judith Moore. No one can feel more fortunate than I do in being surrounded by people such as these, and by the other friends who make life pleasurable and possible. Here, of course, belongs a mention of the man to whom I dedicate this book, and to whom I hope to dedicate my life.

INTRODUCTION

THE WORLD'S

POLICEMAN?

Are we headed into a new Pax Americana? At one point recently, the Pentagon seems to have hoped so. An article on the front page of the March 8, 1992, *New York Times* divulged the existence of a forty-six-page classified Pentagon document arguing that a key U.S. foreign policy goal ought to be ensuring continued world dominance.[1] The Pentagon draft asserted that America's political and military mission after the demise of the Soviet Union should be preventing the emergence of a rival superpower in Western Europe, Asia, or the Soviet republics.

This goal should be achieved by "convincing potential competitors that they need not aspire to a greater role or pursue a more aggressive posture to protect their legitimate interests." To this end, the United States "must sufficiently account for the interests of the advanced industrial nations to discourage them from challenging our leadership or seeking to overturn the established political and economic order." The *Times* emphasized two characteristics of the draft: first, its apparent rejection of collective internationalism (including channeling political action through the United Nations) and, second, the concept of "benevolent domination," according to which world leadership is perpetuated by constructive behavior as well as military might.

The Pentagon has since retreated. The final version of the report muted its original robust call to world dominion.[2] It emphasized collective internationalism and cooperative action to achieve U.S. security goals; gone were the suggestions that the United States would tolerate no rivals. While it was still fairly clear that the Pentagon envisioned a leadership role for the country, the document expressed a "preference" for collective action. The *Times* cited the severe criticism that the initial draft had provoked from foreign nations and domestic policy analysts.

Writing shortly after the initial draft's disclosure, Charles Krauthammer speculated that he might be the only person outside the Pentagon who had anything to say in its defense.[3] In an article provocatively entitled "The Unipolar Moment," he argued unabashedly that the United States should take a dominant role in shaping the new world politics.

> The center of world power is the unchallenged superpower, the United States, attended by its Western allies. . . . American preeminence is based on the fact that it is the only country with the military, diplomatic, political, and economic assets to be a decisive player in any conflict in whatever part of the world it chooses to involve itself. . . .
> We are in for abnormal times. Our best hope for safety in such times, as in difficult times past, is in American strength and will—the strength and will to lead a unipolar world, unashamedly laying down the rules of world order and being prepared to enforce them. Compared to the task of defeating fascism and communism, averting chaos is a rather subtle call to greatness. It is not a task we are any more eager to undertake than the great twilight struggle just concluded. But it is just as noble and just as necessary.[4]

Krauthammer's arguments face an uphill battle for acceptance, as he clearly recognized. The unfavorable reaction to the Pentagon draft should not surprise anyone mindful of the political climate in which the report made its debut. The country was in no mood for international adventures. Public attention was focused on domestic problems, in particular the poor state of the economy. The thrill of the Persian Gulf war victory was long gone, and foreign policy was perceived mainly as a competitor with education, health care, and urban redevelopment for scarce public funds. A contemporaneous poll asked Americans, "Should the United States be the world's policeman?" and 75 percent answered, "No."[5]

In part, the objections are based on prudential concerns. It just seems too distracting, too expensive, and too dangerous to American lives to take on the burdens of running the new world order. We have enough problems at home. Besides, it is popularly believed, our allies take advantage of us; they free-ride on our willingness to pay the costs of collective defense and shut the door on American imports even as we keep our markets open. (And then they complain about U.S. imperialism, some of these critics might be tempted to add.) The more sophisticated versions of these prudential objections are inspired by Paul Kennedy's thesis of "imperial overstretch," which attributes the decline of great powers to extending their ambitions beyond the limits of their resources.[6]

Yet at roughly the same time, the civil war in the former Yugoslavia provoked enough public calls for military intervention that Bill Clinton, then the Democratic presidential candidate, sought to make a political issue of the Bush administration's apparently lackadaisical attitude. Faced with what seemed to be massive human rights violations, the American public was not completely sanguine about simply allowing the conflict to run its own course. The public has continued to support the vigorous enforcement of American criminal laws overseas; Mexican citizens kidnapped in Mexico have been held for trial in the United States, drug barons committing crimes in Colombia have been indicted in Brooklyn, and a former Panamanian dictator was convicted in a U.S. court after the United States invaded Panama to capture him and bring him to trial.[7]

While debate over our proper role in international life is not new to the American political scene, it is newly brought to the forefront by the victory in the Persian Gulf and by the power vacuum left by the unraveling of the Soviet Union. Most popular commentary concludes that being "the world's policeman" is not a role that we should undertake.[8] This is not surprising, perhaps, given the characterization's faintly pejorative connotations. It is at once a bit demeaning (police do not, after all, make the rules; they carry out the instructions of their political superiors, the lawmakers) and presumptuous (who, after all, appointed us?). Cops are "public servants" who do the dirty work of social control; but they are also authority figures who need a mandate to be legitimate. To phrase the question in these terms, then, is to virtually answer it.

The international relations and foreign policy communities are now absorbed with this debate. Paul Kennedy's best-seller was followed by others contesting his thesis,[9] to the point that the single riveting feature of the decade (to Americans, that is) appears to be America's world dominance. Is the role of world's policeman one that we want to pursue? Do we have the resources to enable us to do so if we want to? What are the long-run implications for American prosperity if we continue along this path? If we are going to dominate the world, by what objectives should we be guided? Should we attempt to install democracies around the world? To promote free-market capitalism? Should we promote human rights? Or should we simply pursue our own national interest?

Barely visible beneath the surface of this flood of commentary, polemic, and academic speculation is an issue that is only just now emerging but which informs the whole debate. Is it morally sound for one nation-state to dominate the others? If so, why—and under what circumstances? Krauthammer clearly assumes the answer to be yes, at least when dominance is motivated by the noble goals that he acclaims. Opposition to the Pentagon's draft report was just as clearly motivated, at least in part, by the opposite conviction. Many, including many Americans, believe that it is wrong for the United States to set out deliberately to maintain unrivaled superpower status, cynically buying off potential rivals by keeping them just satisfied enough not to challenge our authority. Only very recently, however, has the question explicitly come to be framed in such stark moral terms. One gets the feeling reading much of the debate that the important issues are the empirical, historical, or prudential ones. Is continued world domination possible? And if so, is it something that the United States should rationally pursue?

The focus of this book, however, is squarely on the moral issues. It is sharply informed by contemporary debate over the role of the United States after the demise of the Soviet Union. A general theoretical issue accompanies the particular one about U.S. power at the end of the century. The issue is not merely whether it is morally reasonable of the United States, in the 1990s and after, to assert its leadership in pursuit of peculiarly American interests or values (whether they be democracy, human rights, or free-market capitalism). The question is also whether and in what circumstances one nation is *ever* entitled to predominate. Our peculiar circumstances in this specific time period and context provide an opportunity to pose the wider issue.

The conceptual wherewithal for posing this general question already exists and is familiar to readers of the international relations literature. In the last few decades, a set of issues collected under the general rubric "hegemonic stability theory" has occupied the attention of a substantial subset of the most important practitioners of international relations theory. A hegemon, stated briefly, is a world leader; it is a state which to some large degree controls world political processes. Hegemonic stability theory addresses the problem of how world politics is altered by a highly asymmetric distribution of world power, in which one state dominates the rest.[10] An offshoot, regime theory, poses a set of related questions about the role of the hegemon in maintaining international institutions. Clearly, our ongoing popular debate about the United States as a world policeman touches many of the same issues as the academic disputes about the nature and extent of hegemony. It seems no coincidence that as the debate over world policing rages in the popular press, "hegemony" fascinates the academics.

While this book in large part takes advantage, then, of the existing terms of debate, there is one important difference between most of the academic literature on international hegemony and the current enterprise. The existing literature is primarily descriptive, analytical, or historical; this project is inherently normative. Most discussions of hegemony focus on the question of the likely empirical effect on international politics of the fact that power is asymmetrically distributed, rather than on the question of whether such a distribution is morally acceptable. This is not to say that writers on hegemony and regimes are oblivious to the normative implications of the phenomena they describe. Some clearly are not. Charles Kindleberger, for instance, acknowledges and applauds the possibilities that hegemony offers for achieving international stability.[11] Robert Gilpin likewise raises the normative issue briefly and declares hegemony legitimate, in part because hegemons frequently provide a beneficial economic order and international security.[12] Others question this assumption of benevolence.[13] Marxists, neo-Marxists, and other leftists attack hegemony with gusto, at least when it is exercised by capitalist powers.[14] Still others avoid categorical evaluations. Robert Keohane, writing about regimes, deliberately flags the normative issues that regimes present, arguing that international organizations can facilitate good purposes or bad.[15] David Calleo recognizes the moral dimensions of hegemony, and asserts that hegemonic power can be used for either exploitative or responsible ends.[16]

But the basic thrust of most of the mainstream international relations literature is not the question of moral acceptability. Aware the writers may be; but their primary focus is generally elsewhere. The question they reserve is the focus of this book. Under what circumstances, if any, is international hegemony legitimate? Does it depend upon the purposes to which hegemony is put? On the processes by which hegemony is acquired? The means or methods it uses? And by what standards should we make all of these judgments?

My argument is that the legitimacy of international hegemony should be evaluated in much the same way that we would evaluate the legitimacy of other authoritative political structures, in particular domestic governments. This point should not be taken as obvious or noncontroversial. Hedley Bull, for example, briefly addressed the question of hegemonic legitimacy but did not draw inspiration from domestic political theory; instead, his principles were specifically geared to the international situation.[17] The literature on international hegemony does not, by and large, rest on an explicit analogy between the hegemon and a domestic political leader. Yet, as I will argue, in many respects principles of domestic political legitimacy have natural parallels in international relations.

Powerful states have the same sorts of moral responsibilities to the states they dominate as to individuals in their power. Political morality is the relevant bench-mark. This is not to say that a hegemon "is" a world government, only that it is similar to a world government in normatively relevant ways. Hegemony is not an all-or-nothing matter; it admits of degrees. In this respect, a hegemon that stops short of possessing complete power to dominate is similar to a domestic government that is not perfectly in control of happenings within its own territory. But to the extent that one state does possess overwhelming international power, I will argue, it possesses *political* power that must be evaluated in *political* terms. For this reason, the standards that we would use to evaluate a world government (or for that matter a domestic government) are relevant in evaluating a hegemon as well.

The metaphor of the world's policeman, then, is illuminating. Police are an arm of the state, not merely private citizens. They are not held simply to the standards of private individuals; their actions must instead be treated as raising issues of political morality. Have they overstepped their legitimate authority? Are the rules they enforce legitimate? Do they employ legitimate methods? Are they sufficiently accountable? Where does their mandate come from? And so on. These same questions must be asked about states that act as world political leaders.

We will be focusing largely on the specific case of American international hegemony. The examples we use will mostly be taken from American foreign policy and will reflect the extensive debate, both contemporary and from the recent past, over whether America uses its unusual powers wisely and well. But the American experience is only one example. There have been other hegemonic powers in the past, and it is quite possible that there will be others in the future. The United States is not the only state that has abused its power on some occasions and put it to good advantage on others.

Chapter 1 sets out the basic argument that we must be prepared to evaluate a hegemon's actions in much the same terms as we would a formal domestic state apparatus. It examines the usual usage of the term *hegemony* and argues that where power is sufficiently asymmetrically distributed, a political governance structure, if not quite a world government, exists. Chapter 2 anticipates an objection to this claim. It addresses the commonly heard argument that normative evaluation is inappropriate in world politics, because international relations is a state of anarchy.

Part 2 then attempts to spell out a liberal political assessment of international hegemony, particularly American hegemony. The usual indicia of political legit-imacy that are demanded in a liberal democracy are typically not present with hegemons. Hegemony seems autocratic, not democratic. Hegemons are not elected, nor can they be recalled. They are not constrained by written constitutions enforced by an independent adjudicative body. Yet there are other political defenses of international hegemony, which may be persuasive in at least some circumstances. Chapter 4 addresses the possibility that hegemony is legitimate because subordinate states have acquiesced; hegemonic power is obtained by persuasion and inducement, not by coercion and threats. Chapter 5 asks whether it would count as a justification that hegemony is exercised in accordance with international law, which is said to be founded on prior state consent. Hegemons also are said to facilitate the provision of public goods that would not be produced in the hegemon's absence; chapter 6 examines this justification of hegemony, analogizing it to domestic theories of hypothetical consent. Chapter 7, finally, asks whether hegemony can be justified by the moral worth of the goals that the hegemon pursues, such as democracy or human rights. Part 3 raises some deficiencies of liberalism in the international arena; it challenges this liberal vision both in terms of whether it accurately reflects liberal premises and in terms of whether liberal premises are suitable in international relations. Chapter 9, then, takes a more critical view of statism and chapter 10 challenges the notion of state consent.

The defenses of American hegemony offered here are, at best, severely qualified. The point is not to argue that American hegemony is always or even typically legitimate (indeed, the arguments offered here will often be very critical) but rather to ask whether there might be some circumstances in which it is morally acceptable. I suspect that some readers will doubt that departure from sovereign equality is ever justified, just as some will remain unpersuaded that pursuit of power and the national interest should ever be derailed by a moral agenda. Most people, though, are probably somewhere in the middle, and here I hope to stake out what a reasonable intermediate position might be. More important, perhaps, this is an effort to focus normative attention on an issue that is usually not deliberately addressed in explicitly normative terms, and to derive the relevant norms from domestic political philosophy. The claim that the issue must be addressed in these terms is more significant than the specific normative conclusions that persons of different political persuasions are likely to reach.

PART ONE

THE MORAL RELEVANCE OF INTERNATIONAL HEGEMONY

1

HEGEMONY

We live in a world of immense, indeed almost unimaginably immense, inequalities. Even within a single nation, there are tremendous disparities in people's access to food, commercial goods and services, political influence, education, health care, and virtually every other ingredient of the good life. The disparities are far greater once we push back our horizons to contemplate transnational comparisons. The life prospects of the middle-class residents of a developed nation bear little resemblance to the life prospects of the dispossessed of the Third World. On this fact there is no dispute, nor could there be.

One of the great disparities that we witness internationally is the disparity in power between the great powers of the world and the lesser. Political and military power are far from equally distributed. If anything, the disparities seem to have increased over the last ten or twenty years. A small group of nations are tremendously influential: the United States, Japan, Germany in conjunction with the European Union nations, Russia, and China.[1] Other nations possess formal equality in international law, but no one mistakes this for equality in fact.

Power disparities are of great consequence to the less powerful nations, who complain bitterly of Western imperialism and neocolonialism. Yet outside the circle of other similarly situated nations their complaints have fallen on deaf ears. In this respect, with rare exceptions,[2] political inequalities have been treated rather differently from economic inequalities. While the powerful nations have shown at least a rhetorical sympathy for Third World poverty, even this modicum of concern does not extend to Third World political powerlessness. The concern for Third World poverty may not (as some would claim) have had much impact on First World practice; but the moral issue of power inequalities, by comparison, has not even received verbal acknowledgment. The fact that states are formally equal under international law is good enough. Yet, as Stephen Krasner has argued, power disparities may better explain Third World dissatisfaction than income disparities.[3]

In fact, in many respects power disparities may be the more intractable of the two; or at least, that can be said of the sort of power that is at issue here: the power states have over one another, rather than the power they jointly have over (say) fighting disease or combating the drug trade. The power that will concern us here is more conflictual than cooperative; it concerns state capabilities to prevail over one another when their values, policies, and preferences collide. It is not the only sort of power; perhaps it is not even the most important sort of power. Quite possibly, all states would be more powerful in a world in which states did not use their capabilities against one another. But in this world they do; and the unequal distribution of power of this sort is both an important source of resentment and a challenge to normative theory.

Power struggles of this sort are more nearly zero-sum (in the sense that what adds to one state's power tends to subtract from another's) than economic disputes. Power struggles are zero-sum because power is relative; anything that increases A's power over B necessarily decreases B's power over A. Economics need not be zero-sum because it is possible for the absolute wealth of both nations to increase. Both A and B can be made economically better off if the pie can somehow be expanded. The rich need not be made worse off by the increased wealth of the less well off; but there is no way to close the power gap without the powerful nations relinquishing power. Thus Robert Tucker, after pointing out that the new egalitarianism of the Third World is centered more on moral and political demands than on economic ones, concludes that "it may well be that the search for status—for recognition as equals and thus for confirmation of independence—can only be satisfied largely through conflict."[4]

Economic and power inequalities are different in another way. The latter are troubling primarily because they create opportunities for subordination, while the former are troubling even without that possibility. Consider the relations between, for example, the United States and Bhutan. Discrepancies in wealth (per capita income, access to health and education, and so on) would be troubling even if the two nations had little or no interaction with one another. One might, analogously, be troubled by comparable discrepancies in political power; by the fact that the United States exercised greater influence than Bhutan does in world politics. But the more serious issue of concern is political subordination—a difference in power that allows the stronger state to dominate the weaker. Power discrepancies are troubling because of their consequences in particular interactions. The U.S. power relationship with Bhutan is less problematic than the U.S. power relationship with (say) Panama because the United States has a history of using its greater power at Panama's expense. Even though the discrepancy may be greater in the former case, the use of the power differential to dominate is greater in the latter.[5]

Economic and power differentials, then, present different sorts of normative problems. Yet economic and power inequalities cannot be divorced from one another. Greater wealth provides the means to greater military and political power, while greater power facilitates the acquisition of greater wealth. There are, of course, counterexamples to this generalization, Japan being the most obvious. Japan's great economic strength has not translated into great military power, largely for reasons of domestic politics. But no one would deny that, other things being equal, more of one tends to lead to more of the other. The focus here is on disparities of power rather than disparities of wealth, with due regard to the ways that the two fit together. And it is on the way that power disparities lead to possibilities for subordination, rather than on the simple fact that some states influence world politics more than others.

There are, of course, Western intellectuals and political activists who take seriously international disparities of political power. Many of these are Marxist or neo-Marxist in orientation, or subscribe to dependency, world-systems, or other leftist approaches to international politics. But if one were to question a randomly chosen person on the street in any town in the United States, one would probably find a far greater consciousness of Third World malnutrition, environmental degradation, and inadequate health care than of the fact that citizens of Third World nations believe themselves completely at the mercy of First World decision makers. One might, in theory, expect a greater concern with inequality of political power from citizens of a democracy; but moral awareness of international political inequalities has not been high.

It is certainly not the case that moral awareness, by itself, solves problems. We are, on some level, morally aware of the tragedy of world hunger; but world hunger persists nonetheless and will continue to persist for many reasons. But while moral awareness is only a small step, it is a first step, and a necessary one. There is, no doubt, a general appreciation that some forms of international political domination are illegitimate; colonialism and conquest, for example, are now widely disapproved. But the current unequal distribution of power is not conceived as morally problematic in the same way; or at least it is not so conceived by mainstream intellectuals or the average citizen. What the Third World calls "neocolonialism" does not stir the consciences of most of the American public the same way as "traditional" colonialism. Despite the domination—the hegemony—of a small number of powerful nations, the American public seems to take for granted that the current distribution of world power is well within the range of the morally acceptable.

HEGEMONY DEFINED

But is this general complaisance warranted? How legitimate is international hegemony? This is the central issue here. We should start with a short explanation of how the term *hegemony* is used. Hegemony, basically, is leadership.[6] Robert Keohane mentions several different possible meanings of the term, more or less defining the hegemon as the "single dominant world power."[7] In the economic context, "hegemony [is defined] as preponderance of material resources."[8] Keohane also cites an earlier work cowritten with Joseph Nye: "Hegemony is defined as a situation in which one state is powerful enough to maintain the essential rules governing interstate relations, and willing to do so."[9] Immanuel Wallerstein writes, "Hegemony in the interstate system refers to that situation in which the ongoing rivalry between the so-called 'great powers' is so unbalanced that one power is truly *primus inter pares*; that is, one power can largely impose its rules and its wishes (at the very least by effective veto power) in the economic, political, military, diplomatic, and even cultural arenas."[10]

Hegemony has both economic and military aspects;[11] indeed, as just noted, they typically reinforce one another. The term can also be used in the Gramscian sense: "moral and political leadership, leadership which is attained through the active consent of major groups in a society."[12] According to Robert Cox, "a hegemonial structure of world order is one in which power takes a primarily consensual form."[13] We will not limit hegemony to consensual uses of power but will use the term in the broadest sense, to include political, military, economic, and psychological dimensions. All of these aspects can be present and significant in a hegemonic relationship. In later chapters we will return to the question of whether it matters that hegemony is primarily either economic or consensual, as opposed to being based on physical coercion.

Two standard examples used to illustrate the concept of hegemony are Great Britain in the nineteenth century and the United States in the mid- to late twentieth century.[14] The Pax Britannica was founded upon the overwhelming economic and naval strength that enabled Great Britain to amass an enormous overseas empire, encompassing nearly one-quarter of the world's people. The extent of British hegemony is disputed, as are the dates of its origin and decline,[15] but the Pax Britannica was clearly over by the end of World War I.

American hegemony dates to the end of World War II. Having largely escaped the domestic destruction visited upon the European powers and Japan, the United States was able simultaneously to expand economically and to help finance the recovery of Europe. For over twenty years it dominated the world economy, supporting the global monetary system through the Bretton Woods agreement. Raymond Aron described this period dramatically in 1966: "After this century's Second World War, the United States . . . found itself responsible for the peace, the prosperity, and the very existence of half the planet. GIs were stationed in Tokyo and Seoul in the Orient, in Berlin in Europe. The West had known nothing like it since the Roman Empire. The United States was the first truly world power, since there was no precedent for the global unification of the diplomatic scene."[16] David Calleo similarly characterized the United States as a sort of "managing director" for the international system.[17] There is currently substantial disagreement over whether the period of U.S. hegemony is definitively at an end, and if so, what will happen next.[18] There is also disagreement over who benefited more from that hegemony, the United States or the nations that it dominated.[19]

Two other illustrations are variations on the general concept of hegemony: the Warsaw Pact and the Concert of Europe. The former is an example of regional hegemony, the latter of oligopolistic hegemony. Both depart somewhat from the simple model of hegemony illustrated by Great Britain and the United States, in the first case because power is geographically restricted, and in the second because it is shared.

The Warsaw Pact illustrates regional hegemony because the states which the Warsaw Treaty placed under the leadership of the Soviet Union were in Eastern Europe.[20] Often compared to U.S. hegemony over Latin America, Soviet domination was both military and economic.[21] Economically, there were extensive trading relations within the Soviet bloc, with the Soviet Union supplying important goods such as oil and the Eastern European nations supplying manufactured goods in return. These economic relations were directed from Moscow, befitting an economic philosophy of centralized planning. Militarily, the Soviet Union was dominant both because it played a leadership role in collective security arrangements and because it claimed a right to intervene forcibly in the other nations' domestic affairs under the Brezhnev Doctrine. Poland, Hungary, and Czechoslovakia were all either invaded or threatened militarily when they seemed poised to stray too far from Soviet hegemonic designs.

The concept of regional hegemony illustrates how hegemony can be less than complete and can exist even in a bipolar world. There can, in this sense, be more than one hegemon; hegemony can be relative to one particular subgroup of states. I will sometimes refer to hegemony as involving "centralization" of power, meaning centralization within the hegemon's sphere of influence. Power, of course, is not *literally* centralized in a bipolar world; there are two centers of power, one per sphere of influence. This qualification—that hegemony can mean regional hegemony and that power centralization occurs within a certain set of states—will not be spelled out specifically except where we consider directly the relevance of the fact that hegemonic power is not global.[22] *Hegemony*, below, will refer to the relationship between a dominant state and its subordinates, even if there are states beyond the hegemon's effective reach.

The Concert of Europe is an instance of oligopolistic hegemony because the leadership role was exercised not by a single nation but by several acting together. After the Congress of Vienna in 1815 the four victorious powers of Europe (Britain, Russia, Prussia, and Austria), later joined by France, coordinated their activities so as to maintain control over various smaller powers.[23] The result was a marked inequality of power. "It is hardly necessary to remark that the supervision of the society of nations by the concerted actions of the great powers, as manifested in Vienna, is absolutely irreconcilable with the notion of political equality. The lesser powers were denied equality of representation; they had no voice in the decisions except as they were required to ratify what the great powers had done; and they had no choice but to accept a settlement which the Concert had agreed upon and which it stood ready to enforce."[24]

What was striking was the great powers' assumption that they were entitled to arrange other nations' affairs as they saw fit, after little consultation with other European (let alone non-European) nations and certainly without their consent. Furthermore, the arrangement was relatively formalized, a fact that led some to compare the Concert to the League of Nations in the next century.[25] "What [the Concert] represented was a formalization of hierarchy as an explicit element within the international order."[26] Whether or not the analogy to the League of Nations is appropriate, reference to the Concert as "a highly significant experiment in supernational control" is not unreasonable.[27]

Regional and oligopolistic hegemony are not such clear examples of hegemony as the Pax Britannica or Pax Americana. Neither really meets the test of hegemony set out earlier, which seems to require that a *single* power assert *global* leadership. But of course even the classic examples offer less than total hegemony, for, as Nye points out, both were geographically limited to some degree, and in both cases the hegemon ruled in conjunction with important allies.[28] It seems reasonable, then, simply to treat hegemony (again as Nye does) as a matter of degree.[29] In its pure form, a single power would exercise complete world dominance, but hegemony might be qualified either geographically or through power sharing.

A key reason that international relations theorists study hegemony is that concentration of power in the hands of one state potentially alters the course of interstate political relations. In particular, an international system dominated by a single state possesses a potential solution to what is known as the public goods problem. Public goods are nonexcludable, in the sense that the producer of a public good cannot prevent others from taking advantage of it and thus cannot capture the full value of what it has created. Air quality, for instance, is a public good in that when an industry cuts down on emissions, the public at large will benefit. Because it cannot prevent others from enjoying the public good, the producer is unable to recapture the cost of production by selling the right to enjoy it.[30]

Public goods such as collective security and monetary stability are important in the international system. But it is commonly argued in the economics literature that such public goods will be undersupplied where there is no centralized enforcement mechanism to compel the recipients of the goods to contribute.[31] Each recipient would prefer to free-ride, allowing the others to bear the costs of providing the good while still enjoying the benefits. So long as there is no mechanism to enforce contributions, too few will contribute and for this reason a suboptimal amount of the good will be produced.

Hegemony offers a partial solution to the problem of providing public goods. Economic theory predicts that the largest participant may have sufficient incentive to produce the good even without a guarantee that others will contribute their shares, for it will also be the largest beneficiary of the good's production. Such activity by hegemons has been observed in the international system. "Since the Industrial Revolution, the two successive hegemonic powers in the global system (Great Britain and the United States) have sought to organize political, territorial, and especially economic relations in terms of their respective security and economic interests. They have succeeded in this hegemonic role partially because they have imposed their will on lesser states and partially because other states have benefitted from and accepted their leadership."[32] Where the hegemon assumes the responsibility of providing public goods, all states in the international system benefit.

This economic conclusion supports what has come to be known as hegemonic stability theory.[33] Under this theory, order in world politics is typically created by a single dominant power, whose continued existence is necessary for continuation of world order. "The hegemon plays a leading role in establishing an institutional environment which is favorable to its own interests (free trade, informal empire) but also accepts costs in being the mainstay of the system providing financial services, a source of capital, and a pattern of military support. According to this conception, the hegemon is the main beneficiary of the system but also the main provider of externalities to the other members: it receives disproportionate benefits but accepts disproportionate burdens."[34] Somewhat akin to the theory of hegemonic stability is "regime theory," which deals with institutional structures or regimes that coordinate behavior and expectations. Regimes may also facilitate the provision of public goods, although there is dispute over how effective they can be absent a hegemon.[35]

We will return later to the question of public goods. The fact that the hegemon may fill this function is one possible justification of hegemony, as some international relations theorists have pointed out.[36] Here I merely note that this alleged advantage of hegemony is reminiscent of one of the reasons economists have long given for having government, namely, that governments make possible the provision of public goods. Governments typically are thought to solve the public goods problem by forcing free-riders to contribute. Whereas the typical argument about hegemony is that public goods will be provided without coercion because the hegemon will find it in its interest to provide them even if the free-riders don't contribute, hegemons can, in addition, be sufficiently powerful to compel the free-riders to contribute to the costs of the public goods. Indeed, hegemons are frequently seen to do exactly that[37] (as for instance where the United States pressured its allies to bear some of the costs of the Persian Gulf war or to open their markets to imports). Hegemony, in other words, functions in some of the same ways and offers some of the same advantages that full-fledged governments do.

HEGEMONY AND GOVERNANCE

Despite the importance that modern international relations theory attaches to them, Robert Keohane warns that hegemons, and the institutional arrangements or "regimes" that they help to create, should not be mistaken for world government.[38] In certain respects this caution is appropriate, for there are ways in which hegemony and world government are rather different. Most obviously, there is no formal institution of "hegemony" which exists independently of the state that exercises world leadership and which authorizes successive hegemons to exercise world power. In this respect, hegemony is quite different from, say, a monarchy or a presidency, in which the authoritative role of "monarch" or "president" exists independently and a series of individuals steps in to fill the function. Hegemons, in this respect, are not like senators, judges, queens, or members of parliament.

Nevertheless, I would argue that hegemony and world government are similar in important ways. Because hegemony is a hierarchical political arrangement, the argument runs, it should be evaluated *as though* the hegemon were a world government of comparable capacities and engaged in comparable activities. The hegemon should be evaluated, in other words, as the world political leader that it is, despite its formal differences from domestic governance structures. It has the same sorts of responsibilities to subordinate states that a domestic government with comparable capabilities would have over those within its power.

The fact that there is no formal pre-existing hegemonic role does not mean that there are no political responsibilities to subordinate states, for not all domestic political actors fill roles that predate them, either. Napoleon and Hitler created their own roles; no titles awaited their arrival. Nor should it matter that there has not been a hegemon at all points in the world's history. Domestic societies also go for periods without centralizing political institutions (the feudal period in Europe provides examples), but this does not mean that when a leader arises, the leadership role is not a political one. The observation that hegemony is not continuous or that there is no formal institutional mechanism for assigning a state to play the role does not defeat the argument that hegemony is a form of political leadership comparable in many respects to domestic governance.

At least one author is willing to characterize the hegemon as actually "governing" the international system. Robert Gilpin likens the international structures by which great powers exercise control to domestic governments.[39] While great powers rarely exercise complete control over the entire international system, he points out, domestic governments rarely exercise complete control either. Gilpin states that at least until recently the most typical form of international system was dominance by a single power—hegemony. "The distribution of power among states constitutes the principal form of control in every international system. The dominant states and empires in every international system organize and maintain the network of political, economic, and other relationships within the system and especially in their respective spheres of influence. Both individually and in inter- action with one another, those states that historically have been called the great powers and are known today as the superpowers establish and enforce the basic rules and rights that influence their own behavior and that of the lesser states in the system."[40] In support, Gilpin quotes E. H. Carr: "International government is, in effect, government by that state [or states] which supplies [supply] the power necessary for the purpose of governing."[41]

Certain international lawyers have made somewhat similar claims. John West- lake thought that the leadership of the great powers during the Concert of Europe had a legal character and was a first step toward a form of international organiza- tion.[42] Thomas Joseph Lawrence saw the Concert in a similar light, in part be- cause the lesser powers had acquiesced. "If . . . the authority of the Great Powers has been acknowledged so constantly for the greater part of a century that it has become a part of the public order of Europe, and it is accepted and even invoked by the smaller states of Europe, any description of it which refuses to recognize its legality seems inadequate if not inaccurate."[43] While ordinarily we might be inclined to equate "legalism" with "formalism," on this occasion the lawyers may have been the "realists."[44] They, at least, looked past the formal commitment to the equality of sovereign states to recognize the hierarchy that existed in reality.

The conceptualization of hegemony as normatively comparable to world gov- ernment is both similar to and different from other recent studies of the gover- nance structures of international politics.[45] One modern school of international relations theory sees governance structures in the coalescence of international relations around international norms (which may or may not also be interna- tional laws). The similarity between that claim and my argument lies in the willingness to go beyond the commitment to a formalistic equality of states and to a sovereignty that puts its possessors beyond the reach of norms. The fact that no single actor is given the formal title of political leader does not, according to either that or the present argument, entail an absence of governance. The differ- ence is that my focus is on the political role of an actor with a preponderance of international power; the focus is narrower than in an investigation of the sorts of normative structures that may be present regardless of whether power is sym- metrically or asymmetrically distributed. In a sense, then, my argument is less ambitious, since it applies only where an additional resemblance between inter- national relations and domestic governance is present: a politically dominant actor.

We need not go so far as to call a hegemonic system a state or a world government. But it would certainly be appropriate to recognize hegemony as a primitive system of governance, or proto-government.[46] Prior to the establishment of true states, individual societies have gone through intermediate phases of political organization in which some of the aspects of a true state are present but a full-fledged state entity does not yet exist.[47] Typically, the leader of a society lacks some of the formalized indicia of control, having only limited enforcement powers and operating at times only through persuasion and inducement. There is no firmly established formal leadership role, and there may be no fixed manner of succession if the leader dies or is incapacitated. "Chieftain" and "big-man" systems are not so different from international hegemony. "Chiefdoms are sociopolitical organizations with a centralized government, hereditary status arrangements with an aristocratic ethos but no formal, legal apparatus of forceful repression, and without the capacity to prevent fission. . . . The chiefdom is far more highly developed than the simpler types of political organization led by 'big men' or comparable leaders."[48] Chieftain and big-man systems have statelike attributes, without quite being developed states. There is some political continuity, although without a large degree of formalization, and there is a mix of centrifugal and centripetal forces.

The hegemon uses similar methods of control to those that a chief or big man would use in dominating members of the tribe. One technique, of course, is physical force. Just as the chief is typically physically stronger or more militarily skilled than the others, the hegemon is militarily the most powerful actor in the international arena. Other techniques involve use of leadership skill, material largesse, and superior knowledge or technology. Because the system is not completely formalized, the leader cannot take the ability to dominate for granted in the same way that a president or a monarch in a politically stable society can. But this is a difference of degree, not of kind; and it is true in both the international and the domestic arenas. Just as a chief may be more or less successful in obtaining a monopoly of power, a hegemon may achieve greater or lesser degrees of predominance. Both hegemony and chieftaincy are political institutions. Both, as Robert Gilpin argues, are systems of governance.[49]

It might seem that international hegemonies are unlike domestic governance systems in that the hegemon is not the leader of the international system but merely a participant. This perception, however, is largely a product of a certain way of conceptualizing international politics; it is a product of formalism and not reality. The hegemon is certainly a participant, but only an a priori commitment to keeping roles discrete prevents recognition that those who fulfill governance roles can also, in other contexts, act as participants. We can look, if we choose, at the international system as a set of formally equal participants, as Kenneth Waltz does, for example.[50] Or we can choose not to subtract actual power asymmetries from the model, acknowledging instead the political governance role that even "participants" can fill.

For in a domestic chieftaincy or big-man system, as in the case of international hegemony, the leader is a participant *as well as* a political leader. An actor that starts in the role of formal equal may be thrust into, fight for, gradually accumulate, or inherit a position of political superiority. Governance roles, in other words, may be created or filled by formally equal participants. In both international and domestic affairs, the political leader plays a dual role, simultaneously a member of society and its head. The fact that a state is a participant in the international system, therefore, does not disqualify it from functioning in a political leadership capacity. Leaders are recruited from the pool of available political actors, which typically are the "governed" of society. "In pre-state societies every man is potentially a chief."[51]

Political equals often become political superiors through a process of gradual acquisition of power. Power becomes concentrated over time in the hands of a small number of participating actors, who solidify control through political, military, and economic maneuvering. Government need not be formed through some formal social contracting process, where participants hand over some of their power at some defined point in time to create a new institutional entity. Domestically, most political orders have probably been created just as international hegemony is created, through accretion—a slow movement from relative anarchy to relatively centralized order, with the process intermittently stagnating or backsliding. It may be difficult to identify precisely when a system of governance comes into being, but at some point the line is crossed and a truly political leader emerges. Considering the sorts of governments to which most of us are accustomed, it would be easy to fall into the mental habit of imagining political institutions as necessarily formal, longstanding and continuous, and deliberately created at some particular time (as by a social contract). But governance can also be the product of relatively fluid institutions, arising organically and of indefinite duration.

Imagine yourself, then, to be an observer of a group of approximately two hundred individuals living on an island. You notice that a small set of individuals—five, say—fairly consistently get their own way. These five operate with the cooperation of about another five or ten individuals, who are somewhat influential in carrying out the chosen five's decisions but have considerably less influence on the decision processes themselves. One actor, in particular, dominates the inner circle. The preferences of the remaining 185 or so are virtually ignored, except occasionally when it is strategically necessary to cater to them for purposes of more effective manipulation. When necessary, the elite five individuals compel the bulk of the population to comply through greater physical power, superior organization, better weaponry, and selective intimidation.

On this island, there are many decisions to be made. The most important have to do with allocation of scarce resources, in particular mining, farming, and fishing rights, and with the protection of existing property interests from theft. There are also questions about whether one individual can use property in a way that disturbs the peaceable activities of others by creating pollution or public nuisances. The enforcement of promises creates contentious issues, as does the redistribution of assets from the fortunate to the less well off. There are questions of whether individuals can be taxed for the common benefit, as well as questions of how the common benefit should be defined.

On all of these matters (and others) the elite make the important decisions, relying on their superior power and on their ability to manipulate existing political cal processes to set the rules as they see fit. They rarely consult the majority and act only to further their own interests. The vast majority of other actors have not been able or willing to organize to end this concentration of power, in part because rebellion would likely be tremendously costly for everyone and also because success is uncertain. The more material assets and political power become concentrated, the harder it seems to resist. And as it becomes more apparent that a small number are in control, no one wants to be the leader of a seemingly hopeless rebellion. An aura of invincibility sets in.

If one in fact witnessed such a society, would one not want to evaluate the concentration of power in normative political terms? Perhaps it depends upon exactly how concentrated power has become. At the outset power may be fairly diffuse, and it is only over time that the circle of powerful actors narrows and the members of the circle become confident of their ability to impose their will. Probably, they will never become totally able to control the situation; the leaders will always have to live with the fact that well-organized and widely shared resistance might either cause revolt or simply block some particular goal. Every political community has those who violate the rules, whether openly or in secret, and success in controlling such behavior varies depending on the skills and powers of political leaders. Obviously, there is a spectrum, but at some point the threshold is crossed. When power becomes sufficiently centralized, a hierarchy exists that must be evaluated in specifically political terms.

My argument is that we would not and should not hesitate to question the legitimacy of the concentration of power in the hands of a small minority of individuals. Liberals, for example, would ask whether there are adequate mechanisms for taking the preferences of the others into account, whether provisions have been made for protecting the individual rights of the unempowered, whether the elite could in some way be held accountable for excesses, and so forth. Monarchists would ask a different set of questions, as would Marxists or proponents of theocracy. But all would treat this society as politically problematic. The situation is not necessarily different merely because states, rather than individuals, are involved and because the island is the whole of our planet. There are those who would argue that the autocracy just described resembles current international society in all important particulars, or even that it understates the situation. Whether one accepts this characterization or not, it is clear that substantial international inequalities exist today, and it is important to ask how well they square with basic political morality.

PERSONAL VERSUS POLITICAL MORALITY

What is at stake in the decision to treat hegemony as a form of world governance? What difference does it make if we subject hegemony to political evaluation, as opposed to some other sort of scrutiny? Why should it matter that the hegemon has political responsibilities derived from normative political theory? The difference is easiest to appreciate by contrasting the two chief alternatives.

The first alternative, typically associated with the school of international relations scholarship known as "realism," denies that *any* sort of normative evaluation of international hegemony is appropriate.[52] International affairs are different from domestic affairs, in which questions of right and wrong make sense. The island nation, in other words, is very different from the global community. Realism is the subject of the next chapter, and so we will leave its investigation until then. Realism is linked to a commitment to the formal equality of states, as a foundation for the characterization of international relations as a state of anarchy. Here, note simply that one of the alternatives to viewing hegemony in light of political morality is to view it as not being within the domain of morality at all. If the rival is realism, then the significance of political morality is evident.

The second alternative sees international affairs in terms of personal morality. This view is the chief traditional rival to realism. Rejecting the notion that states are free from moral constraints, adherents of the second alternative hold that states in international society are subject to the same moral principles that individuals are subject to in domestic society. E. H. Carr describes the traditional dispute in the following way: "Realists . . . hold that relations between states are governed solely by power and that morality plays no part in them. The opposite theory . . . is that the same code of morality is applicable to individuals and to states."[53] Georg Schwartzenberger frames the problem in similar terms: "The problem of international morality can be stated simply. Are groups in international society subject to the same, or comparable, moral principles which govern relations between individuals?"[54]

Personal morality imposes obligations to keep promises, not to injure other people, to provide assistance to others when they suffer from severe hardship, not to lie, to show respect for the others' autonomy, and so forth. There are analogs in international affairs: the obligation to honor treaty commitments, the prohibition on armed aggression, perhaps a duty of international charity, an obligation to respect the sovereignty of other states, and the like. The comparison between states interacting internationally and individuals interacting domestically is sometimes referred to as the "domestic analogy."

The norms of personal morality are symmetric. If Smith owes Jones an obligation to keep promises, Jones owes the same obligation to Smith. Personal morality describes how we should act toward other persons simply by virtue of their common humanity. It assumes a world of formal equals. The obligation not to murder or lie is an obligation that each of us owes to everyone equally, and that everyone else owes equally to each of us. In some respects this symmetric model based on personal morality seems entirely appropriate in the international setting, in which sovereign states are all formally equal. Thus, there seems nothing odd about the fact that international obligations are symmetric under the traditional view of international morality. The United States owes to Angola what Angola owes to the United States and to every other nation in the world.

Personal morality, however, is not very helpful when it comes to evaluating systematic disparities of power or to describing what sort of behavior is appropriate to those that possess such power. It does not capture the special moral nature of hierarchy. The prohibitions found in interpersonal morality cannot be mechanically transplanted into a code of conduct for public officials. Some things are allowed public officials that would not be allowed to private citizens. What would look like theft in the hands of a private citizen may be justified as taxation when done by an officer of the state. Capital punishment may be wrong (as abolitionists argue), but it is not the same thing as murder; it is murder at the hands of the state, which is a different thing (although whether it is better or worse is a matter of some debate.) Putting the awesome power of the state behind an action adds a new and different moral dimension. Hierarchy changes the moral picture; it is necessary to stop and ask whether some particular private moral principle is pertinent to situations of power asymmetry, or whether there are other principles that would better capture public morality. The moral principles that we have evolved to deal with questions of hierarchy fall under the general rubric of political morality.

We noted that a view of international relations which is founded on personal morality relies upon the "domestic analogy" between interstate and interpersonal activities. There is a second possible "domestic analogy," however. Instead of likening interstate activities to personal relations between formally equal individuals in domestic society, we might liken international hegemony to political relations within domestic society. The relations between a hegemon and its subordinates, in other words, can be treated as similar to the relations between a government and its citizens. This results in a "vertical" rather than a "horizontal" approach to international relations,[55] because the key normative feature is the fact that one actor has power over another. The analogy between states and people is not perfect; in fact, in a later chapter we will question the "statist" assumption that states are the appropriate moral entities. For present purposes, however, we will liken power asymmetries between states to those between individuals. Political morality results in a distinctive approach to international relations because it focuses on an aspect of international affairs that private morality does not, namely, hierarchies of power. It employs a different domestic analogy.

If personal morality were the only guide to international affairs, and if political morality had no relevance, then there would be no way to determine when systematic asymmetries of power were legitimate. But personal morality is not, of course, all we have to go on; political morality is also relevant domestically, and by analogy internationally. Political morality supplies the concept of justified hierarchy. One of the most important functions that political theory performs is to specify why, and in what circumstances, power asymmetries are morally acceptable. All political theories except anarchism find hierarchy justified in at least some circumstances. Political theories differ greatly, of course, on what these circumstances are. The answer might be located in liberal democratic notions of consent of the governed and human rights, in Marxist conceptions of proletarian revolution, in theocratic principles about the fidelity of political power to the religious establishment, or in monarchist commitments to hereditary rule.

Political morality, with the concept of justified hierarchy, differs from personal morality in two ways that are simple converses of one another. It offers a basis for criticizing hierarchy, by providing a standard for when hierarchy is legitimate.

But it simultaneously offers a basis for defending hierarchy, again by providing a standard for when hierarchy is legitimate. Hierarchy is neither always right nor always wrong. Precisely because political morality addresses the problem of justified hierarchy, while personal morality does not, it provides a means of differentiating legitimate international hegemony from illegitimate.

CONSISTENCY

This book focuses on the consequences of applying liberal notions of political morality to American hegemonic power. The argument that political morality is relevant to international hegemony is a general one, however, which would apply regardless of what political theory one adopted (liberal, theocratic, Marxist, fascist, or monarchist) and regardless of the country to which the political theory was applied. Why, then, single out the United States and liberalism?

The focus on the United States is partly for purposes of illustration. The United States is currently at the apex of the international system. Admittedly, there are those who argue that its period of hegemony is past, and they may turn out to be correct. Certainly its dominance of the world economy does not compare to the period directly after the Second World War. Militarily, however, its dominance is greater than it was then, due to the collapse of the Soviet Union. And the current absence of superpower competitors translates into influence in many other areas. States that once were able to play the superpowers off against one another now find themselves turning to the United States as the primary remaining source of military and economic aid. United Nations Security Council politics is to a much greater degree determined by American objectives and willingness to act.

The nature and extent of American dominance is currently contested. One's position on this issue is likely to turn on disputed empirical propositions as well as on pragmatic differences of opinion about which aspects of international power matter more. Has the United States really lost its economic or military preeminence and, practically speaking, does economic or military preeminence matter more? The end of this debate is not in sight. It is not necessary, however, to postpone addressing the moral issues until such questions are resolved. The moral question is of interest in its own right, if only as a matter of theoretical political philosophy. Equally important, one's view about the legitimacy of international hegemony is likely to influence whether one thinks hegemony is something that America should eagerly pursue. The conviction that hegemonic power is an important source of international good encourages the systematic cultivation of capacities to intervene; the opposite conviction encourages isolationist tendencies to foster, at most, capacities for self-defense.

There is, of course, the possibility that analyses of American hegemony will become moot within the next decade; by early in the next century such discussions may already seem anachronistic, if indeed they are not already. If so, however, another hegemon may take the place of the United States, and any general principles arising out of an examination of American hegemony can be put to work on the new problems that this new hegemon presents. While the specific occasion for examining international hegemony may pass, the general problem surely will not.

The reason for choosing liberalism as the critical tool (as opposed to some other political theory) is that America is, by and large, a nation of liberals. "Liberal" here is used expansively to include classical laissez-faire liberals such as Adam Smith (and their intellectual descendants, such as Robert Nozick) as well as those who would seek a broader role for state intervention in social life, such as John Rawls or Ronald Dworkin.[56] Admittedly, liberalism is not the typical vehicle for criticism of international political hierarchy.[57] The more usual critical examinations of international power asymmetry come from farther to the left on the political spectrum. Johann Galtung's indictment is a typical example:

> This theory [of structural imperialism] takes as its point of departure two of the most glaring facts about this world: the tremendous inequality, within and between nations, in almost all aspects of human living conditions, including the power to decide over those living conditions; and the resistance of this inequality to change. The world consists of Center and Periphery nations; and each nation, in turn, has its centers and periphery. . . . Any theory of liberation from structural violence presupposes theoretically and practically adequate ideas of the dominance system against which the liberation is directed; and the special type of dominance system to be discussed here is imperialism.[58]

It is to be expected that leftist theorists would be quick to apply their theories internationally, given that Marxism attaches relatively little importance to national borders.[59] Yet such critiques, important as they are, are unlikely to move most Americans. Precisely because they are founded on leftist assumptions, they have little ability to persuade those who do not accept the basic leftist postulates.

This book, in contrast, is an *internal* critique of American hegemony. It is internal to American thought in that it builds upon principles of domestic governance that many Americans already accept. This strategy has one important advantage and one apparent weakness. The advantage is that we need not stop first to build the case for domestic liberalism, but can instead simply start with liberal premises and then proceed directly to ask what international consequences follow from them. The United States should follow liberal principles internationally because it is committed to them domestically.

The apparent weakness is that we seem to be taking a position of extreme moral relativism, in which the only value is consistency. We seem to be saying that the United States should follow liberal principles internationally, while Iran should follow Islamic principles, China should follow communist principles, and Iraq should follow Baathist principles. It seems that we are saying that other nations are above reproach in their international dealings so long as they behave consistently with the principles to which they adhere domestically. Given the truly repellent philosophies that motivate some states domestically, this seems morally quite unacceptable. It also leaves the states with more morally demanding political theories at a competitive disadvantage when they are dealing with the domestically less scrupulous.

The reason that this appearance of moral relativism is no more than that—an appearance—is that we are not claiming that consistency is the only virtue. There are two ways to behave wrongfully in international, as in other, settings. The first is to have the wrong principles; the second is to have the right principles but not to act consistently with them. Here we are focusing primarily on the second sort of moral error; discrepancy between principles and actions. States have domestic political commitments but do not always follow them in their foreign affairs. The fact that one focuses on consistency arguments at one time, though, does not mean that one cannot focus on the question of underlying values at another. Indeed, after trying to describe what a liberal theory of international hegemony would look like, we will return in part 3 to reexamine certain basic liberal premises.

International moralists have long debated the relevance of the "domestic analogy" between interstate and interpersonal ethics.[60] Perhaps it could be argued that the debate over the domestic analogy is irrelevant because the domestic analogy, by itself, does not tell us what interpersonal morality requires. All that it tells us is that interstate relations are like interpersonal relations. But whether interstate and interpersonal relations are similar is an interesting question in its own right, as well as an important part of the debate over international morality. Coupled with a set of principles of personal morality, it provides strong guidance for state actions in the international community.

So, also, with the second domestic analogy, the one that we have been discussing here. The argument that international political leadership is morally similar to domestic governance does not by itself provide the whole answer to questions of international political morality. But it is an interesting argument in and of itself. It provides an important element, further, in the debate over international legitimacy. Coupled with a domestic political theory such as liberalism, it tells whether international hegemony is legitimate and when it has exceeded its legitimate bounds.

CONCLUSION

Helen Milner has emphasized the benefits of linking international and domestic politics, albeit primarily in a descriptive rather than a normative context. Noting that scholars such as James Rosenau had earlier encouraged cross-fertilization, she laments more recent backsliding. "The problem with reverting back to a situation where international politics is seen as unique is that one is less likely to use the hypotheses, concepts, and questions about politics developed elsewhere. International politics must then reinvent the wheel, not being able to draw on other political science scholarship. The radical dichotomy between international and domestic politics seems to represent a conceptual and theoretical step backwards."[61] Milner's argument applies as forcefully in international normative analysis as in the positive side of the discipline.

The primary object of much of the remainder of this book is to spell out a vision of international politics that comports with political values embedded in our domestic politics. It investigates a set of connected themes that surface in common arguments about international justification, asking whether these might ground an adequate justification for international hegemony. The very familiarity of these themes illustrates how international justification already draws on and intersects with the domestic political vernacular. The values embodied in these themes are, in large part, liberal values. It is not possible to develop a defense of liberalism here (indeed, it may not be possible to develop one at all). Domestic liberalism is chosen nonetheless because it is in large part accepted by a substantial part of the American population. To be consistent, I argue, we should evaluate hegemony in terms of how well it fits with these domestic notions.

The individual who rejects domestic liberalism will not be satisfied. But this only serves to demonstrate the point of making the argument in favor of political morality in the abstract as well as in the concrete. Hegemony can be evaluated according to domestic liberal principles, or according to some other domestic political morality. But *it should be evaluated*, and it should be evaluated as a political institution. Before we attempt such an evaluation, however, one obstacle needs to be investigated. We must examine the commonly heard argument that normative analysis is inappropriate because international relations take place in a state of anarchy.

2

ANARCHY

International relations, in the eyes of many, is far removed from domestic politics. Domestic politics is the domain of right and wrong, of principled arguments, of idealistic goals, and of law. International relations is the domain of stronger and weaker, of fighting for national survival, and of compromise with unpleasant and unprincipled reality. It is certainly not the domain of law; from this perspective, international law does not even exist.

When asked to explain the difference, most proponents of this view point to the fact that there is no world government to tame self-interest and ensure international civility. It is safe to behave morally in one's domestic dealings; it is risky (sometimes even suicidal) to do so internationally. International relations specialists express this sentiment by saying that the difference lies in the fact that international relations take place in a state of anarchy.

This chapter rejects the anarchy argument, at least as it applies to the behavior of the world's leading powers toward weaker states.[1] Whatever the relevance of the anarchy argument in a world in which power is evenly distributed, it is not a convincing defense against normative criticisms of hegemony. It is not clear that "anarchy" is even an accurate characterization of a world in which one state predominates. Furthermore, the reasons why anarchy supposedly makes normative appraisal inappropriate do not really apply to a global order dominated by a single powerful state. Regarding the vertical relations between powerful and subordinate states, the anarchy argument has nothing to say. The argument that international morality does not exist is inspired by conflict between roughly equal powers; by the Cold War, by World War II, by the Arab/Israeli conflict, and the like. When the leading state in the world order comes in conflict with a less powerful state, however, the anarchy argument is not plausible at all.

It is true that in its dealings with a less powerful state, even a leading power may be motivated by genuine security concerns; it may be acting to protect its interests against encroachment by a third state powerful enough to seriously threaten long-term security. The United States' actions in Nicaragua or Cuba during the last few decades, for example, can only be explained in terms of its relations with the Soviet Union and its genuine security concerns. But I will argue below that what to do in such cases is still a moral question; it is comparable to the issue of how a domestic government should treat its own citizens in the face of severe threats. Even when national security is at stake, there is general agreement that governments should not have carte blanche over the lives, liberty, and property of their citizens. Arguments of political morality are not defeated simply by raising the specter of national security in the domestic context, and they are not so frail in the international context either. Such cases present a moral as well as a security dilemma.

THE NORMATIVE RELEVANCE OF ANARCHY

International relations theory is dominated by the notion of international anarchy, which is thought to have both positive and normative implications. On the positive side, descriptive models of how the international system operates center on the ways in which conduct is shaped by the absence of a centralized enforcement mechanism.[2] The "international security dilemma" that results from the absence of a central government underlies both traditional balance-of-power analyses and modern game theoretic approaches.[3] The science of international relations deals in large part with the implications of international society's purportedly anarchical structure.

Normative international relations theory must also contend with the concept of anarchy. Here, theory is dominated by a dispute between the so-called realists and their critics.[4] At issue is whether normative analysis of international relations is possible or appropriate. The realists seem to argue that in an anarchy, normative arguments are nothing but moralistic nonsense; states must pursue their interests or they perish, with no room left for idealistic inquiry into matters of right and wrong. Idealists such as Woodrow Wilson or Jimmy Carter, influenced by notions of democracy or international human rights, were supremely misguided because such utopian notions have no place in foreign policy. In this respect, the realists seem to claim, international relations is very different from domestic affairs.

I say they *seem* to argue this because in fact it is not entirely clear that this is what they hold. Some of the realists' critics characterize the argument in this way, and some of the realists' own writings make this characterization plausible. Robert Art and Kenneth Waltz mince no words: "States in anarchy cannot afford to be moral. . . . The preconditions for morality are absent in international politics. Every state, as a consequence, has to be prepared to do that which is necessary for its interests as it defines them. Anarchy is the realm where all can, and many do, play 'dirty pool.' "[5] The "no morality in anarchy" argument is definitely not a figment of the critics' imaginations.

But neither is it a defining element of the realist creed, for it is not altogether certain that all realists are as amoralistic as they are sometimes made out to be.[6] Some realists, such as Reinhold Niebuhr and Hans Morgenthau, were highly principled individuals with apparently clear visions of international right and wrong;[7] we will return later in this chapter to the question of how their vision fits with international morality. As Robert Holmes has pointed out, sometimes the realists seem to be opposed not so much to morality per se as to the particular "moralistic" vision that motivated their adversaries.[8] When they claim that the utopian proposals of their opponents would actually backfire and that their own realist approach to international relations would make us better off in the long run, their arguments seem squarely based upon traditional consequentialist morality. It is possible, then, that what some realists really object to is rigid adherence to moralistic rules, such as absolute prohibitions on war or nuclear weapons. They may merely be claiming that *a proper international morality* would take consequences into account in deciding whether waging war or building nuclear weapons is justified in particular circumstances. It would be a serious error to confuse "morality" with "utopianism," for the debate whether to take practical consequences into account, as opposed to simply following moral rules and prohibitions, is well within the confines of traditional moral theory.

It is not possible to determine what realists, generally, believe about international morality. There is too much variation among realists on this issue, as well as some vacillation on the part of individual realist writers. E. H. Carr claims that not even Machiavelli himself was able to adhere consistently to realist amorality.[9] But it is not really important, for present purposes, whether there is a realist "party line." For one thing, it is not just realism which poses the issue; many scholars who cannot be characterized as realists also start from the notion of anarchy.[10] The "no morality in anarchy" attitude toward international affairs, moreover, has a life of its own outside the academy, in the broader foreign policy community but also in the population at large, where many of the scholarly realists' subtleties are totally left behind. Whatever its connection to realist international relations scholarship, its persistence in the popular mind makes the "vulgar realism" that equates international relations with amorality important to address.

What, then, is the argument? Why would anarchy mean that international relations is off-limits to normative thought? There are two different strands to the argument that in an anarchy there are no norms, a structural one and a jurisprudential one. The structural strand has to do with lack of reciprocity. In an anarchy there is no guarantee that one's own moral and responsible behavior will be met with morality and responsibility by others. If the United States stops building nuclear weapons, what guarantee is there that other states will follow suit? Hobbes, whose name we associate most closely with this argument, said it all: "He that would be modest, and tractable, and perform all he promises, in such time and place, where no man else should do so, should but make himself a prey to others and secure his own certain ruin."[11] A state cannot afford to take risks, according to this argument; it must protect its self-interest, since there is no centralized enforcement mechanism to ensure that other states respect international norms.[12] Because this "security dilemma" argument is based on the anarchical structure of international relations, we can call it the "structural" version of the anarchy argument.[13]

The structural argument is most intuitively convincing when one makes certain assumptions about the psychology of the actors, namely, that they are self-interested and unprincipled. However, this assumption is not strictly necessary. If one knew that all the other actors were altruistic and principled, then one could afford to be altruistic and principled as well. But even if they are altruistic and principled, one may not know it. One has to be prepared for the worst, the structural anarchy argument contends. The mere fact of uncertainty forces even the well-motivated to behave as if the others were self-interested. And others, being aware of this dynamic, will anticipate such behavior and respond accordingly. So one need not assume that the actors in a system are self-interested for the anarchy argument to take hold. One need only assume that they might be and that this fact is generally appreciated.[14]

The second version of the anarchy argument raises the jurisprudential issue whether norms can exist at all when there is no authoritative source for them. In a domestic society, the argument goes, government is the source of rights and responsibilities. But internationally there is no source of norms because there is no government. Where could norms come from in an anarchy? This "positivist" version of the anarchy argument is often coupled with cultural relativism; each state has its own version of right and wrong, and without an international government there is no reason to elevate one state's version over the others. E. H. Carr claimed this observation as one of the chief insights of realism. "The realist," he wrote, "has . . . been able to demonstrate that the intellectual theories and ethical standards of utopianism, far from being the expression of absolute and a priori principles, are historically conditioned, being both products of circumstances and interests and weapons framed for the furtherance of interests."[15]

Insight or not, the power of the cultural relativism argument should not be overestimated. Even if the argument were correct, it would be irrelevant in cases where there was no actual disagreement over values. Often states are in complete agreement about the relevant values, and the conflict is caused by inconsistent desires to possess the same thing (such as a particular piece of territory). Unwillingness to respect the territorial integrity of another state is not caused by a lack of belief in the importance of territorial integrity, but by an unwillingness to extend this conceded value to other international actors, or by a disagreement over the facts to which the value must be applied (for example, who owned the territory first).

Not all (perhaps, in fact, few) international disputes result from one state attempting to impose its values on another. There are, of course, important value differences between nations with different histories and cultures (human rights versus political stability, capitalism versus socialism, Islam versus Christianity or Judaism) and these can cause international tension. But states are perfectly capable of disagreeing, and fighting bitter wars, without any discernible differences in their ideological commitments. Moral righteousness may be obnoxious, but it does not present as great a threat to international peace and prosperity as contempt for generally accepted international norms.

Although the structural and jurisprudential variants of the anarchy argument work in tandem, they are distinct. The structural argument does not assert that no international norms exist; on this issue it is agnostic. It only claims that even if there are such norms, states are not obliged to follow them. The jurisprudential variant is more deeply skeptical, denying that any norms exist at all. While it lends an air of philosophical sophistication to its structural counterpart, the structural argument stands quite sturdily on its own. The structural version is probably the more widely held, perhaps because it requires only minimal assumptions—uncertainty about the motives of other actors and the absence of any means of international enforcement.

For both the structural and the jurisprudential versions of the argument, a great deal hangs on the question of what exactly should count as anarchy. "Anarchy" is what differentiates international from domestic situations. Even vulgar realists rarely argue that morality is never relevant; their claim, instead, is that the morality that is relevant in domestic life is not appropriate for international relations.[16] Their argument therefore depends on the existence of some categorical distinction between international and domestic relations. The definition of anarchy must include all international cases but exclude all domestic cases.

As we look at possible definitions of anarchy, we find that proponents of the anarchy characterization seem to have in mind a world in which power is fairly evenly distributed among states. This is taken to be a defining characteristic of international relations, one which differentiates international from domestic affairs. But definitions of anarchy based on this vision of the international system seem oddly misdirected where there is global political leadership. Hegemony blurs the sharp distinction between domestic and international relations because centralized political leadership does exist. To the extent that anarchy means diffusion of power, it is hard to characterize the current state of affairs as anarchy and therefore hard to argue that international morality is irrelevant. But the main rival definitions—that anarchy is lack of a formal or a legitimate government—undercut the claim that morality is irrelevant to international relations. Formality seems an odd basis for realists to deny the relevance of moral reasoning, and legitimacy clearly presumes the ability to make moral judgments about whether international governance is justifiable.

ANARCHY: WHAT IS IT?

When one contrasts our current state of international affairs with some of the alternatives, it is easy enough to grasp why the world that we inhabit is ordinarily characterized as an anarchy. Anarchy is commonly contrasted with world government. International relations would not be conceptualized as an anarchy if, for example, the United Nation came to possess enough military might to enforce its will. A world empire, likewise, would not be an anarchy.[17] These two paradigms of nonanarchical international political structures are clearly different from the current state of affairs; the world that we inhabit seems anarchical in contrast. But what, precisely, are the relevant distinguishing characteristics? Detailed discussions of what anarchy means are surprisingly rare in the international relations literature. The concept itself is referred to quite frequently, but it usually seems to be taken for granted that the meaning is sufficiently clear and uncontroversial as not to require much elaboration. The two most interesting exceptions to this generalization are Kenneth Waltz's discussion of anarchy in his *Theory of International Politics* and an excellent critique of the concept of anarchy by Helen Milner.[18]

As a neorealist, Waltz is an advocate of the anarchy characterization of international relations. "National politics is the realm of authority, of administration and of law. The international realm is preeminently a political one. The national realm is variously described as being hierarchic, vertical, central, heterogeneous, directed and contrived; the international realm, as being anarchic, mutually adaptive. The more centralized the order, the nearer to the top the locus of decision ascends. Internationally, decisions are made at the bottom, there being scarcely any other."[19] Some of the features Waltz mentions (that anarchy is decentralized and not hierarchical) are also highlighted in the domestic political theory literature. In *Community, Anarchy, and Liberty*, Michael Taylor develops a definition of anarchy. The identifying characteristics that he lists include: widely dispersed capacity to use force, absence of a standing group which possesses or endeavors to possess a monopoly of the use of force, and lack of a means for enforcing collective decisions.[20]

These criteria refer to empirical characteristics that anarchy is thought to possess, and they distinguish our current situation from the two nonanarchical paradigms just mentioned. If the United Nations commanded a standing army sufficient to impose its will around the world, then the world political structure would not be anarchical; since it does not, according to this argument, anarchy prevails. Similarly, if one state were able to establish a world empire, its effective control over other nations would alter the anarchical structure of world politics. Under the empirical view, the defining characteristic of anarchy is the actual distribution of capabilities among the actors in the system.

But there are in addition two other factors that might be taken as indicators of anarchy. One is the absence of a *formal* system of government. The feature which distinguishes this definition from the prior one is its formalism; the actual distribution of capabilities is less important than whether power is vested in the hands of an officially constituted governmental actor. The reason that international politics would not be an anarchy if the United Nations had a standing army is that power would then be in the hands of a centrally located figure, playing a distinct and different role from the various nation-states that it governed. What matters is not merely the ability of a militarily empowered United Nations to impose its will, but the fact of its recognized stature as a government. The same could be said of a formally recognized world empire.

A second alternative indicator of anarchy is the absence of *legitimate* governance. Here again simple de facto power concentration is not the key element; the necessary ingredient is legitimacy. And once again the contrast between the current state of affairs and a hypothetical militarily equipped U.N. is instructive. The United Nations is, more or less, a democratically constituted decision-making body; its members joined voluntarily, and most of its decisions are made through relatively open and democratic procedures. If the United Nations possessed enough military power to compel recalcitrant nations to comply with its decisions, then it would seem prima facie legitimate for it to do so. Thus, so the argument would go, a militarily powerful United Nations would transform the world from an anarchy into a world government, for such a United Nations would be entitled to rule.

The three main competing definitions of anarchy, then, are based on empirical criteria, formal criteria, and normative criteria. The concept of anarchy seems straightforward because we tend to contrast the current state of affairs with hypothetical situations (such as a world dominated by a militarily empowered United Nations) in which *all three criteria* are satisfied. The contrast is sharpest if one compares our present state of affairs to alternatives in which actual distribution of capabilities is concentrated, the concentrated power is vested in an entity with formal governmental status, and that formal government is legitimate. But there may be cases in which some of these conditions are present and not others; in particular, hegemony presents a case in which there is substantial concentration of power, but that power does not reside with a formal world government. It is important, for this reason, to disaggregate the three different sorts of criteria for anarchy. We will consider the empirical, formal, and normative definitions in turn.

EMPIRICAL CRITERIA   The identifying empirical characteristics of anarchy might be thought to include lack of leadership, diffusion of power, chaos or lack of order, and absence of hierarchy. All have to do with the extent to which power is concentrated.[21] Oran Young states that "literally, anarchy refers to the absence of a ruler."[22] Helen Milner likewise considers the possibility that anarchy amounts to chaos, or lack of order.[23] The basic problem with such empirical criteria for anarchy, however, is that they fail cleanly to distinguish domestic from international relations, and in particular that they fail to distinguish hegemonic international orderings from relatively chaotic domestic orderings.

For how apt is it, from an empirical standpoint, to characterize international relations as an "anarchy" when a single state dominates the world order? The more hegemonic an international system becomes, the more orderly and less chaotic it will be. On a purely empirical level, the Warsaw Pact system constituted less of an "anarchy" than the conditions in Somalia before the 1992 intervention or the current situation in Bosnia and Herzegovina. Indeed, the Warsaw Pact system may have been more orderly than conditions in some parts of the inner cities of contemporary America. The extent of diffusion of power in a given international or domestic arrangement is an empirical question, hardly subject to quick generalization. The anarchy argument depends on a sharp contrast between the domestic and international sphere. Anarchy gains its alleged normative significance from the fact that it exists in the latter but not in the former. But domestic and international systems alike lie on a spectrum, from quite diffusely organized to much more hierarchical. And there is a significant area of overlap.

Waltz recognizes that the definition of anarchy must differentiate between domestic and international relations when he discusses the possibility that anarchy is indicated by the presence of violence. "Among men as among states, anarchy, or absence of government, is associated with the occurrence of violence."[24] The problem with this definition, he notes, is that there is at least as much violence within states as between them. Waltz cites a list of civil wars and coups, Hitler's extermination of Jews, and the human rights violations of Idi Amin. He concludes that "if anarchy is identified with chaos, destruction and death, then the distinction between anarchy and government does not tell us much." But he fails to follow this argument to its logical conclusion. The need—and the inability—to differentiate between domestic and international affairs carries over to other empirical definitions of anarchy, not just the "absence of violence" criterion that he rejects. Other definitions of anarchy, such as diffusion of power, fail equally to differentiate certain international orderings—hegemonic ones—from domestic situations.

The same difficulty plagues two other identifying empirical characteristics mentioned by both Waltz and Taylor, the absence of hierarchy and the lack of specialization. As Waltz puts it, "In anarchic realms, like units coact. In hierarchic realms, unlike units interact. In an anarchic realm, the units are functionally similar and tend to remain so. . . . In a hierarchic realm, the units are differentiated, and they tend to increase the extent of their specialization." But in hegemonic international orderings, as in most domestic societies, there are both hierarchy and functional differentiation. Waltz sometimes seems to acknowledge this; he concedes that there are large power disparities between the strong and the weak. And although at one point Waltz states that anarchy means lack of role differentiation, he also recognizes that the different capabilities of states shape the roles that they play.[25] As Milner argues, Waltz does not insist that states are interchangeable; he recognizes the different functions of the greater powers and the lesser.[26] Again, it is precisely in cases of hegemony that the realists' attempts to distinguish domestic from international orderings break down. It is when one portrays international systems exclusively in terms of evenly distributed power that these definitions are most convincing.

There is a tendency, in defining anarchy, to idealize domestic society while casting international relations in the worst possible light.[27] It seems to be an article of faith that the two are significantly different, and so the object of any definition of anarchy must be to identify the distinguishing characteristic. But this article of faith distorts both sides of the comparison. It is a commonplace in the writings of scholars such as Hedley Bull that there is a great deal of order in international affairs. This is particularly so where a single state dominates the international system. It is also true, however, that there is a great deal of violence and disorder in domestic relations. The difficulty in defining anarchy so as to place all domestic cases firmly on one side of the line, and all international ones firmly on the other, may simply be that the two sets of cases overlap, with hegemony squarely in the area of intersection.

One would not want to deny that the average international situation displays less order and concentration of power than the average domestic situation. It may very well be that the two sets of cases overlap at only the extremes of their distributions; the most organized international systems resemble the least organized domestic ones. Conceding this point, however, it remains the case that we cannot categorically differentiate international from domestic systems on the grounds that the former are anarchic while the latter are not. The point is that a hegemonic world order should be evaluated in the same way as a domestic order with a comparable degree of power concentration, not that all international situations should be treated the same as all domestic ones. The true explanatory variable, in other words, should be the degree of centralization of power rather than whether some particular leader's power crosses international borders.

FORMAL CRITERIA   For the anarchy argument to be successful, it must be based upon something more than the absence of these simple empirical characteristics. What then distinguishes hegemony from domestic governance? The missing ingredient might seem to be a formal one. There is a fair degree of power concentration in today's world, but it is not in the hands of a formal government. There is hierarchy but it is informal; formally, states are assumed to be equal.

This seems to be the notion of anarchy favored by Robert Gilpin, who explicitly rejects the identification of anarchy with lack of order. "Relationships among states have a high degree of order," he writes, "and . . . although the international system is one of anarchy (i.e., absence of formal governmental authority) the system does exercise an element of control over the behavior of states."[28] Gilpin, as we have already noted, is somewhat unusual in that he does not hesitate to use the word *governance* to describe the hegemon's relationship to the international system.[29] Yet he nonetheless characterizes the international setting as an anarchy. Anarchy, then, must reside precisely in lack of formality, for if both domestic and international systems are systems of governance, then the only relevant difference making the latter anarchic must be the fact that its governance system is not formalized. As Oran Young puts it, "Political anarchy is the condition of any polity that is lacking in formal institutions of government at the system level."[30]

Another way to put this point is that while power may be *concentrated* in a hegemonic system, it is not *centralized*. Centralization seems to require more than concentration of power; it suggests that power must be located in the hands of an entity with some special, central status. Why does it seem that the hegemon is not "central" in this sense? The answer must be that while the hegemon possesses concentrated power, it lacks the special status that would locate it at the center (or, perhaps better put, the apex) of the international political scene. It does not occupy the right formal position; it is a player in the world political system and not a referee. Under this interpretation, to borrow a phrase from Nicholas Onuf and Frank Klink, the world is "formally but not substantively anarchical"; for the substantive fact of hierarchy is conceded but no formal relevance attaches.[31]

So, to continue this argument, it would be a different state of affairs if exactly the same amount of concentrated power were placed in the hands of an institution such as the United Nations. Currently, the existence of the U.N. does not resolve the problem of international anarchy because it has no way to enforce its decisions. But if we could combine hegemonic power with the formal authority of the U.N., we would have true world government. And with the anarchy problem resolved, morality would resurface in international relations.

The first difficulty with relying on such a definition of anarchy to support the argument against international norms is that it hardly seems compatible with realism. The argument depends upon a contrast between formal equality and formal hierarchy; actual differences in capabilities are disregarded. Realism, however, prides itself on its attention to the realities of the situation. Helen Milner captures the problem nicely: "To deal with . . . issues [of international power concentration], Waltz has to relinquish his more legalistic notion of the international system as one of sovereign equals. At times, he indeed does this. . . . Waltz himself then does not find the assumption that all states are equal and thus that power is highly decentralized to be either empirically true or heuristically useful. *As a good realist*, he focuses upon the few strong powers in the system."[32]

Milner is concerned primarily with the role that anarchy plays in the positive (rather than the normative) theory of international relations. But the point applies equally well to the use of the anarchy argument to defeat normative scrutiny. The realists are pulled in opposite directions by two opposing inclinations. One is the tendency to treat the international system as a collection of formal equals, with equal capabilities and a resulting diffusion of power. This is the world of formalism, of formal equality—and of anarchy. The other is realistically to describe and analyze a world which bears little resemblance to this simple formal model.

A second problem is that if formalization is called for, there is no obvious reason that the formal model chosen has to be one of formal equality. One could as easily decide to formally conceptualize the hegemon as a world political leader. Surely that choice is not precluded by the mere fact that the most powerful actor doesn't calls itself by the name "world government." A decision to formalize international politics in one way rather than another is a choice about which aspects of reality to recognize officially; formalizations highlight certain favored features while casting others into the shadows. Equality is one way of formalizing international relations, but it deliberately leaves out of the picture the power asymmetries that exist in fact. It is one possible choice out of many, and the anarchy characterization leaves the choice largely unexplained.[33]

The decision to treat all states as formal equals may be influenced by the standard economic model of the marketplace, in which all buyers and sellers are conceived as formal equals even though some are vastly more economically powerful than others. Of course, even in the market context itself this model may be misguided, as leftist critics of microeconomic reasoning would probably claim. But there is an important reason why this model is even less appropriate for international relations than for market relations. Market relations take place within a legal system which *imposes* a structure of formal equality.[34] All buyers and sellers are granted the same legal rights—to buy, to sell, and to own property— and the model of formal equality is reinforced by these legal norms. The formal equality of the market, therefore, is a consequence of an overarching normative structure that prescribes formal equal roles for all of the actors; and the existence of such a structure is precisely what the anarchy argument denies in international relations.[35]

The insistence that the most important characteristic of international relations is formal equality—lack of formal governance—seems to reflect a belief that the formal equality of the international system is some tangible thing that is really "out there," as opposed to a consequence of how we choose to conceptualize the world.[36] But formal equality is not really "out there"; it is an artifact of the way we think, not a reflection of the way things are. It is a mental habit and, like most habits, tends to take us captive. This tendency must be resisted. The question then remains whether there is good reason to treat the leading world power differently from a comparably centralized domestic system.

NORMATIVE CRITERIA AND "SELF-HELP" SYSTEMS A third possible definition of anarchy relies on normative criteria, in particular the absence of a *legitimate* government. Helen Milner concludes that legitimacy is the "linchpin" for Waltz; that it is lack of legitimacy that is distinctive in world politics.[37] No state is entitled to command; no state is obligated to obey. As Waltz puts it, "Nationally, the force of a government is exercised in the name of right and justice. Internationally, the force of a state is employed for the sake of its own protection and advantage. . . . Nationally, relations of authority are established. Internationally, only relations of strength result." Waltz alludes to the Weberian definition of the state when he writes: "The difference between national and international politics lies not in the use of force, but in the different modes of organization for doing something about it. A government, ruling by some standard of legitimacy, arrogates to itself the right to use force. . . . An effective government . . . has a monopoly on the *legitimate* use of force."[38]

Normative considerations also permeate other efforts to define anarchy, such as the characterization of international anarchy as a "self-help" system. "Self-help," says Waltz, "is necessarily the principle of action in an anarchic order." Where there is government, individual actors can turn to the state for protection. Where there is no government, actors must provide for their own defense. This has a number of consequences, in Waltz's view. "In a self-help system, each of the units spends a portion of its effort, not in forwarding its own good, but in providing the means of protecting itself against others. . . . The conditions of insecurity—at the least, the uncertainty of each about the other's future intentions and actions—works against their cooperation." In any self-help system, the actors worry about their survival, and this worry conditions their behavior.[39] Where government exists, the individual actors can afford to relax and can gain the benefits of cooperation. States use self-help, in other words, because there is no legitimate government to turn to. Where there is such a legitimate government, it and it alone is entitled to use coercion.

It might seem that self-help is a different sort of criterion than absence of legitimacy, because the latter is unabashedly normative, while the former seems more descriptive. But a closer look at the concept of self-help reveals normative elements lurking within. If "self-help" were understood at the most purely descriptive and literal level, then some particular order would be a self-help system whenever the actors in it needed to rely on their own devices to protect any of their interests. The mere fact that some of the actors' interests were not safeguarded through authoritative political processes would mean that they must protect those interests on their own and that the system relied on self-help. In such situations, the argument would continue, moral criticism is inappropriate because one cannot count on government to protect those interests.

But it is not the case that the lack of official protection for actors' interests necessarily turns an arrangement into a self-help system. If it did, then domestic society would be a self-help system as well, since there are many interests that domestic governments do not protect. The anarchy argument assumes that the difference between the domestic and international systems is that our interests are provided for by government in the domestic but not the international context. But this contrast is misleading. It is certainly not the case that domestic government provides each of us with everything we might want. The domestic citizen lives in great insecurity; about being fired from his or her job, getting heart disease or cancer, going bankrupt, losing a beloved spouse or lover, and so on. The domestic citizen, moreover, must rely on self-help if he or she wants to amass a fortune, become a famous neurosurgeon, or be awarded a MacArthur fellowship. In any society, the government provides certain protections and guarantees the fulfillment of certain interests but leaves others to individual initiative. As to matters where no official guarantees are provided, the sole remedy is self-help.[40]

A literal interpretation of the concept, then, does not capture the difference between domestic and international affairs. For the distinctive nature of international relations cannot simply be that there are some interests that must be protected or pursued through one's own devices; the same can be said of domestic society. What seems, instead, to make international relations distinctive is the nature of the interests at stake. The classic version of the security dilemma involves a situation in which a truly significant state interest—perhaps even its continued existence—is threatened if the state plays by the rules. This is the situation in which the anarchy argument is most seductive. Yet, it is when we try to specify the cases where the self-help argument is most compelling that the normative considerations that underlie it come in focus.

For whether the self-help argument is persuasive depends on whether the interests in question are legitimate. Where the interests are clearly illegitimate, the fact that only self-help will work is beside the point. It is true that the only way that Saddam Hussein might hope to acquire Kuwait was the use of military force; self-help was the only means for achieving his goals because the world community would never have cooperated in his conquest. But such examples form no part of the anarchy argument's appeal. If Iraq were entitled to Kuwait, then the fact that no world government existed to facilitate its acquisition might lead to the conclusion that Iraq was entitled to use any means in its possession. But if one starts from the premise that annexation of Kuwait is illegitimate, then nothing follows from the fact that no authoritative processes exist to facilitate its annexation. It does not matter that self-help is the only way to achieve a goal if the goal itself is reprehensible. Indeed, even if a world government did exist, Iraq's only method for obtaining Kuwait's territory would probably be self-help. Yet this fact alone would not turn world government into a self-help system.

The basic logic of the security dilemma takes the following form: This nation is legitimately entitled to some interest (such as continued existence); the world's political processes cannot guarantee us that interest; therefore we are entitled to use any means, fair or foul, to guarantee it ourselves. The security dilemma logic is simply one version of the classic claim that the end justifies the means. As such it is not unique to international relations; it can be employed whenever there is a legitimate end that cannot be achieved by legitimate means. Now there are those who deny that the end can ever justify the means, and they will also reject the claim that a state is entitled to use any means at its disposal to protect its own security. To those who are open to the possibility that the end justifies the means, the anarchy logic makes perfect sense. Note, though, that the logic itself rests on moral premises (and controversial ones) about ends and means. Most important for present purposes, moreover, even people who believe that the end justifies the means find the argument appealing only where the end itself is acknowledged as worthy. In this respect the self-help argument necessarily rests both on moral beliefs about ends and means and on unexpressed normative premises about what ends are worthy of protection.

To put it another way, a system is self-help where there are interests that are worthy of protection but do not receive it. The term *self-help* is reserved for situations in which the powers that be fail to protect what are perceived as morally compelling claims to security or property. A hegemonic system should be characterized as self-help if and only if legitimate interests go unprotected. To show that some system is a self-help regime, one must show that there is a discrepancy between what a governance system *does* provide and what it *should* provide. In most domestic societies, the discrepancy is not too large, so the term *self-help* is not employed.

We noted earlier that there has been serious disagreement over whether it is fair to charge realists, as a group, with amoralism. One of the reasons for that disagreement should now be clear. Certain of the classical realists, such as Hans Morgenthau, were highly sensitive to the question that we have just been addressing, namely, the legitimacy of a state's interests. Their opposition to the Vietnam War was founded in large part on the conviction that no legitimate interests of the United States were at stake in that war, and that it was therefore wrong of the United States to get involved.[41] While the ends can justify the means, this is so only if the ends are themselves legitimate. This objection cannot be met by citing goals the realists would have deemed illegitimate, such as promoting world capitalism, extending U.S. dominion over Asia, or maintaining corrupt allies in power in South Vietnam. In the realists view, U.S. actions should be tied to goals such as the territorial security of the United States, which they recognize as valid. The normative limitation to the furtherance of *legitimate* objectives provides the necessary critical purchase to ground an attack on U.S. policy.

Not all realists have been inclined to distinguish between legitimate interests (which self-help may be used to defend) and other interests (as to which self-help is inappropriate). Indeed, the willingness to insist that interests be legitimate may be limited to classical realists, whose philosophical compunctions found no particularly friendly reception among later "neorealist" writers. Waltz and Art, for example, claim that every state must be free to define its own interests as it sees fit.[42] But by resisting the claim that states should be entitled to use self-help only to pursue legitimate interests, such arguments make it impossible to differentiate international from domestic affairs. For in both international and domestic politics some interests go unprotected, and indeed the same would be so internationally even if a world government were created. Vulgar realism offers no explanation for why this makes the current international system, but not domestic society or world government, a self-help system. If "self-help" does not incorporate a distinction between legitimate and illegitimate interests, then individuals, like states, are entitled to define their interests however they choose; individuals, like states, will be aware that not all of their interests are guaranteed by authoritative political processes; and individuals, like states, will be entitled to use all means at their disposal to promote those unprotected interests.

Calling international society "self-help," then, is a normative judgment to the effect that current governance mechanisms are normatively inadequate. Implicit in this characterization is a notion of what legitimate governance (whether domestic or international) would look like, and a belief that it would protect certain interests that currently go without official protection. While a hegemon may effectively protect its own interests and enforce the norms it finds advantageous, international affairs is nonetheless self-help so long as the hegemon does not guarantee sovereignty, territorial integrity, enforcement of international agreements, and other things that would be secure if a legitimate world government existed. International affairs are not called self-help merely because on *some* issues the only remedy is self-help; the same could be said of domestic affairs. They are called a self-help system, instead, because self-help is required even on issues as to which enforcement should be available. The self-help characterization, in other words, is another way of saying that no *legitimate* international government exists.

LEGITIMACY AND WORLD ANARCHY

But definitions of anarchy that turn on legitimate government and self-help pose problems of their own. The first is that they do not really differentiate domestic from international society. As Helen Milner points out, many domestic governments are utterly lacking in legitimacy.[43] This is, of course, the same difficulty that plagued the empirical definitions of anarchy: an inability to categorically distinguish international from domestic systems.

Waltz's reasoning is somewhat curious in this respect. As mentioned earlier, Waltz considers and rejects the possibility of defining anarchy in terms of the presence of violence. He rejects the definition because there are violent domestic regimes such as the Soviet Union under Stalin, Germany under Hitler, and Uganda under Idi Amin. One paragraph later, however, he concludes that the difference between the two settings must be that domestic governments are legitimate and use force in legitimate ways, while no legitimate international government exists.[44] This is a peculiar conclusion to follow immediately on the heels of references to Amin's Uganda, Stalinist Russia, and Hitler's Germany.

This is also where Waltz argues that the difference between domestic and international systems turns on self-help. "An effective [domestic] government . . . has a monopoly on the *legitimate* use of force, and legitimate here means that public agents are organized to prevent and to counter the private use of force. Citizens need not prepare to defend themselves. Public agencies do that."[45] But, as with a definition based on legitimacy, the categorical distinction between domestic and international affairs does not hold up. Jews, gays, leftists, and gypsies must certainly have experienced Nazi Germany as a self-help regime, one in which they were unfortunately quite poorly positioned to help themselves.[46] Waltz's generalization to the contrary, public agencies certainly did little to defend them. The legitimacy and self-help criteria are quite unable to fill the role that Waltz envisions for them: to differentiate domestic from international politics.

Once again, there is a tendency to cast the best light on domestic affairs (by presuming legitimacy) but the worst on international affairs (by presuming illegitimacy). Waltz seems to be using a double standard for determining whether some state of affairs is an anarchy: one standard for domestic systems and another internationally. Domestically, he asks only that a government of some sort exist; legitimacy is then conclusively presumed. Amin's Uganda, Stalinist Russia, and Hitler's Germany pass this test. Internationally, however, he requires actual legitimacy. Waltz is trying to show that international and domestic order are different, that the former is anarchic and the latter is not. But he does this by imposing a different, and more demanding, test in the international setting than the domestic.

There is, in addition, something very odd about the way the entire argument fits together. Morality, presumably including political morality (since Waltz does not say otherwise), is said to be irrelevant in anarchy.[47] Anarchy exists where there is no legitimate government. Putting these two principles together, we find that morality is irrelevant wherever there is no legitimate government. But where morality (including political morality) is irrelevant, the political institutions that do exist (such as hegemons) *do not need to be legitimate*. This means that one can never criticize a government as illegitimate, because if one is correct that the government is illegitimate, then moral standards do not apply because there is a state of anarchy. The argument in effect uses the fact that the world political leader is illegitimate to argue that it need not be legitimate. Note how strange this argument would sound in the context of domestic governance. Because Hitler's government was illegitimate, Germany was an anarchy and therefore political morality was irrelevant. Because South Africa's apartheid government is illegitimate, it is an anarchy; thus it need not be legitimate. The argument is equally strange in the international context.

A final problem with legitimacy-based definitions returns us directly to the claim that there are no norms in a state of anarchy. The reason that there must be norms even in a state of anarchy (as Waltz defines it) should by now be obvious. The definition of anarchy is itself normative; how then can it be argued that normative analysis is inappropriate in international relations? The definition is normative because it relies on the concept of *legitimacy* in international government. Certainly, if it is possible to assess whether an existing international structure is legitimate, it must be possible to evaluate international concentrations of power. Even if no other issues are subject to normative scrutiny, it must be possible to evaluate the legitimacy of hegemony, because the anarchy characterization presupposes an ability to distinguish legitimate from illegitimate world government. One need only apply the standards of "legitimacy" that Waltz himself contemplates.[48]

HORIZONTAL AND VERTICAL RELATIONS

Much of the difficulty with all of these definitions of anarchy can be traced to the failure to differentiate horizontal relations between states of roughly equal power from vertical relations of subordination between a powerful state and a powerless one. The moral responsibilities of less powerful states is a different issue from the moral responsibilities of the more powerful. It is necessary, in other words, to distinguish between personal morality and political morality. The realist argument that international morality cannot exist in a state of anarchy is best equipped to deal with relations between equals.[49] Because international affairs is portrayed as a system of formal equals, the realists feel no need to concern themselves with vertical relations of power. The anarchy argument that they craft, for this reason, is not well suited to address such interactions.

The clearest evidence that the anarchy argument is formulated with relations between equals in mind is the empirical definition of anarchy that realist authors such as Waltz have offered. Waltz claims that international morality is nonexistent or irrelevant because international relations is a state of anarchy and anarchy means lack of hierarchy or diffusion of power. He then contrasts international with domestic affairs, characterizing only the latter as "vertical."[50] The world that he seeks to model, clearly, is a world of equal players. He does not seek to capture in his analysis the fact that some players are powerful enough systematically to dominate others militarily.

Of course, all model building is a process of simplification; sometimes much greater clarity and insight can be achieved by focusing on a few features of a complicated real-world situation and disregarding the rest. But the problem here is whether the features which have been selected for incorporation into the model include all of the really important ones, or whether on the contrary other key features have been left out. One of the features that Waltz has chosen not to include turns out to be central for normative purposes: the power differential between the leading states of the world and the subordinate ones.[51] The anomalous aspects of the anarchy argument that we have identified above stem from the fact that the model does not differentiate relations between equals from subordinate / superior relations.

Take, for example, the odd fact that (according to Waltz and others) morality is irrelevant in anarchy, but that the way to determine whether anarchy exists is to make an essentially normative judgment (namely, whether there is a legitimate government). Clearly, Waltz expects us to be able to make normative judgments about whether some dominant power is exercising legitimate power over the other states; a negative answer to this question is key to the anarchy characterization. And states are expected to act on the outcome of this determination, for the existence of anarchy and therefore the applicability of international morality turn on this factor. But Waltz does not presume an ability to make normative judgments about how to deal with other states of roughly equal power. That ability would exist only within a legitimate governance system and not in a state of anarchy. Implicitly, then, Waltz is treating these two sorts of normative judgments as very different, for the first type is always possible (even in an anarchy), while the second is not.

It makes a certain amount of sense to differentiate the normative question of whether morality exists between coequal actors from the (equally normative) question of whether a legitimate government exists. Certainly a difference exists in the domestic context. If a domestic government were sufficiently illegitimate and oppressive, individuals might be absolved of some or all of the responsibilities that they would ordinarily have. For example, Nazi Germany was for its Jewish citizens enough of a Hobbesian "anarchy," or self-help regime, that they might well be thought entitled to disregard many aspects of conventional morality in order to preserve their own lives. Their obligations to the state itself, in particular, were at an end, but so might be their moral debts to other private citizens. Where one's life is at stake, the end may justify the means. Yet accepting this argument in no way commits one to the notion that morality as a whole was irrelevant in Nazi Germany, and especially not to the notion that the government itself should be immune to arguments of political morality. While the situation of the Jews and gypsies might well be described as "anarchy," the government could not plead "anarchy" itself as a reason for disregarding basic morality.

The same distinction between the morality of powerful and powerless actors applies internationally. The fact that the dominant power is illegitimate may provide an excuse to lesser powers, who find themselves caught in an anarchic self-help regime. The dominant power itself, however, cannot make the same "anarchy" argument to deny its own moral responsibilities. It is misleading, perhaps, to talk about the existence of international morality as a whole; powerful actors may have moral obligations even when the less powerful do not. The "no morality in anarchy argument" seems to apply equally to all normative judgments, but even vulgar realists cannot mean it that way, given their assumption that it is possible to evaluate international governance.

This distinction between the responsibilities of the more and less powerful state makes sense when one keeps in mind what the anarchy argument is all about. When the subject is horizontal relations between states of roughly equal power, there are important reasons to ask the question that Waltz asks, whether there is a legitimate source of authority. When a state is considering taking action and wants to know whether it is doing the right thing, it may be important for it to know whether it is subject to some legitimate government. If it is, it should then ask whether that government has promulgated any standards that cover the contemplated action, and if so, what they provide. To determine that there is no such superior authority is to remove one set of potential factors from consideration: the norms of superior authority. For this reason, it does indeed make sense, in examining whether a state is bound by international norms, to ask whether they were promulgated by a superior body. A state should ask whether there is any body to look up to as authoritative.

But this is not the only normative issue in international relations. A state might have moral obligations for a different reason; not because there is some superior authority which has promulgated rules, but because it is more powerful than other actors and has a responsibility to exercise power in a morally legitimate way. These latter obligations do not depend on the presence of some powerful third party to promulgate and enforce them. If they did, then governments would never have moral responsibilities in their domestic dealings, because there is no powerful third party to oversee their dealings with their citizens. All of political morality would have to be abandoned, even as it applies to a state's domestic affairs.

Vertical domestic relations are similar to vertical international relations in that there is no authoritative neutral third party to arbitrate disputes.[52] Where citizens claim a right against their domestic government which the government refuses to recognize, there is no independent authority to whom they can turn to resolve the difference. There is no guarantee that if they behave morally then the government will do so as well. (Nor is there a guarantee to the government that if it behaves properly, so will it citizens.) Similarly, in the international arena there is no authoritative mediator for hegemon/subordinate disputes. Both domestic and international vertical relations are, in this sense, equally in a condition of "anarchy." It would be possible to claim, with Machiavelli, that that principle is inapplicable to domestic relations as well as to international ones. This position has the virtue of consistency. But it makes no sense to treat international vertical relations as anarchical, and thus not subject to norms, while insisting that domestic vertical relations are norm-bound.

MORAL DILEMMAS AND SECURITY DILEMMAS

I said earlier that there were two main strands to the anarchy argument, one a jurisprudential claim that without centralized government there is no source of norms, the other a structural claim that states find themselves in a security dilemma. Neither of these is persuasive as applied to vertical relations.

This is particularly clear with regard to the jurisprudential argument. If we were to apply the jurisprudential argument to domestic vertical relations, then there would be no way of determining whether domestic governments were legitimate. Where would the standards come from? The only positive source for norms is the government itself. But it makes no sense to apply standards that the government itself has promulgated; this would allow a state to bootstrap itself into legitimacy. Standards of legitimacy have to come from somewhere outside the government, but the jurisprudential argument denies that such sources exist.

Indeed, in both the domestic and the international contexts, applying the jurisprudential argument to vertical relationships would lead to infinite regress. The relationship between two actors is said to be governed by morality only if there is some legitimate third party of higher authority. But how do we know whether the third party is legitimate? There must be some source for the norms by which legitimacy is to be judged. But where do these come from? By the anarchy argument's own terms, they must come from some higher body. But this means that there must be some higher power, a fourth party, to promulgate the norms by which to evaluate the third party. And so on, ad infinitum. The jurisprudential argument simply cannot accommodate the fact that we need to make, and customarily do make, moral judgments about political actors at the top of the hierarchy (whether domestic or international.)

The second part of the anarchy argument is structural; it points to the security dilemma with which states are confronted in the international arena. This argument, really, is the crux of the matter, the central element of the realist critique of international morality. The argument is that states cannot afford to follow international norms, because they will be subject to the predations of other states that do not. International relations is the realm of self-help. Yet this argument also is unpersuasive as applied to vertical relations.[53]

For the same argument could be made about a domestic government; it also has no third party to turn to if it is threatened from within. If the structural argument is taken seriously, it will always immunize actors at the top of the hierarchy from moral scrutiny, because these actors have no higher power to turn to if they are threatened.[54] But this seems perverse; if anything, the more powerful actors should be subject to higher moral scrutiny, not lower. The actors at the top of the hierarchy are powerful enough that they do not need such assurances before they can be required to act in a morally defensible way. The absence of a powerful third party to protect them means that they must fall back on self-help, but that is not too much to demand of the most powerful actors.

Precisely because it is the leading world power, the hegemon is far less susceptible to threats from other nations. Hedley Bull was merely stating the obvious when he wrote: "Great Powers have been secure against the attacks of small Powers; and have had to fear only other Great Powers, and hostile combinations of Powers. We have only to think of the security enjoyed by Great Britain in the nineteenth century to appreciate that the insecurity which is a feature of the Hobbesian state of nature, insofar as it exists in international society, is not distributed equally among all its members."[55] There are few circumstances in which the hegemon must genuinely fear for its national security. Particularly in its vertical relations—relations, that is, with the weaker powers over which it predominates—it cannot usually claim to be putting its national survival at risk. Consider, for example, the American invasions of Panama and Grenada. Panama and Grenada hardly posed tremendous security risks for the United States. The security dilemma argument tends to show, once again, that the anarchy argument is directed at relations between comparable powers, for the security threats with which the argument is concerned come largely from equals.

Here, however, the question must be raised whether it really makes sense to treat even a hegemonic power as relatively immune to security risks. For one thing, an alliance of smaller powers might be enough to threaten even the world's leading state. In addition, we have used the term *hegemony* to include regional hegemony; this means that there may be other hegemonic powers in other parts of the world with comparable military capacities. Although the United States was the world's leading power after the Second World War, it was still subject to genuine military threats from the Soviet Union. The same was true of Great Britain in the last century; despite its great power, it would have had to fear a coalition of other European nations. To call some state a hegemon is not to say that it is so powerful as to be completely immune from security risks.

Vertical conflicts between the greater and lesser powers, moreover, are shaped by these horizontal conflicts between rough equals. Take, for example, the American mining of Nicaraguan harbors. Superficially, this example seems similar to the invasions of Panama and Grenada; the hegemon was operating within its sphere of influence. But of course our activities in Nicaragua were much more a product of American/Soviet relations than of our attitudes toward Nicaragua itself. At issue is not just a vertical relation between a powerful and a less powerful state, but a horizontal one between rough equals. The same is true, of course, of the Cuban missile blockade; while immediately directed against Cuba, the motivating conflict was the rivalry between the United States and the Soviet Union.

But the fact that genuine security risks can arise in vertical relations does not mean that such relations are off limits to international political morality. Domestic governments also are vulnerable, despite the fact that they are substantially more powerful than any of their individual citizens. Their vertical relations with their citizens are often colored by horizontal threats from other powerful nations; and they are vulnerable to purely domestic threats, such as organized rebellion by their subjects. The fact that some problem raises national security concerns does not put an end to moral discussion; it is just the beginning. The problem with the structural anarchy argument, in other words, is by now a familiar one: it fails to maintain the sharp distinction between domestic and international affairs on which the anarchy characterization seems to depend. There are also *domestic* problems in which the continued viability of government is at stake. And these pose moral issues. In both domestic and international politics, the question whether the end justifies the means (or whether it does so in some particular case) *is a moral question.*

During the Second World War, as Robert Holmes reminds us, the American government feared a Japanese invasion on the West Coast, and thousands of Japanese-American citizens were interned in camps because it was believed that national security was at stake.[56] "If the overriding concern is with the preservation of the state," he argues, "what does it matter whether a threat is external or internal?"[57] The Japanese internment example, of course, arose in the course of a war; but there are also purely domestic crises that threaten the very existence of states. In Peru, for example, the government is threatened by a domestic movement, the Sendero Luminoso. Similarly, the Algerian government has recently faced fundamentalist Islamic movements that threaten (the government claims) the very existence of democracy in Algeria. The stated fear is that if the fundamentalists are voted into office, they will abolish the constitution and democratic electoral processes. The Italian government is unable to control Mafia activities; American police are unable to control the drug trade. In all of these cases, a choice must be made about whether to adopt tactics that offend individual rights and democratic values or whether to act less forcefully and remain vulnerable to the consequent risks. In all of these cases, we face the difficult moral question of whether the end justifies the means.

The moral difficulties raised in such situations are enormous. Should the government apply moral principles straightforwardly, even though the heavens may fall? Should it balance the national interest that it is trying to protect against the rights of innocent persons? Is it ever permissible to suspend democratic processes to protect democracy in the long run? How certain must one be of impending disaster before taking action? There are no easy choices in such situations. But the strategy of simply ignoring the moral issues is as extreme, and unacceptable, as the simplistic moralism that the realists condemn.

CONCLUSION

The anarchy argument that moral principles do not apply to international relations relies on oversimplified notions of morality, of international affairs, and of domestic politics as well. It oversimplifies morality by equating it with simplistic moralism. Moral theory rarely deals with easy problems that can be resolved by application of simplistic moral rules. Its traditional domain, instead, is difficult dilemmas in which principles and interests conflict. There are, of course, differences of opinion about how to accommodate competing interests consistently with morality; one might take the utopian position that self-interest and security are irrelevant and that abstract and unyielding principles are all that matter. But a moral person need not; wholesale rejection of morality is therefore out of place.

The anarchy argument also oversimplifies international relations. Its version of the international system is that power is diffuse rather than centralized, that equality rather than hierarchy is standard. Certainly there is diffusion of power at some times and in certain parts of the international system. But at other times and places, hierarchy is a better description. It is a mistake to generalize from the former cases, ignoring the latter. International relations theory needs to deal with both. It is equally mistaken to become mesmerized by one's own formalizations, which capture elements of sovereign-state equality but leave unmentioned consistent power differentials.

The anarchy argument, finally, oversimplifies domestic politics, probably in order to maintain the sharpest possible contrast with international relations. Domestic political relations are portrayed as centralized, ordered, hierarchical, and legitimate. Sometimes they are. But they are also sometimes chaotic, illegitimate, disorderly—and anarchical. Domestic regimes, moreover, can be vulnerable internally in many of the same ways that they are vulnerable externally. The "security dilemma" which realists describe between states is not unique to international affairs. States also face security risks in their dealings with their own citizens, and political morality must face the question of what to do in such circumstances.

The anarchy argument is phrased as an objection to applying moral principles to international relations. But in fact it is corrosive of all morality, domestic as well as international. Its logic would lead to the conclusion that the strongest actor in the system is never subject to moral censure. It seems to suggest that moral principles are irrelevant whenever no authority exists to ensure satisfaction of one's preferences, even though domestically there are many sorts of interests that are not guaranteed by states. Where security is at stake, it seems to hold, moral principles are completely irrelevant—even though security concerns also arise domestically. The anarchy argument essentially holds that whenever a genuinely difficult issue arises, morality just drops out of the picture. But the prime objective of morality, including political morality, is to deal with genuinely difficult problems.

Of course, the simple claim that political morality applies to international relations does not tell very much about what moral principles there are or what they require. These principles must be specified and their international application clarified before any concrete results will emerge. What would political morality require in the international context? What are the moral responsibilities of a liberal democracy that finds itself the sole world superpower? The bulk of the work is still before us.

PART TWO

A LIBERAL THEORY

OF INTERNATIONAL

HEGEMONY

3

GLOBAL

LIBERALISM

How is it possible to justify international hegemony? Hegemony seems quintessentially autocratic, based on power rather than principle. It self-evidently violates the autonomy of the less powerful nations and is incompatible with the principle of sovereign equality of states.[1] If any principles might be taken to be constitutive of the international normative order, they would be sovereign autonomy and sovereign equality. How could an international order that violates both of these principles ever be morally acceptable?

In domestic politics, we should keep in mind, the same conundrum arises. Hierarchies abound, despite our domestic commitments to analogous principles of personal autonomy and equality. Despite the general acceptance of those principles, all but a small group of anarchists agree that domestic political hierarchies are in some circumstances justifiable. The central question, of course, is why and in what situations a justification exists. Domestic political theory attempts to answer these questions, and the next four chapters carry over into the international arena some of the answers that domestic liberalism offers.

It is, of course, contentious to define what "liberalism" means in domestic politics. We will consider below a varied menu of liberal approaches, from libertarian to Rawlsian. Two common themes link the theories we will characterize as "liberal." The first is the emphasis on democratic participation, with governance resting on some form of popular consent. The second is the protection of a particular set of substantive human rights from oppression even by majorities. Both of these are important but different, and they play out in different ways in the international applications below. There are important philosophical debates about what forms of participation are needed, what substantive rights must be protected, and how to balance these considerations when they come in conflict. Providing a definitive account of liberal theory, though, is not my project.[2]

My object instead is to explore liberalism's potential as a justification for international hegemony. To what extent can U.S. hegemony be explained in terms that are consistent with its domestic political values? In important respects, the next four chapters will draw on conventional notions about what would make American hegemony morally justifiable. At the most immediate level, we will simply try to collect and systematize existing intuitions about international morality, developing their strengths and fitting them together into a coherent pattern. We will be working with the responses that come immediately to mind when American initiatives are challenged. In fitting these together, I will borrow from conventional liberal ideas about the relationship between domestic citizens and their governments, pointing out how these are reflected in existing arguments about international morality.

In important respects, however, a deeper critical agenda will emerge. First, we will see that none of the rationales examined here is itself without problems. While it is important to build as strong a case as possible for all the rationales discussed, it is also important not to overlook their failings. To some degree, in fact, it is the deficiencies of each that drives us to consider the next. Second, we will return in part 3 to take a critical look at the entire project. The next four chapters assume that what is needed is an explanation for the relations between the hegemon and weak states that mirrors the explanation for relations between government and citizens. It assumes, in other words, that liberalism can be satisfied in a model which treats states as the relevant actors. Indeed, the tendency to treat states as the relevant actors is strongly entrenched in existing commonsensical notions of international justification. Part 3 suggests that this statist model may itself be incompatible with liberalism, and for reasons that highlight liberalism's own weaknesses.

Before turning our attention to the critical argument, however, the positive case for a liberal theory of international hegemony must be presented. It is possible to deduce what sorts of factors would make hegemony most consistent with liberal principles by starting with a case in which American intervention was widely approved when it was undertaken: the U.S. action in Somalia. Even many of the usual critics of American overseas involvement were relatively accepting, at the time, of the U.S. efforts to establish order and bring relief supplies to that country.[3] There are several aspects of the Somalian intervention that explain why it was far less controversial when initiated than American interventions elsewhere. The first is that it seemed generally to be welcomed by the Somali people. Not all of them wanted U.S. intervention, of course, because it threatened the existing power structure of the Somali warlords. But the vast bulk of the population seemed to welcome it, and there was no Somali government in place to object. The importance of this fact to the legitimacy of American actions is suggested by the way the United States has tried to depict the population as welcoming in some past interventions (the Panama invasion, for example) and the state itself as having asked for our assistance in others (as in Vietnam). The change in American attitude toward the intervention in Somalia during the first year after its initiation is explainable in part, moreover, by the changing American perceptions about whether the Somalian people wanted us there. What matters, then, under this justification for American hegemony is the consent of the target state and its people. Chapter 4 deals with what we will call contemporaneous consent.

The intervention in Somalia was also both multilateral and supported by the United Nations. During the Persian Gulf war, President George Bush had made much of the fact that the United States was working through legitimate international channels; it had obtained the approval of the Security Council and the publicly offered basis for acting was violation of the U.N. Charter and other international norms prohibiting territorial aggression. These international norms and institutions are authoritative because they were established in advance by the entire world community. The U.S. intervention in Somalia, similarly, was justified because it followed procedures that were agreed to beforehand by the involved parties. Chapter 5 addresses what we will call *ex ante* consent.

Whether or not the world community has agreed to American leadership, it can nonetheless be argued that it is enormously beneficial to the world community that some strong state take charge. In Somalia, it can be claimed, what matters is not so much whether other states agreed to strong state leadership as the fact that strong state leadership was necessary for the public good. The benefits of international peace and stability require international governance for the same reasons that the benefits of domestic peace and stability require domestic governance. Somalia, in fact, itself illustrated the costs of anarchy. Whether or not American leadership was agreed to, it was a rational solution to the problem, a solution that rational states would have agreed to. I will deal with this argument in chapter 6, under the rubric "hypothetical consent."

Finally, chapter 7 addresses the simple claim that intervention in Somalia was justified by the urgent need to save large numbers of people from death by starvation. The human suffering there was simply beyond the comprehension of most Westerners; it challenged us as human beings to do something to help. I will deal with these straightforward arguments of human rights and basic subsistence needs under the category of substantive morality. What matters here is not so much what anyone has agreed to, but what basic moral principles require. One feels that it is simply not morally acceptable to sit by while people die for utterly preventable reasons.

Each chapter starts by trying to build the positive case for the theoretical justification that it deals with. Only when the positive case is complete will the discussion turn to the theory's weaknesses. In all four cases, the weaknesses are substantial; despite the arguments' intuitive appeal, their foundations are seriously flawed. But it is necessary to spell out the positive cases in some detail before turning critical. Despite their flaws, these four arguments in some sense capture important parts of the liberal political argument. They resonate with liberal values, and it is important to understand their successes as well as their failures. There are reasons for the appeal of the arguments.

It is not possible to consider all the philosophical subtleties of these various forms of liberal argument. The subtleties have occupied many pages of scholarly journals, and many of the questions that the scholars raise remain unanswered. Rather than attempt a sophisticated contribution to the domestic political theory literature per se, we will concentrate on the general contours of the relevant debates and on how those debates impact on international morality. With each of the theories we describe, we will ask how it applies to international situations, show that it conforms to some extent with existing intuitions about international justification, and acknowledge that the international applications have problems that would be largely familiar to domestic political theorists.

Liberalism, in some respects, presents international hegemony with its greatest challenge. Liberalism includes a strong commitment to equality; hierarchies are suspect. This does not mean that hierarchy cannot be justified, for liberalism recognizes hierarchy as valid in many instances. It simply means that justification must be given and that the justification must comport with liberal principles. Liberalism also includes a commitment to liberty, which makes the coercive power of the hegemon prima facie problematic. It would be far easier (and less interesting) to justify international hegemony in terms of a more authoritarian political philosophy, one in which hierarchies were treated as God-given. To the extent that liberalism succeeds in justifying international hegemony, the hardest case has been made.[4]

The commitment to liberalism, though, is only provisional. Part 3 adopts a stance that is more critical of liberal premises, and in particular of liberal notions of state identity and consent. These two notions are key to the liberal arguments that we will be investigating in part 2, and they deserve extra scrutiny. But their importance cannot be properly appreciated without first developing the liberal point of view itself. The next four chapters, accordingly, set out both positive and negative features of American hegemony, but from a perspective internal to liberalism. There is a surprisingly strong liberal case to be made for American hegemony—not a completely convincing one, to be sure, but one that is more convincing than might be expected given the appeal of the norms of sovereign autonomy and equality.

4

CONTEMPORANEOUS

CONSENT

Consent is a potent and obvious liberal tool for rationalizing America's vast power in contemporary international relations. It is a potent rationalization because where genuine consent exists, it comes fairly close—perhaps as close as any theory could—to settling the major normative issues. For liberals, it is not clear why anyone would have a right to object to American leadership so long as all nations consent. There is no coercion where American actions are entirely consensual.

Consent is also an obvious rationalization, because there seem to be many occasions when the United States uses persuasion and inducement rather than force. Indeed, it would seem that persuasion and inducement would be the favored techniques of foreign policy, for obtaining the agreement of other states typically reduces domestic controversy, deflects unfavorable international opinion, and minimizes the danger of provoking an international incident. It would certainly be an exaggeration to defend all American actions as consensual; it is easy to think of important situations where other nations objected to U.S. actions. Yet consent is a good place to start; and we will return to nonconsensual exercise of power in the chapters that follow.

The sort of consent investigated in this chapter is contemporaneous consent: consent that is given at roughly the same time as the American action in question. In the next chapter, we will examine ex ante consent, which consists of prior generalized consent to norms of conduct. From a normative perspective the two are rather different. Most of what is termed "consent theory" in political philosophy deals with ex ante, rather than contemporaneous, consent; discussion of traditional consent theory, therefore, is postponed until the next chapter. Here we will deal with a much simpler notion, one which does not involve the use of coercive power.

Indeed, it might even be said that instances of contemporaneous consent do not pose problems of political legitimacy at all. They look more like instances of market exchange, which many liberals would characterize as an economic rather than a political phenomenon. Why, then, should we even have to discuss contemporaneous consent? Contemporaneous consent, it might be said, does not pose a problem of political justification precisely because it is not coercive. There is some merit to this suggestion, but there are reasons not to follow it.

For contemporaneous consent is an important phenomenon to investigate even if this argument is correct. There are two ways to view the issue. One might say either that contemporaneous exchange is not political, because it is not coercive, or that contemporaneous exchange is political but justifiable, because it is not coercive. The former claim restricts the domain of political criticism; it "solves" the problem by declaring certain issues off limits. The reason, of course, is not totally arbitrary; certain actions need not be justified because they are consensual. But the effect, nonetheless, is to restrict the domain of inquiry. If we take the second path, in contrast, we have not made everything hinge on prior definitional fiat. But one must still explain why it matters that the actions are agreed to. The end result in either case would be the same; whether consensual actions are acceptable because consent means that something *need not be justified* or because consent means that something *is justified*, the operative normative issue is whether consent was given.

This claim—that legitimacy is assured when contemporaneous consent is given—is the subject of the present chapter. It is a plausible claim, especially to those who by and large are comfortable with liberalism. Those who do not consider themselves liberals, especially those who incline toward a more critical stance, are less likely to be satisfied with consensual explanations. We will examine two different sorts of criticisms of justifications based on contemporaneous consent. Some criticisms are internal to liberalism; while taking liberal premises seriously, they doubt that contemporaneous consent is always an adequate justification. Others are external; they attack the heart of liberal premises. This chapter focuses largely on the internal critique in order to determine what a liberal should conclude about American hegemony. But we will try in addition to identify the major places where an external critique would engage with liberal assumptions, and we will return to these issues in part 3.

DIPLOMACY, BRIBERY, AND SANCTIONS

There are, roughly speaking, three overlapping ways of using power that could plausibly be characterized as consensual.[1] They are: diplomacy or persuasion, bribery or positive inducements, and sanctions or negative inducements. These three are typically tied together, for successful diplomacy often relies on inducements (positive and negative) and inducements are usually communicated through diplomatic channels. Access to all three of these instruments of power, moreover, is typically correlated with a state's economic strength. Now that there is general agreement in the international community that military means of settling disputes are in most cases illegitimate, greater attention has been paid to economic means.[2] All three instrumentalities, in other words, are linked to the notion of exchange.

DIPLOMACY The United States has often worked its will through diplomacy. Diplomacy is used to persuade other nations to cooperate with American goals, sometimes merely by demonstrating to other nations the advantages that cooperation is claimed to offer. While bribery and sanctions often lurk in the background, diplomacy proceeds in part by altering the participants' perceptions of their own interests.

In some circumstances, diplomacy consists of persuading two or more nations to resolve their differences with one another. In others, diplomacy involves persuading a state that if it follows some line of decision, it will become internationally isolated. Sometimes diplomacy means convincing reluctant parties that they must be willing to negotiate with one another face to face. Often it means convincing them that they must be willing to compromise if they are to have a chance to secure their objectives. The marshalling of facts, the making of arguments, the application of pressure to try to understand the other's point of view as well as one's own—these are tools of diplomacy.

A good example of American diplomacy is the Camp David peace accords between Egypt and Israel. The accords, signed in 1978 and 1979, were a product of the Carter administration's efforts to reach a comprehensive settlement of the

Middle East conflict. While the accords have not (at least not yet) become the basis of a full-fledged resolution of the dispute between Israel and the Arab countries, they did manage to put an official end to the state of war between two of the disputants. Israel agreed to withdraw from the Sinai Peninsula; Egypt agreed to establish normal diplomatic relations with Israel and to allow Israel freedom of navigation through the Suez Canal.[3] The United States is currently continuing its diplomatic efforts in the Middle East; another somewhat comparable example of diplomacy was the Vance-Owen peace talks seeking to end the fighting in the former Yugoslavia.

Even when diplomacy seems to be operating for the benefit of the parties that the United States brings together, we should not overlook how it expands American power. Most obviously, the United States would not be trying to bring the parties together if their reconciliation were not somehow to U.S. advantage. The eventual agreement can be shaped to reflect U.S. interests if the United States is active in bringing it about. More intangibly, diplomacy adds to a nation's prestige in the world community. U.S. diplomacy increases the chances that, when the next crisis emerges, the world community will look once more to the United States as a mediator. While the power advantages of diplomacy may sometimes seem remote or inchoate, they are nevertheless considerable.

BRIBERY The Middle East peace talks have also, over the years, illustrated two other methods of advancing U.S. objectives without the use of force: bribery and sanctions. Bribery is an often used method for "persuading" another nation to cooperate with U.S. goals. In the Camp David process, for example, Egypt received substantial U.S. aid guarantees in exchange for its willingness to break with other Arab nations and make peace with Israel.[4] Similarly, the United States has used development aid and favorable trade status as "carrots" in inducing other countries to cooperate in reducing supplies of drugs, pursuing terrorists, and allowing emigration to Israel.

An excellent example of U.S. bribery of other nations in pursuit of its foreign policy objectives is its cash payments for maintenance of American military bases on foreign territory. For many years, for example, the United States maintained two military operations on Philippine soil, one at Subic Bay and the other at Clark Air Force Base. The presence of large numbers of American military personnel on Philippine territory was a sensitive issue for the Philippine government, for many Filipinos saw the bases as a continued expression of American imperial attitudes toward the Philippines, which had from 1898 to 1946 been an American colony. The financial advantages to the country were, however, substantial. In addition to the business the bases created for the local economy (a mixed blessing, without a doubt, given the nature of businesses that tend to thrive near military bases), the United States provided payments of hundreds of millions of dollars annually. The political unpopularity of the bases finally triumphed over the financial benefits in 1992, as the Philippine Senate decided to terminate the arrangement.[5]

SANCTIONS The mirror image of bribery, of course, is sanctions. Bribery involves positive inducement, while sanctions involve negative inducement. Not all sanctions should be characterized as consensual; whether sanctions can be justified on a theory of contemporaneous consent depends on what the sanctions are. If the United States deprives another nation, against its will, of some benefit to which that state is entitled, then the sanction cannot be justified under a theory of contemporaneous consent. But sometimes sanctions involve deprivation of a benefit that the other nation is not already entitled to. Contemporaneous consent explains why the United States may threaten to cut off a benefit that it is currently providing, or to cancel one the other nation is hoping to receive but which the United States has no obligation to supply.

This point is illustrated by the dispute over loan guarantees to Israel. American guarantees have enabled Israel to obtain loans at a more favorable rate of interest, but they have been criticized as helping Israel to free up additional domestic funds to build settlements in the occupied territories. In 1992 the Bush administration wished to take more forceful steps to dissuade Israel from further building in the occupied West Bank; the settlements, the administration felt, were substantially undermining the Middle East peace process. Supporters of the Israeli settlement policy, both in Israel and in the United States, protested bitterly what they saw as coercive intervention in domestic Israeli affairs. Of course, from the perspective of the Bush administration, the United States was not engaged in making illegitimate threats. It was simply stating that it did not plan to provide a benefit that Israel wanted, a benefit to which some of Israel's supporters (according to the Bush administration view) had come rather inappropriately to feel a virtual entitlement.[6]

Another example of the use of sanctions concerns the continuing dispute over whether the United States should deny the People's Republic of China most favored nation status on the grounds that it had not sufficiently improved the human rights climate in the country.[7] After Tiananmen Square, domestic pressure groups urged Congress and the President to sanction Beijing for the crackdown by holding back on trade liberalization. From the U.S. point of view, such sanctions would not have been "coercive" because China had no preexisting right to most favored nation status. The issue was mooted in 1992 when the Bush administration blocked congressional efforts to deny MFN status to penalize the Chinese on human rights grounds. In 1993 the Clinton administration decided to continue MFN status, with a warning to China that its human rights record would have to improve within the next twelve months.

These three techniques of foreign policy—diplomacy, bribery, and sanctions—are ubiquitous. "Wielding money as a club to induce other states to alter their internal or international policies can be a tricky proposition, but it is frequently adopted. In recent years, the United States has, for example, denied trade benefits to Paraguay because of systematic human rights abuses there, invoked 'Super 301' trade sanctions against Japan because of its failure to adopt policies that would lead to higher levels of American exports, and suspended aid and other payments to Panama because of acrimony with the Noriega regime."[8] Other mixtures of incentives and persuasion include debt-for-nature swaps, the 1990 arrangements to provide loans and credits to the Soviet Union in exchange for its approval of NATO membership for a unified Germany, and the withdrawal of financial assistance after Yemen opposed the U.N. resolution approving the use of force against Iraq during the Persian Gulf war.[9]

Even if distinguishable in theory, diplomacy, bribery, and sanctions are rarely separable in practice. Diplomacy, obviously, typically involves incentives as well as factual arguments and persuasion. Israel and Egypt agreed to the Camp David accords in part because of the advantages they received from each other, but also because of the benefits they sought from the United States. Bribery and threats to withhold inducements are two sides of the same coin; an offer to provide a benefit if the target state cooperates is frequently also a threat not to provide the benefit if it does not. Whether a particular example is characterized as diplomacy, bribery, or sanctions, the basic underlying motivation of the parties is typically the possibility of a bargain.

What matters most for present purposes is the fact that opportunities for consensual exercise of international power are substantial, particularly for a state such as the United States which has substantial largesse to distribute. Contemporaneous consent is a potent liberal justification for the accumulation of international power. It is also a substantial tool in practice for achieving one's international objectives.

CONSENT AND INEQUALITY

Characterizing some particular foreign policy maneuver as consensual lends an air of egalitarianism that is substantially undeserved. "Bargaining" has connotations of symmetry, of quid pro quo, of benefits for all. As Kenneth Boulding puts it, "Exchange in its pure form is almost the antithesis of imperialism. It implies equality of status rather than inequality, for if A gives B something and B gives A something, they both stand at that moment on a equal footing. . . . The unctuous servility, for instance, of the merchant or the shopkeeper in the face of the king or aristocrat serves only to disguise and to make palatable the fundamental equality of the relationship."[10] But there is hardly universal assent to this description. Bargaining frequently takes place in a world of uneven resources and opportunity costs. The weaker party is likely to be consistently at a disadvantage, needing the benefits the stronger can provide much more than the stronger needs benefits from the weaker. Whether one chooses to call this phenomenon "heteronymous exchange"[11] or simply unequal bargaining power, the point is actually underscored by the very example that Boulding gives. For the "unctuous servility" he refers to strongly suggests that the inequality of the parties is the fundamental truth about the relationship, rather than an attempt to disguise the fundamental truth of party equality.

Even a strictly liberal analysis should recognize that the very subject matter of the exchange itself might be the power relationship between the parties. The weaker might be paid precisely to assume a subordinate position to the stronger. Employment contracts, for example, are voluntary bargains, but that doesn't mean that the employees of General Motors are the management's peers. The whole point of some consensual arrangements is to create or maintain a role of subordination: employees are hired to do what the management tells them to. From the fact that an arrangement is consensual, nothing should be assumed about whether the parties to it are equals, either before negotiations or after the agreement is concluded.

The tools of consensual foreign policy management are only available to nations, such as the United States, with considerable resources. The United States is of course not the only nation that uses inducements to achieve its foreign policy objectives; indeed, such activity is not limited to superpowers, as the wealthy Arab nations' use of the oil weapon clearly illustrates.[12] Nor is the United States the only nation that has engaged in diplomacy. To be truly successful in the use of these methods, however, one needs something to offer in exchange. A country that has limited resources above what it takes to survive is unlikely to be able to conceive grand strategies and carry them out through these methods.[13]

Two examples illustrate the potential of consensual methods for creating and sustaining international inequality. The first is the nuclear nonproliferation regime. The United States was the first nation to build nuclear weapons, with the Soviet Union following shortly thereafter. The current list of states with acknowledged nuclear weapons capability includes the United Kingdom, France, and China in addition to the original two.[14] Given both the threat of nuclear warfare and the possibilities that nuclear material might fall into the hands of terrorists, nonproliferation has been an important priority both for current nuclear weapons states and for states not themselves desiring to go nuclear but concerned about others that might.

Nonproliferation is currently the subject of a treaty regime that sharply distinguishes between nuclear and non-nuclear states. The main objective of the treaty regime is to keep the "nuclear club" from expanding. Non-nuclear states are supposed to be given access to peaceful nuclear technology in exchange for their cooperation. Whatever other prospects the world community may have for disarmament by existing nuclear weapon states, the nonproliferation regime itself does not endeavor to strip them of their nuclear weapons capabilities. Instead, it projects a two-tiered system into the indefinite future.

The regime is consensual in the sense that the primary means of preventing further spread of nuclear weapons is the withholding from non-nuclear states of something to which they have no prior entitlement: nuclear technology and materials.[15] No coercion is involved; the existing nuclear states, it is claimed, simply fail to provide weapons development assistance. But it is also clearly inegalitarian, in that it establishes a two-tiered system of "have" and "have-not" states. As one author emphasizes, "A major source of resentment towards U.S. nuclear policy on the part of non-nuclear weapon states involves the discriminatory nature of the present two-tiered nuclear order and the perceived reinforcement of the international status quo by U.S. nonproliferation policy. Although proliferation itself usually is not condoned as a means to reduce international inequities, there is a tendency on the part of the developing states to view U.S. nuclear policy in terms of North-South politics in which the less-developed Southern nations are denied their fair share of the product of the nuclear technology revolution."[16] A consensual arrangement may be inegalitarian if the parties to it agree to the creation or maintenance of unequal powers.

A second example involves the International Monetary Fund. The IMF was set up after the Second World War to provide relatively short-term credit to nations experiencing financial difficulties, on the theory that in the past nations experiencing difficulties had tended to react with fiscal and trade policies having destabilizing effects on the international financial system. It was not originally intended primarily as assistance for developing nations, and indeed many of its grants of credit have gone to developed Western nations such as the United Kingdom. Currently, however, many would-be borrowers are developing states, and serious tension has arisen over the practice of conditioning grants of credit on agreement to domestic financial restructuring that would, in the eyes of the IMF, make the receiving country more financially sound and thus better able to repay.

The conditions imposed are strongly influenced by principles of conventional capitalist economics. The restructuring that the IMF requests typically includes such terms as trade liberalization, elimination of domestic subsidies, higher taxes, and currency devaluation. The fact that the conditions are imposed by the Western nations that have a dominant voice in running the fund does not make the medicine any sweeter. Conditionality has often been met with heated rhetoric about neocolonialism and capitalist domination; on occasion, governments agreeing to such conditions have become extremely unpopular at home.

The arrangement is clearly consensual in the sense that nobody requires a nation to request credit, and if some country doesn't like the terms it is offered, it is free to turn them down. But it is also inegalitarian. Most obviously, voting power to approve requests is assigned to member nations based on how much currency they have contributed; Western nations, and particularly the United States, have very substantial ability to veto grants of credit of which they do not approve.[17] Left-oriented critics of the fund have pointed to this aspect of its processes as proof of its iniquity:

> From its inception the Fund has been dominated by the wishes of its largest member, the United States of America. Until 1956, this dominance was so absolute that decisions were made effectively by the U.S. Secretary of the Treasury, to the point that the Fund's staff had no authority to negotiate conditions for the drawings. . . . It is still safe to assume that no major decisions are taken against the strong wish of the United States. . . . The Fund, like the World Bank, is nominally a part of the United Nations system. It has, however, its own constitution and is in no way subject to the one-nation one-vote principle of the UN General Assembly. The Fund is controlled by its member states in proportion to the size of their quotas. It is thus ruled firmly by the rich countries.[18]

Furthermore, the critics claim, the fact that dollars were denominated the reserve currency allows the United States to manipulate the system by its control over the value of the dollar.

> A particularly controversial result of this system of employing the dollar as the international reserve currency and unit of account is that the U.S. has been able to run a virtually unlimited deficit in its domestic budget and to finance it largely by obliging foreigners to hold dollars. . . . The restrictive consequences of the world's reliance on the supply of independently generated U.S. dollars for its liquidity is becoming intolerable, especially for the poor African countries whose access to dollars is extremely limited. . . . The very manner in which the system is structured enhances global inequities and should therefore be characterized as unethical.[19]

As with our example of nuclear nonproliferation, the IMF illustrates the comfortable consistency between the fact that some arrangement is consensual and the fact that it is inegalitarian. While entry into an institution may be a deliberate and freely made choice, the structure and rules of the institution do not for this reason necessarily provide for the equal treatment of all. The fact that people enlist in the Army says little about the nature of its chains of command. For that matter, it might be called "consensual" to self oneself into slavery. Consent may perhaps justify inequality, but it does not justify denying that inequality exists.

THE LIMITS OF CONTEMPORANEOUS CONSENT

Arguments based on consent are deceptively simple. Their theoretical power lies in the suggestion that perhaps nothing really needs to be justified; coercion is not involved. Yet, the examples that we have given of consensual hegemony—military bases, aid to Israel, nuclear nonproliferation, and IMF lending—suggest that there may be more to it than that. These have all been the source of much controversy, and the targets of U.S. power have frequently objected, sometimes quite vociferously, to overbearing American attitudes and actions.

Some question the morality of linking issues to provide a quid pro quo. Thus, for instance, two authors arguing that development aid should be used to induce abstention from nuclear weapons development by poorer nations recognize that linkage presents difficulties: "Some will no doubt complain that it is improper to 'bribe' other states in this way, that injecting cash or conditioned in-kind benefits so overtly into the statecraft of sovereign nations impermissibly cheapens the vaunted traditions of international relations. In the same vein, some will resent this type of application of economic leverage, considering it to be just as aggressive and improper as a direct application of coercive military power. We look upon these transactions as business propositions, however. . . . 'Immorality' is not inherent in all unconventional arrangements between willing sellers and willing buyers."[20]

In addition, some international instruments can be read as condemning any efforts to achieve foreign policy goals through economic means. Several U.N. General Assembly resolutions speak of "economic coercion" as though it were comparable to military methods,[21] although the consensus seems to be that these resolutions consist more of inflated rhetoric than of legal norms.[22] Overall, the Third World (in conjunction with the former Soviet Union) has been the strongest proponent of prohibitions on economic coercion. Yet when the Arab states sought to use their domination of the international oil market to punish supporters of the state of Israel, no Third World voices were heard protesting.[23]

At a minimum, it is fair to say that even those who would prohibit economic coercion outright have not been able to define it. On the other hand, the reaction that such "consensual" uses of power have provoked is strong and negative enough to motivate a closer look at whether consent might be a more problematic justification than at first appears.

CONSENT BY STATES An initial problem is that it is not always so easy to decide whether effective consent has been given. Even where the leader of a state has agreed to certain terms, there may be questions about whether that leader is truly representative of the people of the state. The legitimacy of the government of the consenting state is, for this reason, of obvious importance. Contemporaneous consent should not hold the citizens of a nation to an agreement made by a dictator, against their wishes and against their interests, for international agreements affect individual people as well as states, and a truly unrepresentative government is not authorized to relinquish their rights.[24]

For example, the United States cited consent as the basis for its involvement in the Vietnam War; the South Vietnamese government had invited its participation. The Soviet Union, similarly, cited the consent of the Afghan and Czech governments to justify its invasion of those two countries. In neither case was the government in power adequately representative of the people of the country; a puppet government cannot give consent to the very outside forces that are responsible for keeping it in power.

Similarly, critics of the IMF have doubted the representativeness of various governments that have agreed to the fund's conditions for obtaining credit. It is charged that right-leaning governments are only too happy to obtain credit on such terms, for IMF conditions typically hurt the worst off in society.[25] It is, claim critics, socialist redistributive programs which tend to be targeted by IMF conditions; for the IMF often requires states to raise taxes and reduce subsidies, while adopting trade liberalization policies that seem to advantage multinationals at the expense of protected local industries. Whether these charges are factually accurate is open to debate; there are reasons to believe that IMF policies can actually be advantageous in some respects to the poor, in the long run and even sometimes in the medium run.[26] Nonetheless, critics allege the existence of a local "fifth column" in cahoots with foreign interests, and of a government effectively functioning as its puppet.[27]

Here we are squarely confronted by a serious problem. "Consent" requires someone to do the consenting, but who should it be, the state or its citizens? If "the state" is responsible for granting or withholding consent, then this effectively means the regime that controls the state, which may or may not authentically speak for the state's people. This issue plagues all of the varieties of consent theory that we will describe below—contemporaneous, ex ante, and hypothetical—although the issue takes slightly different shapes in different contexts. The question is whether we can justify using a simplified "state-actor" model rather than asking, in each instance, whether the state is an effective representative of its peoples.

The argument that we cannot justify using such a model turns on the fact that states are artificial entities which are not necessarily entitled to moral solicitude. It is *people* who experience the consequences of strong-power hegemony; and it is the effects on *people* that must be justified.[28] Furthermore, it is far from clear that a state-actor model can be reconciled with liberalism, and it is the possibility of a liberal justification, specifically, that we are exploring. The liberal focus on the autonomy and rights of individuals seems inconsistent with treating state consent as conclusive.

But other considerations argue that we should set this question aside for the time being, in order to see whether the remaining aspects of the liberal justification for hegemony can be developed. My object is to explore the possibility of a liberal explanation of an existing institutional practice—American hegemony. That practice itself, however, seems to presume that world politics will be conducted by state actors; for American foreign relations is largely directed at other governments and not at their individual citizens. If we develop a consent-based theory that circumvents state governments, it may have great theoretical appeal but it will not count as a justification for existing institutions. For the time being, then, we will search for the best possible liberal explanations for consent between states.

Ultimately, we will return to the question whether this exclusive focus on states is warranted. The problems of reconciling this focus with liberalism are indeed formidable. What is striking, however, is how easily the remaining portions of the consent-based arguments follow, once this assumption is made.

CONSENT AND COERCION Complaints about "consensual" uses of American power have not been limited to situations where the government in question was not an effective representative of its people. The representativeness objection relates to the process by which consent is expressed; other objections relate to the substance of the agreement which is reached. The greater number of accusations that U.S. actions are not as consensual as they seem are directed to the substantive terms to which other states appear to agree. Consent is illusory, it is argued, because the bargain struck is so one-sided.

This refrain has been sounded over and over in the controversy surrounding IMF conditionality. One leftist critic of the IMF system, Cheryl Payer, argues that the system is unfair because it traps poorer nations in an endless spiral of borrowing, inability to repay, and the resulting need to borrow even larger sums. The inability to pay, it is claimed, arises from the fundamental economic unsoundness of the IMF's recommendations, which do not promote economic self-sufficiency:

> The system can be compared point by point with peonage on an individual scale. In the peonage, or debt slavery, system, the worker is unable to use his nominal freedom to leave the service of his employer. . . . The worker cannot run away, for other employers and the state recognize the legality of his debt; nor has he any hope of earning his freedom with his low wages, which do not keep pace with what he consumes, let alone the true value of what he produces for his master. . . . Precisely the same system operates on the international level. . . . If they remain within the system, the debtor countries are doomed to perpetual underdevelopment, or rather to development of their exports at the service of multinational enterprises, at the expense of development for the needs of their own citizens.[29]

The basic thrust of the argument, that agreement is not consensual if states have no genuine choice, is the same when Filipinos dispute the legitimacy of U.S.

military bases, or when Israelis protest the tying of U.S. aid to cessation of settlement activity in the West Bank.

The argument that some exchange relations are in fact not free and voluntary fits neatly with our earlier observation that even voluntary relations can be highly inegalitarian. While some would say that even an *inegalitarian* relationship is legitimate if it is freely entered into, once the relationship is stripped of its claim to *voluntariness*, it is far more difficult to defend. Critical theorists have been quick to note the normative problems this combination presents: "Formally free and equal agents will always find themselves trapped in heteronomous influence relations because of the asymmetrical opportunity costs that necessarily obtain in systems of exclusive property rights, like international relations. That the structure of opportunity costs is quite stable means that relations of influence are stable too—stable enough to warrant description as relations of super- and subordination."[30] To this set of problems one might add the charge that powerful nations are often able to subvert the value systems of the weaker states, so that it is no longer even clear whether the weaker ones really want the terms that they agree to. Infant formula is considered more modern, hygienic, and prestigious than breast feeding; rural workers spend their meager earnings on Coca-Cola and American cigarettes; and state leaders waste precious tax dollars on prestige projects such as subsidized national airlines. Comprador classes in society become addicted to Western commercial products, culture, and political ideals, and the one-sidedness of the bargains that weaker states are compelled to make is no longer apparent even to them.

Here we must consider carefully the standard liberal response. In essence, it turns on two claims: that if the relevant actors agree to some particular terms, then by hypothesis they believe that they will be better off with the agreement than without; and that other states should not paternalistically attempt to second-guess that assessment. It is true that parties sometimes agree to conditions that they do not like because they are in desperate straits, and this might seem to be a form of duress that would obviate the assumption of voluntariness. But according to the standard liberal economic argument, the very fact that the weaker nation finds particular terms hard to resist is an argument in favor of the agreement rather than against it; for the harder it is to turn down an agreement, the more likely that the agreement is truly advantageous. It is particularly those who are in desperate straits who most need credit, foreign aid, or military bases.

Precisely this argument has been made in response to leftist critics of the IMF. The consequence of disallowing conditionality, it is claimed, will be that wealthier states will not be willing to support the fund and to make possible the loans that it provides:

> If membership in the Fund becomes onerous to creditor countries, they will cease to support it and direct their business elsewhere. . . . Membership in the Fund is undoubtedly still valuable to industrial creditor countries, but not so valuable or indispensable that the Fund could be forced to reduce their net benefits without risking the loss of their support and subscriptions. . . . The irony is that as some of the least masochistically inclined developed countries have walked away [from international organizations commandeered by developing nations] these organizations have also become less interesting to developing countries because little useful business could continue. The high road is therefore not something developing countries can force developed countries to travel. It is useless for them to man the toll booths, draped in holy cloth, for there will be no traffic or sacrificial tribute.[31]

This is not a debate that can be resolved within liberal theory. The criticisms of contemporaneous consent that we have sketched are clearly external to the liberal tradition. If the basic terms of liberalism are accepted, then the challenge is clearly misguided. Conversely, once one moves away from liberal premises, the liberal response has little force. The debate in international relations is precisely parallel to the critical theorists' rejection of liberalism in the domestic context. These arguments, then, form no part of a liberal theory of American hegemony.

But other criticisms of consent have a solid grounding in liberalism itself. Within a basically liberal philosophy, the difficulties with contemporaneous consent are limited in scope but fairly convincing where they apply. We will consider three: the issue of prior entitlement, the problem of inalienability, and the existence of monopoly.

PRIOR ENTITLEMENTS The argument from prior entitlement is based on the fact that one can legitimately sell only that which one already legitimately owns, and one should threaten to withhold only that which one does not already owe. To withhold what is rightfully the property of another, or to place conditions upon its return, is not consensual bargaining; it is extortion. That is why "your money or your life" is not a choice at all.

Developing countries have long drawn attention to their prior histories as colonies of today's developed nations. Some were plundered for gold, others for furs and timber, and still others for slaves. In some cases underdevelopment was systematically promoted by the colonizing nation, which wished to preserve the colonies as markets for their own goods; both colonial trade with other developed nations and indigenous industry were discouraged. This history of colonization provides a foundation for a claim for reparations; softer terms of credit and other forms of concessional aid are appropriate to help former colonies escape the conditions that the colonizers created. Their historical claims, it is argued, give developing nations an entitlement to aid that developed nations cannot now condition on compliance with capitalist restructuring.

Entitlement arguments need not be based on historical claims to reparations. Regardless of the cause of its poverty, a developing nation may assert that developed nations have an obligation to redistribute their wealth to help the least advantaged. Such claims may be based on a philosophical objection to the current distribution of wealth as morally arbitrary, or on the simple argument that every individual has a right to basic subsistence.[32] To the extent that a nation successfully argues for an entitlement to the resources of the United States, it can defeat the liberal claim that agreements are fair because they are mutually beneficial. The United States is simply not entitled to place conditions on turning over resources that are not properly its own in the first place.

Assumptions about entitlements may help to explain Israeli complaints that tying loan guarantees to cessation of settlement activity in the occupied territories illegitimately infringes upon Israeli sovereignty. We have already noted the accusation, made by some proponents of tying, that Israel treats U.S. aid (wrongly, in their view) as a form of entitlement.[33] An entitlement argument could perhaps be founded on America's historic ties to the land of Israel, although for obvious reasons it would be politically risky for Israel to state the argument in such a direct form within earshot of the average American taxpayer.

Claims of this sort are even closer to the surface in other disputes over "consensual" exercise of U.S. power. The fact that some military bases are located in countries over which the United States once exercised colonial sovereignty (Cuba and the Philippines, for instance) lends credibility to the argument that such agreements are coercive. The United States owes reparations to these countries, so the argument would go, and should not condition aid upon the use of their sovereign territory. Objections to IMF conditionality sometimes rest, at bottom, upon the argument that wealthy countries have a moral obligation to forgive loans to poor ones and are thus not justified in imposing conditions upon further loan restructuring: "If the Western governments were genuinely concerned about the effects of the debt burden on development, they could declare the debts forgiven, or at least, as Laurence Whitehead has suggested, refrain from vindictive sanctions when the suffering debtor finally repudiates the debts. The fact that forgiveness of debts is never considered in the contemporary world indicates that the much-deplored debts are in fact serving a useful function above and beyond the money to be repaid. They help to keep the potentially rebellious borrower in line."[34] If one assumes that the poor countries are entitled to loan forgiveness, then the refusal to extend forgiveness functions quite straightforwardly as an illegitimate method of ensuring debtor country subservience.

The argument from entitlements is also buried somewhat deeper in other disputes over conditionality. It is frequently claimed that IMF conditions violate the domestic sovereignty of debtor nations, a claim that we will turn to directly in a moment. The IMF version of the story is that such conditions are necessary to ensure repayment.[35] It is possible, of course, that the IMF is simply mistaken about the conditions being necessary for creditworthiness. But if it is correct, then debtor countries' insistence that the loans be made without conditions is effectively an insistence that the loans be made with no assurance of repayment. And this can only be justified on the grounds that the receiving nations are entitled to the moneys as gifts.

The problem with many arguments about prior entitlements is that, once stated straightforwardly on their own terms, they are not very credible. It is interesting to note that when the Western nations protested the Arab oil embargo, it was argued in some quarters that the Arabs were behaving in an impermissibly coercive way because these nations did not have an unqualified sovereign right to the oil that happened to underlie their territories.[36] This is not a position that one would have expected the Western nations, especially oil-producing ones such as the United States, to have adopted.[37] Other arguments against the Arab trade sanctions in this case run aground on the generally conceded principle that nations have a sovereign right to trade—or not to trade—with whichever nations they please.[38] Some difficult cases of economic coercion may be resolvable on grounds of prior entitlements, but objections in most other cases must have some different basis.

INALIENABILITY   There is another argument that may be buried in the objections to IMF conditionality: The IMF is requiring developing nations to give up rights that are inalienable. Control over a nation's intrinsically domestic affairs—its sovereignty—cannot be ceded to other nations, the argument would go, and decisions about a nation's fundamental economic and social structure are intrinsically domestic. When a debtor nation protests that the conditions the IMF proposes infringe on its sovereignty, there may be more at stake than the simple claim that the burden imposed is too onerous. The qualitative nature of the burden may be as important as the burden's size and weight. Where a debtor nation protests that it cannot be required to give up its sovereignty, the reason may be that it views its sovereignty as inalienable.

The analogy between IMF conditionality and peonage, mentioned above, suggests that inalienability may be the real issue. In the domestic law of liberal societies, individuals are not allowed to sell themselves into slavery or other comparable forms of servitude. The reason is that one's freedom is inalienable. Regardless of one's voluntary consent, there are some things that simply cannot be bought and sold; one cannot sell one's kidneys or corneas, one cannot sell one's children, and one cannot sell oneself into a life of slavery or prostitution. In liberal societies, there are basic limits on freedom of contract. And so it may be argued that, as between nations, sovereignty cannot be put up for sale.

There is considerable rhetorical appeal to this way of putting the argument. The rhetorical appeal comes from the analogy between personal autonomy and the independence of states. Those things that are most likely to be inalienable between persons are things that are most intimate and most tightly bound up with personal identity. Liberals do not object to the marketability of real property or personal possessions—cars, jewelry, stock certificates, condominiums.[39] But should people be able to sell their body parts, children, or sexual services? Such things are supposed to remain within an individual's own control. Similarly, to say that state sovereignty is inalienable makes use of the rhetoric of "inalienable rights" to explain why some domestic functions must remain with the state. Decisions about the most intimate of state domestic relations cannot be made by outsiders, even outsiders that are willing to pay.

It is not surprising, then, when other nations make the choice to turn down aid tied to strings they find offensive. In July 1992, for instance, Mexico decided that it would no longer take American assistance to fight the narcotics trade. As the New York Times reported, "The Mexican Attorney General, Ignacio Morales Lechuga, said in an interview on Friday that the Government had no intention of relaxing its efforts to stop illegal drugs. But he said Mexico would bear the costs because it was no longer willing to tolerate what it considered the unwarranted interference that comes with American aid. . . . In part, Mr. Morales Lechuga said, Mexico had lost patience with the regular debate in the United States Congress over whether Mexico is doing what it should to help stop drugs. 'We do not like the fact that our conduct in the fight against narcotics trafficking is debated outside Mexico,' he said."[40] Similarly, India recently told the World Bank that it would not be needing a $450 million loan to complete a vast irrigation and hydroelectric project.[41] It decided that it was simply unwilling to comply with the bank's environmental and resettlement requirements.

Before we allow ourselves to be carried away by the inalienability argument's rhetorical appeal, we should consider its limitations. The first is really an extension of the earlier argument about prior entitlements; the claim that a state cannot give up an inalienable right requires that what would be given up actually be a right. Although not all rights are inalienable rights, all inalienable rights must be rights. For a state to rely on an argument about inalienability, then, the thing that it refuses to give up must first be found to fall within its legitimate prerogatives.

The case of most favored nation status for China illustrates the point.[42] Assume that China argues that most favored nation status cannot be conditioned upon its compliance with human rights norms because sovereignty over its own domestic affairs is inalienable and cannot be traded away to Western nations. To say that it has an *inalienable* right to violate human rights norms, however, requires that it have a *right* to violate human rights norms. And this is exactly what the Western nations dispute. They claim that China has an obligation to respect basic freedoms such as freedom of speech, religion, assembly, and political association.

Another illustration returns to the earlier example of tying Israeli loan guarantees to cessation of settlement in the occupied West Bank. It has been claimed that the linkage is objectionable because Israel cannot be required to relinquish its sovereignty, to which promotion of the settlement activity is closely tied. Yet many have argued that Israel is prohibited by international law from building settlements in the occupied West Bank even with its own money. If it is true that Israel has no *right* to build in the West Bank, then it can hardly have an *inalienable* right to do so. Deciding whether there is an inalienable right requires a determination of what the parties are entitled to do. Only once one knows whether a party has some particular right can one proceed to the subsequent question of whether those rights are inalienable.

There are important differences, for this reason, between inducements for a state to comply with international norms and inducements for a state to do something that international norms do not require. The former cannot support objections of inalienability, while the latter may. South Africa could not complain that trade sanctions violated its inalienable right to maintain a system of apartheid, because apartheid is prohibited by international law. Debtor nations have a better claim, in contrast, that IMF conditions violate their inalienable sovereignty, because they are not typically violating international norms with their chosen economic schemes.[43] A nation that so wishes certainly has a right, in the eyes of the international community, to adopt a socialist economic system, to subsidize commodity prices, and to overvalue its currency; showing that it has a right is the first step in the argument toward showing that it has an inalienable right.

There are other problems with the inalienability argument. Even if a state has an inalienable right to do something, this does not mean that other states have an obligation to assist it. Assume for the moment that Israel's critics are wrong in their belief that continued settlement activity violates international norms.[44] Even if Israel has a right to build, and even if this is an inalienable right, it does not follow that the United States (or any other nation) must give Israel the money to do so. The right to do something, even where it is inalienable, does not automatically carry with it a right to subsidies. This is an important consideration in the case of loan guarantees because the point of linking them to settlement activity is that some fear that aid to Israel effectively frees up funds that otherwise would be used for other domestic purposes, allowing the funds to be used for settlement building.

To put it another way, the question must be raised whether settlements could be built if U.S. aid were not given.[45] If the answer is no, then there is no inalienability objection to conditioning aid upon not building settlements. In such circumstances, the cause of the failure to build settlements is the lack of adequate Israeli funds to build without U.S. aid, rather than any conditions that the United States places on receipt of aid. The United States is not obliged to give Israel assistance necessary to make it possible for Israel to build, even if Israel in theory has an inalienable right to do so. In contrast, if Israel were intending and able to build on its own, and if it had an inalienable right to do so, then conditioning aid on relinquishment of that right would be morally objectionable.

These are big ifs, of course, and we have said almost nothing about what makes a right "inalienable." There is something of a rhetorical tendency to turn every right into an inalienable one. But the mere fact that something is a right— even an important one—does not make it inalienable. States have sovereignty over their natural resources, but this does not mean that they cannot sell those resources. While the "right" to control over resources means that those resources cannot be taken away involuntarily or without compensation, the very right to control the resources seems to include a right to sell them or give them away.[46] Similarly, a state's right to decide what to do within its own territory does not automatically entail the absence of a right to base that decision upon the incentives offered by other states. There may be a rhetorical tendency to treat all rights as inalienable, but this tendency should be resisted.

This argument leads to a suspicion that only those governmental functions that are most closely tied to state sovereignty should be treated as inalienable; the right to sovereignty over territory, the right to ultimate authority over the state's citizens, the right to political independence. It is easier to give examples of situations where inalienability was violated than to state general criteria.

For example, China was forced to relinquish an inalienable right when it ceded jurisdiction to Western nations that formed extraterritorial enclaves on Chinese soil in the nineteenth century.[47] The inalienable rights of the Baltic states were violated by Stalinist Russia when they were forced to accede to Soviet domination during the Second World War.[48] The same would be said of the rights of other peoples subject to colonialism in Asia, Latin America, and Africa. Note, however, that most of these examples could as easily be explained on the grounds that the states in question were literally forced to go along; there was no colorable claim that these agreements were voluntary. For a state is not likely under ordinary circumstances to relinquish a truly inalienable right of sovereignty voluntarily.

It would be unwise for weaker nations to seek to expand the category of inalienable rights indefinitely, for inalienability is a two-edged sword. The argument, if successful, is very strong, for it means that states are literally disempowered from using the rights in question as a medium of exchange.[49] A state protesting IMF conditions may not be better off asserting that its sovereignty over domestic economic issues is inalienable, for having relinquished the capacity to make economic concessions, it may find itself without a bargain. The danger of refusing to compromise one's sovereignty is that the other party to the transaction may not find it worth its while to trade.

Whether this result ensues depends on whether there are other terms that the stronger nation would accept that would be more satisfactory to the weaker. Refusal to comply with the conditions that the stronger party presents involves an element of bluffing. Weaker nations that refuse to comply with IMF conditions are betting that a bargain more to their liking can be struck; that the IMF will not just walk away. One factor that can make this conviction more plausible is the existence of monopoly power.

MONOPOLY POWER   Whether the stronger nation will be willing to negotiate further and ultimately agree to other conditions more to the weaker's liking depends on whether these other terms would still make the arrangement beneficial to the stronger party. If a debtor nation refuses certain IMF conditions as too great an infringement on its sovereignty, there may still be conditions that will satisfy the most powerful IMF members, although to a lesser extent. The riskiness of the strategy of rejecting proposed IMF terms that are too burdensome depends, therefore, on the margin of profitability of the rejected deal. If the proposed but rejected terms are very close to the minimum terms that the stronger states would accept (the "reservation price"), then it is unlikely that some alternative terms can be found that will please the stronger party less but still be satisfactory. If the margin between the reservation price and the rejected terms is greater, then the chance of agreeing to some alternative set of conditions is enhanced.

Classical economists assume that in a totally free market in which there are many buyers and sellers, the margin will be small. Competition between sellers forces the price down; where the margin for one seller is substantial, other sellers will attempt to undercut it. It is for this reason that economists tend to assume that regulations designed to protect the weaker party to the transaction will backfire. If the margin is already quite small, then any shift of terms in favor of consumers will drive sellers out of the market. Regulation cannot effectively force sellers to sell at below cost, and it is assumed in a free market that sellers are already selling quite close to cost.

The situation is different, however, where instead of a free market with many buyers and sellers there is a market dominated by a single seller.[50] In such circumstances, the monopolist can keep the price above the one which would prevail in a competitive market. The profit margin can be higher, because there is no competitor to undercut prices that are kept artificially higher than the point at which the seller would be willing to sell. In such cases, regulations which shift the terms in favor of the consumer will not necessarily have the effect of driving the seller out of the market; so long as the price remains above the seller's reservation price, the seller will still find the transaction profitable.

Although the IMF might find attractive certain conditions that would infringe a debtor nation's sovereignty, it is nonetheless possible that it would settle for less. One cannot assume that the original terms it has provided are as low as it can afford to go, meaning as lenient as possible while still providing adequate security for the loan. If there were a standard market price established by competition, one might argue that the IMF could not go any lower; for if were possible to go lower, then competitors would already have done so and this would be reflected in the market price. But it is not at all clear that there is a functioning market, or competitors.[51]

Similarly, weak nations cannot always count on competition and a free market to set prices for other sorts of consensual agreements. If the Philippine government wishes to demand greater compensation in return for the use of its territory for U.S. military bases, and if the United States is the only nation that wants a military base in the Philippines, the government can't count on competition to lift the price as high as possible.[52] For this reason, it is possible that the weaker state will actually be able to obtain terms more to its advantage if it is incapacitated from accepting certain kinds of conditions (for instance, because certain kinds of infringements on sovereignty are deemed inalienable). The United States will not necessarily be driven from the market, because it may not have already been offering the most generous terms that it would be willing to accept. The existence of monopoly power alters the conditions of bargaining so that an incapacity to agree to certain disadvantageous terms may be to the weaker party's advantage.

During the Cold War the United States did not have monopoly power on issues such as military bases, because a country that felt unsatisfied by American terms might turn to the Soviet Union to try to get a better deal. Many of them tried, and sometimes succeeded. The result was a lessening of the extent to which the great powers could take advantage of the lesser ones; for under such circumstances, superpowers would compete: "[Where there are many powers in the core,] competition within the core for influence over a given peripheral state is a distinct likelihood. What makes this possibility important . . . is that such competition should, in principle, eliminate all heteronomous influence relations within the international system, and therefore eliminate the system's core-periphery structure.[53] This would be true not only for military bases but also for various sorts of grant and loan assistance.[54] In exchange for support in the United Nations, for ideological commitments to capitalism, or for logistical assistance in low-intensity regional conflict (such as in El Salvador or Nicaragua), a developing nation might bargain for financial assistance, arms, or support in its own domestic or international policy objectives. In the absence of competition from the Soviet Union, the United States is now freer to set the terms as it sees fit.

The United States, metaphorically, is now the only bank in town. Where there are many banks and they all require extensive security for a certain type of loan, then it is reasonable to be cautious about prohibiting demands for that sort of security. Where there is only a single bank, then that bank has no incentives to make its demands as reasonable as possible. The analogy is closest in the case of IMF conditionality, where the metaphor of "the only bank in town" may well be accurate. Analogous reasoning applies, however, in any circumstances where the United States is in a monopoly position and seeks to extract concessions out of the weaker parties with which it deals.

This argument about monopoly seems to resemble the characterization as inegalitarian that we made earlier, but it is actually different. The IMF is inegalitarian in the sense that it is dominated by states that contribute a large share of the fund's capital. But what matters here is not the internal structure of the fund so much as whether there are any other private or international agencies set up to offer loans of this sort.[55] If there were two or more such lending institutions, there would be competition even if all of them were structured in an inegalitarian way. Conversely, where there is only a single lender, competitiveness does not turn on whether its structure is egalitarian.

Where monopolies are present, the fairness of the terms of trade cannot be taken for granted. The simple fact that a nation agrees to some terms does not establish that they are fair, or that stronger states would refuse to deal if they had to offer terms more advantageous to the weaker. Consent is not a complete liberal justification, for this reason, in circumstances of hegemony. The issue is not merely whether the weaker party perceives a benefit in agreeing to terms that it does not like, but whether the benefit that the stronger party obtains is considerably and systematically larger. A hegemon is able to capture the lion's share of any gains from trade.[56]

THE RELEVANCE OF NORMS

Phrasing the issue in terms of consent seems to raise as many questions as it answers. Consent may seem a simple concept, but it is hedged with limitations. Some of the relevant issues, such as the presence of monopoly power, are empirical ones, easy enough to understand if not always easy to resolve. But others are normative. What counts as consent, what it is fair to consent to, and what rights cannot be traded away all seem to be determined by the background norms of the international community.

The question, for instance, whether it is fair to require Israel to cease settlement activity as a condition for obtaining U.S. loan guarantees depends on a whole series of normative issues. Does the United States have a background obligation to support the state of Israel—does Israel, in other words, have a prior entitlement to U.S. aid? If so, then attaching strings to the aid is unfair. Does Israel violate international norms by building settlements? If so, then the United States has no obligation to provide it with the means to do so. Even if Israel has a right to build settlements if it chooses, is this an inalienable right—a right that the United

States should not ask it to relinquish? The concept of consent, itself, does not help to answer these questions. These are questions that must be answered before the "consent" characterization is even relevant.

We asked a similar set of questions with regard to the conditionality of loans to developing nations. Do they have a prior right to international wealth redistribution? If they do, then developed nations cannot demand a quid pro quo, and in particular they cannot demand that the recipients show creditworthiness. If not, then conditions would seem to be permissible—but only if the conditions do not infringe on attributes too essential to sovereignty. Analogous questions arise for other consensual uses of power; intervention at the invitation of a local official, establishment of military bases, debt-for-nature swaps, compromise settlements of all kinds. Whether the methods used are diplomacy, bribery, or sanctions—in most cases, the three work in combination—contemporaneous consent is the beginning of the inquiry, not its conclusion.

Norms are needed, then, to specify what should be counted as consent. At least for liberals, disagreements over whether particular instances of consent are legitimate most likely turn on disagreement over these underlying normative issues, for few dispute the appeal of consent theory in principle. But what is the source of these norms? They cannot themselves be a product of the consent process, since they specify whether a particular example of consent is valid. If international hegemony is to be founded on consent, then, it must turn in addition on the satisfaction of these norms, for they structure the process of bargaining.

Norms are also relevant for a different reason. We have seen that contemporaneous consent by itself is not *sufficient* for legitimacy unless the underlying norms are satisfied. But it is also possible that there may be cases in which contemporaneous consent is not *necessary*. The norms of the international community may justify the exercise of hegemonic power even where the target state does not agree. Contemporaneous consent, in other words, may be too restrictive a theory of international legitimacy. To see why, we must turn to a second theory of hegemonic legitimacy, which is related to the consent theory that we have been discussing but which goes a good deal farther. That is the theory of ex ante consent.

5

EX ANTE

CONSENT

The apparently straightforward explanation offered in the last chapter—that some instances of American hegemony might be based on the consent of other states—raises a problem: Consent can be determined only within a general framework of norms of international conduct. What is the source of these norms?

Here we might take a suggestion from domestic political theory. Consent in the domestic setting must also be determined within a general framework of norms setting out the property rights of the parties, for much the same reasons that consent in the international setting depends upon norms setting out the parties' entitlements. Domestic theory must also, then, address the issue of where these norms come from. To justify these norms, some domestic theories turn to a particular sort of consent theory, ex ante consent. The backgrounds norms that structure the parties' legal and political relationships can be justified on the grounds that the parties agreed to these norms in advance.

The importance of these agreed upon norms extends beyond their role in shaping the contemporaneous agreements into which states enter. They also function as an independent source of legitimacy for the use of international power. In domestic society, prior entitlements shape private agreements (they form, in other words, the foundation for contract law), but they also shape rights and obligations in other ways (for instance, by providing a foundation for tort and criminal law). In the international community, similarly, once such norms are recognized as legitimate in determining property entitlements, their importance goes beyond contractual arrangements between states. Once these norms are recognized, they provide a justification that is independent of contemporaneous consent, a basis for general enforcement of the norms against the states that violate them.

As an illustration of the overlapping but different roles that prior entitlements play in contemporaneous and ex ante consent, consider Russia's claims to the Kurile Islands, which it has occupied since the Second World War.[1] Japan has been reluctant to promise financial aid to Russia until the territorial dispute is resolved. The legitimacy of the Russian claim is relevant in determining whether Russia might exchange its territorial claims for financial assistance from Japan.[2] If Russia had occupied Tokyo after the war and used its occupation to extort aid from Japan, it would not be able to justify its extortion on the basis of contemporary consent. It would be exchanging something that it did not properly own.

But the legitimacy of the Russian claim would also be relevant for other purposes. If a third nation were to invade the Kurile Islands, this would then be an offense against Russia; Russia's ownership of the islands, in other words, would be the basis for a claim alleging violation of international law. The justification for international sanctions would not lie in any contemporaneous consent, but in prior background agreement that each state's territorial sovereignty should be respected. The norms of territorial integrity are relevant to international exchanges but also independently define international rights and obligations even in the absence of exchange. International obligations follow directly from such norms, and these norms, it can be argued, are founded on prior general agreement among states. Once ex ante consent is recognized as an independent basis for international norms, therefore, its importance goes far beyond its role in structuring acts of contemporaneous consent.

The United States has been increasingly ready to rely on vindication of general norms resting on ex ante consent as a justification for its international actions. The most spectacular recent instance in which U.S. actions were justified by ex ante consent was the Persian Gulf war, in which the United States and its coalition partners justified going to war by the need to uphold Kuwait's territorial integrity. Holding Iraq to the norm of territorial integrity might be justified by the general support that the norm has in the world community, and in particular by the fact that Iraq had committed itself to that norm by agreeing to the U.N. Charter. When the United States casts itself in the role of enforcer of international law, the explanation for its claimed right to do so rests in part on the fact that the nations of the world have, by and large, agreed to these international norms. As we will see below, some international legal scholars have self-consciously appropriated consent theory as the basis for international legal norms.

Moving to a theory of ex ante consent does not resolve all problems of reliance on prior norms. For the general principle that states ought to comply with their prior commitments itself must rest on something. States, after all, might change their minds about whether they want to submit to some particular international norm. Why should they not be allowed to? It is easy enough to think of reasons for the principle that commitments must be honored; the reliance of other actors in the system, the practical advantages of being able to bind oneself, and so on. What is clear, though, is that the principle is a normative judgment and that it cannot itself be explained in terms of prior consent without indulging in circular reasoning.

Two things might be said in response to this objection. The first is that while ex ante consent requires prior adoption of the premise that previous commitments should be honored, this is a relatively thin commitment. The only principle not itself justified in terms of consent, in other words, is one that is fairly innocuous and widely held. There is enormous intuitive appeal (in the usual case) to the notion that voluntary assumption of an obligation to obey rules is an adequate basis for those rules. Whether there are any relevant limitations to this general principle in the case of international hegemony is a topic that we will turn to later in this chapter.

Second, ex ante consent is a peculiarly liberal theory. Resting as it does upon voluntary assumptions of obligation, it is a strikingly appropriate way to approach international power from within the liberal framework, which is the framework we are currently investigating. The object just now is not so much to defend liberal political assumptions as to examine whether international hegemony is consistent with them. The fact that liberal theory ultimately falls back on normative premises about the binding nature of commitments must be granted. But the problem, if it is one, is for philosophers of domestic politics to address.

CONTEMPORANEOUS AND EX ANTE CONSENT COMPARED

Both contemporaneous and ex ante consent are based on the same notion, voluntariness. For this reason, they have important elements in common. To some degree, the distinction between contemporaneous and ex ante consent is artificial because the two necessarily overlap. Take International Monetary Fund loan conditionality, for example. The powerful nations dominating the IMF agree to approve a loan, and in exchange the receiving nation restructures its economy. But whether the restructuring precedes the loan, or the loan precedes the restructuring, one side or other (or both) must make commitments about performance in the future. If the restructuring occurs first, it is because there is an expectation of assistance; if the assistance comes first, it is because of the commitment to restructuring. There are probably very few cases of purely contemporary consent, because it is rarely possible for the two performances to occur instantaneously.

At a minimum, however, there are important differences of degree. The differences fall roughly into two categories: differences relating to the timing of agreement and performance, and differences relating to the generality of what is agreed to. Timing is perhaps the more obvious difference. While some of the examples in the previous chapter involved agreement taking place prior to performance, the delays were relatively short, with the two sides performing roughly at the same time. This is important for enforcement purposes, because with roughly contemporaneous or overlapping performances, the remedy for noncompliance on one side is withholding of performance on the other.[3] The United States may pay out financial aid on the assurances that it will be allowed to keep its military bases, but if the nation on whose soil the bases are to be located has a change of heart, the United States will be able to withhold future assistance.

In contrast, commitment to international norms extends indefinitely into the future. With such open-ended commitments, there is a higher probability that one side or the other will decide that the bargain struck was a mistake. Ex ante consent raises enforcement issues that are far more serious than those raised by contemporaneous consent. One state may be called upon to respect a norm with little guarantee of reciprocity by the other, whose performance lies far in the indefinite future. Where one state is called upon to respect a World Court judgment, for example, it does not know whether other states will do the same if they find themselves in its shoes in the future.

The differences in the generality of what is agreed to are also important, even if they likewise are only a matter of degree. Instead of a debt-for-nature swap in which environmental protection of a specific parcel of land is exchanged for forgiveness of a particular loan, the parties might all agree to stop degrading the environment in some particular way. Generality is a matter of degree because a nation might agree to protect the black horned rhino on a specific parcel of land, to protect the black rhino nationwide, to outlaw participation in the world-wide traffic in black-rhino horns, or to prohibit the sale of products from all endangered species.

Even if it is just a matter of degree, though, generality is important. Just as the increase in time lag between agreement and performance creates greater enforcement difficulties, so does increased generality. It is usually more difficult to determine what very general rules require in particular cases than to determine what very specific terms require. The greater the generality, the more likely that some particular application will be different from what particular parties thought they were agreeing to. Where consent was very specific, it is more likely that a state would have clearly focused on what it would have to do, and would have appreciated the costs of performance at the time of agreement and therefore be genuinely willing to perform.

For this reason, there is greater likelihood of breach with ex ante than with contemporaneous agreement. Ex ante consent raises issues of enforcement that do not arise, or do not arise in as serious a form, with contemporaneous consent. As a result, ex ante consent raises the prospect of genuine coercion.

EX ANTE CONSENT, COERCION, AND HIERARCHY

With ex ante consent comes the necessity for coercion, albeit coercion that is legitimated by prior agreement. Contemporaneous consent does not require the use of force, but ex ante consent does. With contemporaneous consent there is agreement at the time of performance, but with ex ante consent the agreement precedes performance, in some cases by a long time. The time period between agreement and performance means that one of the states may have had a change of heart. A norm that seemed to be a good idea at one time may appear less advantageous as circumstances change; or a rule that looked good in the abstract may look different as the circumstances of application become clearer. Perhaps most important, one of the states may already have received the benefit of the other states' compliance and have no incentive now to carry out its own end of the bargain. In such cases coercion may be required.

Coercion need not involve physical violence, for there are other sanctions for rule violation that fall short of military force. For example, it may be possible to freeze the assets of states that violate international norms, as the United States did when its embassy was seized in Tehran. But note that even sanctions stopping short of military force are coercive if they involve withholding a benefit that the violating state is otherwise entitled to. Such negative sanctions are different from simple refusal to provide a benefit that the granting state is entitled to withhold.

norms are authoritative. If international law norms are themselves derived from prior agreement, then consent seems to supply a justification for enforcing them. U.S. power could in this way be explained in terms of ex ante consent, at least so long as the United States limits its role to enforcement of international law.

Traditionally, two alternative foundations have been offered for international law: natural law and positivism.[8] The natural law tradition of international relations draws on the same sources as the natural law tradition of domestic jurisprudence; it was strongly influenced by Catholic thinkers such as Thomas Aquinas. Early international lawyers such as Francisco Suarez and Francisco de Vitoria applied natural law reasoning to issues such as just war theory and the rights and duties of the Spanish colonizers of the New World. Natural lawyers suggested that international law followed from basic universal principles of morality.[9]

The main competitor to natural law has been positivism. Positivism defines "law" without reference to morality. In international law, the positivists have been concerned to found international law, instead, on the consent of states.[10] Since states could consent to immoral rules, or fail to consent to moral rules, in the positivists' eyes there is at most a contingent connection between international law and morality.

In chapter 7 we will return to the role that substantive morality plays in justifying international hegemony. Natural law theories of international law will then become relevant. Here, the more relevant theme is the positivists' claim that international law must be founded on state consent.[11] Positivism is undoubtedly the dominant view in contemporary international legal circles. While pure moral reasoning may account adequately for certain international norms, such as human rights protections, many of these norms can be accounted for on the philosophically less troubling basis of state agreement; and some international norms, such as trade agreements or protection of foreign ambassadors, are better explained in terms of common acceptance. Positivism, in addition, seems to allow international lawyers to avoid recourse to controversial moral judgments.

The positivists' insistence that international law must be founded on state consent is based on the intrinsic sovereignty of states.[12] Natural lawyers might be content to turn to philosophical principles or to God as a source of superior authority, but in the absence of such sources the only grounding for norms is the states themselves. By agreeing to a norm in advance, a state binds itself without relinquishing any of its inalienable sovereignty. Some purport to find philosophical embarrassments in this reliance on state sovereignty; for if a state was truly sovereign, it would seem to retain at all times the right to abandon its prior commitment to principle.[13] This objection parallels the argument raised earlier that even ex ante consent must ultimately turn to moral principles, for it rests on the premise that states cannot repudiate their commitments.[14] But despite the logical puzzles inherent in the sovereignty argument, positivist international lawyers such as Oppenheim have steadfastly recognized prior agreement as the sole basis for international legal obligation.

State agreement is typically manifested in one of two ways: by treaty or through custom. As Oppenheim puts it, "As the basis of the Law of Nations is the common consent of the member-States of the Family of Nations, it is evident that there must exist, and can only exist, as many sources of International Law as there are facts through which such common consent can possibly come into existence. Of such facts there are only two. A State, just as an individual, may give its consent either directly by an express declaration, or tacitly by conduct which it would not follow in case if did not consent. . . . Treaties and custom, are, therefore, exclusively the sources of the Law of Nations."[15] Treaties, of course, represent the most explicit agreement one is likely to find; certainly consent is more explicit here than in most domestic law situations, where individual citizens have rarely explicitly undertaken to obey the law. Treaty law covers a wide variety of topics, ranging from protection of human rights or the environment to chemical warfare prohibitions, trade policy, international enforcement of judgments, and fisheries management. While there is often disagreement about what particular treaties require in particular circumstances, their jurisprudential status is relatively secure.

Customary law is more difficult, both in its jurisprudential foundations and in the practical difficulties in ascertaining what it requires. The practical difficulties in determining what norms states are supposed to have implicitly agreed to are evident. But so are the theoretical assumptions underneath the notion. Customary law is said to be founded on the actual practice of states; states consent to customary norms tacitly, through conduct rather than contract. But how widespread must a practice be before it can be treated as customary law? And how long-standing? What if one custom prevails among one group of states and another custom prevails among the rest? Customary international law inhabits a shady world of inference, interpretation, and implication.

Despite such difficulties, the basic object of the positivist theory is clear: States are not supposed to be bound against their own wishes. This principle is embodied in other principles, as well, such as the rule that General Assembly resolutions (which require only a two-thirds majority, rather than unanimity) are not legally binding.[16] The underlying philosophy of this positivist approach to international law is the same philosophy as that underlying the theory of ex ante consent. It is the notion that the only secure foundation for individual obligation is individual agreement.

ENFORCEMENT PROCEDURES

The substantive norms themselves are only half of the story. The argument that they are the product of prior state consent is well known in international law. But if the United States is to rely on ex ante consent as a justification for its international authority, it must do more than show that the norms it is enforcing were agreed to. It must also show agreement on the role of the United States as enforcer.

This additional part of the argument does not have an analog when the basis for international power is contemporaneous consent. With contemporaneous consent, reaching agreement and enforcing the agreement are not widely separated in time; there is no separate "enforcement" phase. And there is no need for a distinct "enforcer"; each state protects its own interests, by failing to reciprocate if its partner's performance is not forthcoming. It is because ex ante consent contemplates separate, and coercive, enforcement that separate issues of enforcement legitimacy must be addressed. The fact that agreement has been reached on some particular substantive norm does not by itself say much about what the remedy for violation should be, or about which states or institutions should be involved in imposing the remedy.

The difference between agreements and the remedy for breach is apparent in domestic substantive disputes, as well. Even where it is clear that some norm has been violated, it does not automatically follow that all individuals have rights to impose sanctions or that they may impose any sanctions that they personally find appropriate. The norms that regulate who is the proper individual to impose penalties, and what the penalties should be, must also be satisfied. In domestic society, that authority is typically reserved for the state; individual enforcement is illegitimate "vigilante justice."[17] The analogous question in the international context is whether stronger states such as the United States are entitled, in effect, to "take the law into their own hands."

This question is particularly acute given the connection between enforcement powers and hierarchy. We noted earlier that ex ante consent is tied to hierarchy in a way that contemporaneous consent is not. Because ex ante consent necessitates coercive enforcement, its effectiveness depends upon the stronger powers in a system. Treating the stronger parties as the natural ones to enforce community norms, however, grants the stronger parties a superior place in the hierarchy. The hierarchy that ex ante consent theory encourages raises legitimacy problems with U.S. actions. Why should the United States, one is tempted to ask, be entitled to appropriate the role of "world's policeman"?

In theory, the problem could be avoided by assigning enforcement to some institution other than the individual state actors. In theory, a United Nations could be established that would have its own military forces, supported by its own compulsory taxing authority.[18] In practice, of course, no such institution currently exists.[19] To the extent that the U.N. has access to military force, the reason is that member nations have been willing to contribute personnel and resources. So long as the U.N. must act through its powerful members, as it did in the Persian Gulf war, the problem of hierarchy remains, for a small group of nations enjoy a privileged place in the scheme of international enforcement.[20]

To say that hierarchy poses an issue of legitimacy does not mean that the problem is insoluble. Indeed, the very fact that enforcement falls unavoidably upon the strongest members of the system is itself a suggestion about why their special powers may be acceptable.[21] Put simply, without the support of the strongest powers it is likely that no enforcement mechanism would exist. If hegemonic enforcement is the best that is available, perhaps all rational states should be willing to settle for it. We will return to this theme in the next chapter, when we examine what hypothetical rational states would agree to. More relevant in the present context are the ways in which existing states actually *have* settled for it. For if the standard here is whether states have agreed to some set of norms and institutions in advance, it can be argued that in fact they have.

There are two arguments in support of this conclusion. The first is that the United States may be acting at the request of the victim of the international violation. Presumably, there are some self-help remedies that a victim might use to protect itself and to remedy an injury it has suffered. Most obviously, a state would have a right of self-defense in case of military attack. But if it has a right to defend itself, then there seems to be no valid objection to its requesting assistance from other, stronger parties under a theory of collective self-defense.[22]

The relevance of the victim's request lies not so much in the fact that there is consent between it and the United States.[23] While this would be true, and would be an example of contemporaneous consent, it is not the aspect of the remedy that is most significant here.[24] For in addition to the issue of whether the United States is justified in acting vis-à-vis the victim, there is the issue of its actions vis-à-vis the violator. Here the answer has two parts. First, the substantive norm that was violated was agreed to ex ante by all involved states, including the violator.

Second, the enforcement process is itself justified because all states recognize the remedy that the victim would have, and the victim has simply asked the United States to exercise the remedy on its behalf.

The second example of prior consent to particular enforcement mechanisms consists of the general acceptance of the role of the Security Council. States that are members of the United Nations have agreed, by accepting the U.N. Charter, to the Security Council playing a dominant role in the maintenance of world order. While the General Assembly is not entitled to impose coercive sanctions, its role being limited to the adoption of nonbinding resolutions, the Security Council is vested with the authority to impose both economic and military sanctions in response to threats to world peace.[25]

These two justifications for U.S. enforcement action—collective self-defense and U.N. approval—are connected in that the U.N. Charter explicitly recognizes rights of self-defense and of collective self-defense.[26] The two may differ in that some remedies authorized by the Security Council might not independently be appropriate self-help remedies.[27] But the two are likely always to overlap in practice, because any international incident that provokes Security Council action would probably also give rise to a right of self-defense.[28] Both, of course, were possible bases for the actions of the United States and its allies in the Persian Gulf war.

In early August 1990, immediately after the Iraqi invasion of Kuwait, the Security Council met and passed a resolution that characterized the invasion as "a breach of international peace and security," a precondition of Security Council jurisdiction under section 27(3) of the Charter.[29] Soon thereafter it imposed extensive mandatory trade sanctions.[30] In late November, when its actions seemed to have had no effect, the Security Council acted once more, adopting resolution 678, which gave Iraq until January 15 to comply and "[authorized] Member States . . . to use all necessary means to uphold and implement [its earlier resolutions] and to restore international peace and security in the area." There is some dispute whether this resolution was itself an enforcement measure under the Charter, or whether it simply authorized states to act in collective self-defense on Kuwait's behalf.[31]

Shortly after the deadline expired, the United States and its allies attacked, pushing the Iraqi army out of Kuwait and well back into Iraqi territory. The council imposed stringent conditions in the wake of the resulting cease fire. Iraq was required, among other things, to destroy its existing chemical and biological weapons, to submit to extensive inspection of its nuclear facilities, and to pay reparations for its invasion of Kuwait.[32] Two days later the Security Council passed an additional resolution[33] purporting to protect the Kurdish minority from Iraqi attack. This resolution was the basis of the subsequent allied establishment of a security zone within Iraqi territory, although the resolution itself purported to recognize the "territorial integrity and political independence" of Iraq.

The norms that Iraq violated in its invasion of Kuwait were central ones in the contemporary international community. The invasion violated both norms of substance and procedural norms concerning how to deal with international conflict. The substantive norms were ones prohibiting seizure of another nation's territory. The procedural norms were ones requiring peaceful resolution of disputes, for although Saddam Hussein claimed to be retaking territory that was rightfully Iraq's, it is clear as a matter of international law that military aggression is no longer considered to be an acceptable method of setting international boundaries. As Oscar Schacter points out, there have been innumerable occasions in world history in which disputes have been settled through force; but this was the first such instance since the inception of the United Nations in which one state sought to devour whole another U.N. member state.[34] The Charter of the United Nations, of which Iraq was a member, prohibits such unilateral recourse to force.

Of equal importance with Iraq's prior agreement not to commit aggression was the fact that the allied response was in accordance with international law. The Security Council clearly had jurisdiction over the matter and the resolutions were passed by the necessary majorities.[35] While there might be doubt over whether the United States was acting as an agent for the United Nations, or whether the United Nations had simply authorized private members to act on their own initiative, the means of enforcement seemed clearly legitimate under the Charter. There are certainly disputes over whether the United States subsequently overstepped its delegated authority, for instance by its imposition of a "no-fly" zone, particularly in light of the recognition in resolution 687 of Iraqi territorial sovereignty. The basic contours of the remedy, however, seem within the U.N. Charter authority, and for that reason within the scope of Iraq's prior consent.

If the Security Council's role is established by state consent, it should not for that reason be taken to be egalitarian. A small number of countries, most notably the United States, have permanent seats on the Security Council and a veto over its actions, resulting in an entrenched aristocracy of states. Other states have two-year limited and rotating terms on the council; without a veto, their powers are not as extensive as those of the permanent members. When the United States acts at the behest of the council, then, it can cite the general consent of the world community to its special powers. Or at least it can do so as long as it faithfully adheres to the decisions that the council has arrived at, rather than using the decisions opportunistically, as a springboard for its own chosen goals. But Security Council authorization, and ex ante consent, do not make the system egalitarian. As might be imagined, the "great power veto" was the subject of much controversy when the Charter was drafted.[36] As Sen. Arthur Vandenberg put it in his diary at the time, "This 'veto' bizness is making it very difficult to maintain any semblance of the fiction of 'sovereign equality' among the nations."[37]

The collective self-defense justification for U.S. intervention is likewise not egalitarian. The stronger states, obviously, are the ones that are best positioned to defend their own rights. And a weaker victim that has strong allies is much better able to vindicate its rights than a victim whose friends are all as weak as it is. When the justification for action is self-help and the assistance of one's allies, the formally equal system of self-defense that states agree to turns out to be highly inegalitarian in practice. It should be noted that the practical inequality of a self-help system still stops short of the explicitly authorized formal hierarchy of power established by Security Council voting rules. However, contrary to what might at first appear, this lack of formalized hierarchy makes the inequality inherent in collective self-help *more* suspect rather than *less*. For in the context of the Security Council, it can at least be argued that the weaker nations explicitly agreed to a hierarchy of enforcement powers.

THE LIMITS OF EX ANTE CONSENT

Some of the problems with justification based on ex ante consent parallel problems raised in our earlier discussion about contemporaneous consent. For example, there is the question whether a state's leadership can consent on behalf of its people, if the leadership is not popularly responsive. In addition, there is the issue whether it should be presumed that an agreement is in a state's best interests simply because the state agreed to it. These are problems with consent generally, no different here than in the previous chapter. But there are also ways in which ex ante consent raises additional and different issues, making ex ante consent more legitimate in certain respects but more problematic in others. Most important is the fact that ex ante consent involves consent to general norms of conduct rather than to a specific quid pro quo.

Generality is important for several reasons. On the one hand, agreement to general rules may be less well informed than agreement to a specific exchange. It is harder to anticipate the consequences of open-ended norms that extend into the indefinite future than to anticipate the consequences of a contemporaneous exchange. One might, for this reason, be more concerned about the fairness of ex ante agreements. Where states know what they are consenting to, it is more reasonable to assume that the norms are in their best interests. The less they are able to predict the long-run consequences, however, the less confident we should be about the meaningfulness of their acceptance.

On the other hand, the very fact of generality imposes certain safeguards. A formal rule that imposes equal obligations on all parties is less likely to be completely lopsided. The fact that the other parties to the agreement are willing to live with a certain limitation on their own conduct tends to show that it is not too severe and that the benefits outweigh the costs.[38] This argument about formal equality should not be overstated. It is clear that rules which are general in form can, in some cases, be vastly more advantageous to some parties than to others. Such is the import of the familiar aphorism about the rich, as well as the poor, being forbidden to sleep under bridges. Formal generality is not an air-tight protection. But, imperfect as it is, it is a protection that simply does not exist in the case of contemporaneous consent.

The most important problem with ex ante consent relates to enforcement. Sometimes pressure is required to motivate states to comply. Whether the pressure is military or economic, it must typically be supplied by the stronger states in the system, for weaker states are not well situated to bring pressure to bear on violators. There is no guarantee, however, that stronger states will find it in their interest to compel compliance. Sometimes, in fact, the stronger states will actually take the side of the violator (or even be the violator). And even when they sympathize with the victim, it can be costly for them to throw their weight behind the community's norms. The stronger states will not always be willing to bear the costs of enforcement.

When the United States, for example, contemplates sanctions against China for human rights abuses or for its occupation of Tibet, it first carefully calculates the costs of alienating the administration in Beijing. When it considers military intervention in Bosnia, it weighs the potential loss of American lives and the practical difficulties it will face in eventually extricating itself. In addition to economic and military costs, there may be political costs; for intervention to enforce international norms can in some circumstances alienate important domestic constituencies. Pressuring the Israeli government to accept the return of deported Palestinians risks offending committed domestic supporters of the state of Israel. The U.S. relationship to the alleged violator is very likely to color the chances that action will be taken.

The relationship between the United States and the *victim* is also relevant to the probability that the United States will intervene. The costs of taking action will seem more worth bearing if the benefits are expected to accrue to the United States or its allies directly. While America's allies are likely to turn to the United States for help when their rights are threatened, other states may be reluctant. And even if such other states are willing to ask, it is always possible that the United States will refuse to get involved or will demand something in return.

And we should not overlook the possibility that the United States may itself be the violator. A system of enforcement that relies on willingness of stronger states to stand behind international norms has little to offer when the problem involves foxes guarding henhouses in the first place. The United States stood behind the norm of territorial integrity when Iraq invaded Kuwait. When Cuba, Panama, and Grenada were invaded, however, the United States was not part of the solution but the source of the problem.

The world's most powerful states, and in particular the United States, may be the only possible source of pressure to comply with international norms. But they have motives and incentives of their own, and it cannot be taken for granted that they will be willing to incur the costs associated with enforcement. In this respect, the problems of international enforcement are simply an exaggerated form of the problems of domestic enforcement, for domestic governments also sometimes pick and choose which violations warrant official attention. Powerful groups in society are better situated than marginal ones to flout the law and then deflect attempts at sanctions.[39]

General norms, then, have all the strengths of generality; the fact that obligations are imposed on all actors equally provides some assurances that the norms are fair. The problem, though, is that they may not be complied with in all cases. If so, the desirability of the rule, in practice, turns more on the aggregate costs and benefits of those situations in which the rule is honored than on the aggregate costs and benefits of the situations to which it should theoretically apply. It does not matter how beneficial the rule would have been to some case if it had been followed, if in fact the rule was not followed. When we evaluate the actual pattern of applications of a rule, the benefits may be much lower than when we evaluate the benefits of the rule in theory, if it were universally respected.

Not only is the overall benefit potentially lower; the distribution of benefits and burdens is likely to be significantly skewed. Weaker states and those without strong allies will bear more of the costs of respecting the rule, while the strong states and their friends will receive more of the benefits. Despite the advantages of generality, the chief disadvantage lies in the potential for discriminatory enforcement. While states may consent ex ante to general norms, and while they may even consent to enforcement by the world's strongest powers, they do not thereby consent to an unfair pattern of enforcement. They do not consent to being compelled to obey the rules when adherence is in the stronger states' interests, while being unable to secure the benefits of compliance when the stronger states choose to look the other way.[40]

It is clear that much opposition to the U.S. assumption of an international enforcement role is based upon perceptions that the United States intervenes selectively, to promote its own interests and the interests of its allies. Palestinians complain that the United States takes an active enforcement role in combating terrorism by sympathizers to their cause, while ignoring international-law violations by the state of Israel. Israel responds, of course, by arguing that the United Nations has passed many resolutions condemning Israeli actions but looks the other way when the Arab states violate human rights. Some Bosnian Muslims claim that the United States and its European partners would take a more active role in defending them if they were not Muslim and their attackers Christian. Saddam Hussein asks why the United States cares so deeply about the national self-determination of the Kuwaitis, but is so hostile to the national self-determination rights of Palestinians.

While one might dispute some of these accusations on factual grounds, it is hard to dismiss the claim that U.S. decisions to intervene are often, if not always, based on self-interest.[41] Indeed, some voices within the U.S. polity argue loudly that decisions to intervene should be made on precisely this basis.[42] Given that, as a political matter, U.S. decision makers tend for obvious reasons to be responsive to American voters—rather than to the victims of international-law violations in the other nations—it should not be a surprise to find patterns of selective enforcement. There is no doubt, however, that such discrimination undercuts American claims to legitimacy.

If the United States wants to cite ex ante consent as a justification for its enforcement powers, then, it has a responsibility to enforce international norms in a less selective way. It cannot simply pick and choose, depending on whether compliance is in its interests or in the interests of its allies. This is not to say that enforcement must be an all-or-nothing matter. We will return in chapter 7 to the issue of when less than 100 percent enforcement is defensible. The fact that there may sometimes be principled reasons for staying out of an international dispute does not, however, mean that the United States should be free to make the choice based on its own selfish interests. Or at least if it does act selectively, then when it does intervene its decisions cannot be justified by the fact that it is enforcing international norms agreed to by the community, for the rule as enforced is not the rule that was agreed to.

THE PLAUSIBILITY OF ACTUAL CONSENT

A further problem is whether actual consent can realistically be said to exist in most cases. The consent that exists in many circumstances is not explicit; it is tacit, inferred, or implied. Now, there are certainly circumstances in which it is reasonable to infer consent that is not made explicit. There is no magic contractual formula that states must follow in undertaking commitments. But there must be some limits to the theory's elasticity. The difficulty is whether, in the attempt to explain all international norms as consensual, we have diluted the concept of consent to such a degree that it has been drained of most of its normative meaning.

This problem does not exist in the same way for contemporaneous consent. There, actual consent is typically quite clear. Usually it is explicit. Specific terms are individually bargained for and it is relatively clear to both parties what is at stake. Ex ante consent, however, is more indeterminate. The problems of ambiguity are most acute with customary international law, when one nation claims that another agreed implicitly at some time in the past that it would or would not undertake certain sorts of actions. With debt-for-nature swaps or loan conditionality, it is in the interests of all parties to make the understanding clear. And if one side stops performing, claiming that there was no agreement, the other side can cease performance also. When one party's performance precedes the other's by a lengthy period, the party that has not yet had to perform will have incentives to dispute whether any tacit agreement took place.

The sorts of actions that are thought to indicate ex ante consent make disagreement natural.[43] Where there is no treaty commemorating the alleged agreement, what might count as acceptance of a norm? Should it be enough that the state in question has acted in conformity with the rule in previous circumstances? That is taken by international lawyers to be one indication of consent. But conformity might, of course, simply be a result of the fact that it happened to be in the state's interests to behave that way in the past. Thus international lawyers add the requirement that conformity should have been a result of the state's belief that it was bound by the norm in question.[44] Obviously, though, it is hard to determine why states happened to act in accordance with some rule in earlier situations. Indeed, given the diversity of reasons that states do the things that they do, it is not even clear whether the question itself is well defined.[45]

There are also problems about what to do when states have simply had no past involvement with the rule in question. Are we to infer that they consented to norms that other states treated as binding, simply because they sat watching silently and did not object? Hans Kelsen gave the example of a state which has never had access to the sea but then by treaty acquires a territory situated between its old territory and the sea. "Previous to the acquisition of the new territory it had no opportunity to apply the norms of maritime law. . . . It had no opportunity to contribute, by its actions, to the custom by which these norms of international law have been created. . . . If these norms of international law are considered as applicable to the state concerned from the very time it became a maritime state, these norms of customary international law cannot have been created by all the states upon which they are binding."[46]

It should be kept in mind, as well, that the genesis of many international norms lies in practices antedating the existence of an effective world forum, such as the United Nations, where objections might be registered. In reality, the international norms that we currently accept as having passed the tests of time and of state acquiescence are largely a product of the mutual understandings of a small group of powerful Western nations, understandings that non-Western nations surely had a right to ignore. The fact that other nations did not object as the norms were formulated is not something to which we can, realistically, attach much normative importance.

Even more difficult to explain from the perspective of actual consent is the fact that states that have newly come into existence are held to norms that predate them. New states are not allowed at birth simply to list which norms they accept and which they don't. States that were in existence at the time the norm is formulated at least possessed the theoretical right to object to the norms. "Persistent objectors" are not, according to legal doctrine, supposed to be bound to rules that they have consistently rejected.[47] New states, however, do not have even this option. As they come into existence, they are automatically burdened with all of the norms that await them. Oppenheim explained this result in terms of tacit consent: "New States which came into existence and were through express or tacit recognition admitted into the Family of Nations thereby consented to the body of rules for international conduct in force at the time of their admittance. It is therefore not necessary to prove for every single rule of International Law that every single member of the Family of Nations consented to it. . . . The admittance includes the duty to submit to all the rules in force."[48]

Given such evident readiness to infer consent from virtually any positive sign (indeed, from virtually any ambiguous sign as well), it is clear that the "consent" that is required for purposes of ex ante consent is a consent of an exceedingly attenuated sort. The problem, of course, is no more acute in international relations than in domestic politics, where consent-minded liberal philosophers have inferred consent from such unexpressive activities as walking on the highways or simply failing to leave the state in which one was born and raised.[49] As Brierly noted, "The attempt to build the state out of a social contract has been abandoned by political philosophy for at least a century, and the attempt to base international law on the consenting wills of individual states alone is merely a survival in the international field of this discredited doctrine."[50]

The problems may perhaps be less serious in international than in domestic relations, for some norms at least are founded on express agreement to treaties; consent this explicit is rarely found domestically. Even so, it is not possible to stretch consent to justify all the substantively desirable international norms that might come in useful. Kelsen stated the general problem bluntly: "It is certainly possible to assume that a state is bound by international law only if it recognizes this law as binding upon it, just as it is possible to assume that an individual is bound by national law only if he recognizes this law as binding upon him. . . . But there is hardly a writer ready to accept all the consequences of such an assumption."[51]

With all these evident inadequacies in basing obligation on ex ante consent, one reassuring thought should not be lost sight of. Most of the objections to consent theory that note the implausibility of tacit consent are relevant to the issue whether ex ante consent is a necessary condition, not to the issue whether it is a sufficient condition. Even if some inferences of tacit consent sound far-fetched, this does not mean that those inferences that are reasonable are morally irrelevant. This means that we need not abandon ex ante consent as one approach to justifying acts of international hegemony. We only need to recognize that it cannot be stretched to include all instances that some might like.

International lawyers have long recognized a fundamental tension in the foundations of international law, as to whether it is founded on consent or on natural law. The positivists have stressed the process by which norms are adopted; they insist that sovereign states can only be bound by their own agreement. Natural lawyers emphasize the consistency of international law with fundamental morality. It is clear that the two are only contingently equivalent. While states might consent to morally correct norms, they need not; they might agree to norms that had no moral foundations or they might fail to agree to norms that were morally required. For norms that are truly desirable as a moral matter, some authors (like Oppenheim) would simply tinker with the definition of what should count as acceptance, on the apparent assumption that surely if one looks carefully enough one can find some indications of state agreement. The concept of consent then gets stretched beyond recognition as one tries to make the two approaches reach the same results.

But it would be better to approach the problem candidly, acknowledging that consent does not necessarily produce all of the results one might ideally hope for. One must then face the problem directly of what to do when there is simply no plausible indication that consent was actually given. Those who feel compelled to remain faithful to a process-based analysis will turn their backs on norms without the proper consensual pedigree. Those whose first loyalty is to substantive morality will recognize that there must be other ways to justify one's international activities.

We will investigate two approaches that contain important elements of substantive morality. The first, hypothetical consent, aims to incorporate substantive desirability into the process of consent. It is something of a hybrid. The second turns unashamedly to value judgments, dispensing with the need for state agreement and resting instead on the necessity of doing what is morally right.

6

HYPOTHETICAL CONSENT AND THE PROVISION OF PUBLIC GOODS

At first it might seem puzzling that some legal scholars have stubbornly persisted in claiming consent as a justification for norms to which states obviously have not and could not have consented. It defies common sense, for instance, to claim that a newly formed state is bound to preexisting rules by consent even where it has vigorously denounced those rules on its entry into the international community.[1] But there is a certain odd logic to using consent to explain why new states should be bound, and why norms are binding in other cases where actual consent is clearly lacking. When the question is raised whether a new state should be held to international norms, it somehow makes sense to conclude that the new state would have consented if it had only been present at the time the rule was formulated. This is an explanation based on hypothetical, rather than actual, consent.

Take, for example, the norm that states should grant immunity to diplomats from other states. It is a longstanding norm and it clearly predates most contemporary states.[2] It is nonetheless unsurprising that some might attempt to justify the norm in terms of consent—hypothetical consent, if actual consent cannot be demonstrated. The inference of hypothetical consent is appealing for two reasons. First, the desirability of the norm is obvious. States need to communicate with one another, and particularly in an era before electronic communications, this was typically done through exchange of diplomats. Virtually all states both send and receive diplomats; the rule of diplomatic immunity, for this reason, does not discriminate in favor of one state or against another. Whatever advantage might be gotten from harassing the diplomats of another state is likely to be short-lived, for future diplomatic exchanges will be deterred. All in all, the rule seems likely to work out fairly and well, and it seems that it is the sort of norm that states would want to have.

Second, there is an obvious explanation for the fact that the newly created state did not agree to the norm at the time the rule was being formed: the state simply did not exist. This is important because it negates any inference that might otherwise be drawn from the fact that the state did not agree. Under some circumstances, the fact that a person or state does not affirmatively agree to an arrangement might be taken as an indication that the person or state rejects the arrangement. To bind the person or state in such a case would violate its autonomy. But where the state did not yet exist, or where it was not in effective communication with the community in which the norm arose (as with non-Western nations that later found themselves bound to Western custom), the fact that it did not affirmatively agree does not indicate disapproval.

Here the fact that states could not under the circumstances reasonably be interpreted as having participated in the negotiations is used, paradoxically, to support the consent argument rather than to defeat it. The question is what to make of the fact that no position one way or the other was ever taken; should silence be taken as indicating a failure to accept the norm, or as indicating a failure to reject the norm? If the standard is actual consent, then the fact that a state could not have agreed counts against a norm rather than in favor of it. Under this view, it is unreasonable to expect silent states to have come forward to reject international norms, so that silence does not indicate approval. But it can be argued with equal plausibility that it is unreasonable to expect that they would have come forward with their approval; for this reason, silence does not indicate rejection either. The lack of opportunity to express a position means that no inference can be drawn either way.

These two parts to the argument work together to support the claim that rational states would have agreed if they had had the opportunity. The fact that the arrangement in question is substantively desirable suggests that it is something that reasonable states would agree to. The fact that they did not have an opportunity to pass judgment on the arrangement means that their failure to agree is not a rejection and can be disregarded.

These are the basic outlines of the claim that norms of international behavior can be justified under a theory of hypothetical consent. And the same hypothetical-consent argument that can be made in support of particular norms of international behavior (such as protection of diplomats) can also be made in support of international hegemony as a general matter. As with the argument that states would have agreed to particular norms, there are two parts to the argument that states would have agreed to hegemony in general. The first concern—substantive desirability—asks what benefits hegemony confers on the world at large.[3] Why does it make sense to think that hegemony is something to which other states would have agreed? There is, as we will see below, a large literature dealing with this topic, for some have argued that hegemony is normatively acceptable because it helps to ensure the provision of public goods such as international peace and security. The second concern—the explanation for lack of actual consent—requires us to spell out in further detail why there is so little explicit and consensual institutionalization of this supposedly beneficial arrangement. Here we need to examine the likely impediments to adoption of substantively desirable international agreements.

There are two different sorts of arguments about how an agreement that appears substantively desirable might nonetheless not be adopted. The first relies on standard rational choice theoretic reasoning about the transaction costs of bargaining and about collective behavior. There are a number of different practical and strategic obstacles to reaching agreement within a group even when agreement is in the interests of the group and to the benefit of all of the group's members. The fact that an agreement was not reached does not, therefore, prove that it would not be of benefit to the parties or that they do not want it. We will call this the "market-failure" explanation.

The second is more ambitious. It is based on the possibility that actors might be prevented from reaching reasonable agreements by the interests that they currently have. An arrangement that would be generally recognized as reasonable and fair when viewed abstractly and impartially may not produce consensus because the selfish interests of the parties stand in the way. This is a different concept of hypothetical consent, for it asks what hypothetical fair-minded individuals would agree to, not what currently existing states would want. We will call this the "partiality" explanation for why desirable arrangements are not adopted.

What both conceptions of hypothetical consent have in common, though, is that each tells a story about why the allegedly desirable agreement was not in fact reached, and about why that fact should not matter even in a theory that, in some sense, privileges party agreement as a basis for political institutions. In an ideal world, both theories argue, the agreement would have been reached; that is the foundation for imposing it. The difference is that under the market-failure explanation, "ideal" is defined in terms of lack of transaction costs while under the partiality explanation "ideal" is defined in terms of lack of bias in favor of one's self-interests. The market-failure formulation tells us to try to approximate what the actors would do in a hypothetical ideal process of negotiation. But the partiality explanation is doubly hypothetical; for it tells us to approximate what hypothetical ideal actors would do in a hypothetical ideal process.

THE LURE OF HEGEMONY

International hegemony has received remarkably good press in recent years in the political science community.[4] Cha_____ _____ _____ the fact that hegemony sometime_____ _____ twisting, preferring to depict int_____ responsible leadership.[5] A bit more_____ of good: "The danger we face is n_____ omy, but too little, not an excess of domination, but a superfluity of would-be free riders, unwilling to mind the store, and waiting for a storekeeper to appear."[6] The claim is not so much that smaller states have affirmatively indicated that they do prefer great power hegemony, but that if they were rational, they would. "All other things considered," writes David Lake about other states' foreign policy, "states should prefer more hierarchic external relations."[7]

This conclusion might strike some as counterintuitive. It would ordinarily be assumed that states do not like hierarchy any more than people do, at least when they do not expect to end up at the top of the hierarchy. Indeed, it is sovereign equality that international legal norms are designed to protect; unsurprisingly, it is subordination—not lack of hierarchy—that strikes most observers as problematic. The key to the conclusion that hegemony is generally beneficial to the world community lies in the economic theory of collective action and in what has come to be known as hegemonic stability theory.

According to this theory, the chief advantage of hegemony relates to its effect on promoting collective action. Even where all states would benefit, there may be practical problems in creating the optimal amount of public goods. Economists have long predicted that public goods are more likely to be supplied when there is a single large actor that will be able to capture a large share of the benefits produced by the public goods. International relations theorists argue that the presence of a hegemon for this reason increases the chance that public goods such as international peace or fiscal stability will be secured.

The public goods problem that concerns both domestic economists and international relations theorists arises roughly as follows.[8] There are some goods—so called "public goods"—that everyone is able to enjoy regardless of whether he or she has contributed to their creation. They are "nonexcludable," meaning that there is no technically feasible method for limiting their enjoyment to the subset of the population that shared the cost of providing them. Public goods are also "joint," meaning that their enjoyment by one individual does not preclude their enjoyment by others; public goods don't get used up. Classic domestic examples of public goods are pollution-free air, which is available to all who breathe and is not consumed by those who use it, and lighthouses, which are visible to contributors and noncontributors alike and whose use by one does not interfere with use by others.[9] Other examples of public goods include crime reduction, preservation of endangered species, outdoor public art, and public streets.[10]

Public goods give rise to collective action problems because nonexcludability undercuts the incentives for contributing to their production. Why bother to pay the costs in time or money when one might simply wait for others to supply them? There is always, in other words, a temptation to free-ride; but if large numbers succumb to the temptation to loaf while others work to provide the good, then the goods will not be provided, or will be provided in a less than optimal amount.[11] Paradoxically, this difficulty can arise even if everyone would value the public good more than his or her own proportional cost of supplying the good. In such circumstances, it might seem collectively rational for everyone to contribute, but the group behaves in a collectively irrational way. It is these collective action problems that hegemony is thought to help resolve.

For economists argue that collective action problems are less acute where there is a single large actor rather than a large number of small ones. Because the single large actor, being large, stands to gain more from the provision of the good, it cares more about whether the good is provided. Therefore it is willing to contribute to the good's creation, even if that means allowing other smaller actors to enjoy the good for free. The problem of free-riding is most severe in larger groups, according to this reasoning, but even in small groups there is, as Mancur Olsen puts it, "a surprising tendency for the 'exploitation' of the great by the small."[12]

Without going into the mathematical reasoning for this result, we can illustrate the point by an example. In a world where there is no effective intellectual property protection, computer software is a public good. Once the creator puts the program on a disk, anyone can copy it (nonexcludability) and this does not interfere with use by others (jointness). Yet a company may find it worth its while to invest money in producing computer software even though others will take advantage of the programs it produces, so long as it is large enough that it will get enough use out of the program to recoup its cost of production. Although it would prefer to be able to charge other users for pirating the program, at least it doesn't lose money when they do because their use does not interfere with its own. If there were no companies large enough to be able to recoup the costs of production, however, the software would not be produced.[13] And even where there is one large company, there may be some valuable programs that do not get produced because they are not of sufficient benefit to that company.

The extension of this argument to international relations has given rise to hegemonic stability theory, according to which public goods will not be provided in the absence of a single powerful actor, the hegemon. Robert Keohane describes the two central tenets of hegemonic stability theory as, first, that order in world politics is typically created by a single dominant power; and second, that the maintenance of order requires continued hegemony.[14] The hegemon's ability to solve collective action problems and provide public goods is the feature of hegemony that could make it potentially attractive from a hypothetical-consent point of view, for this capacity makes hegemonic governance desirable.[15] To quote Charles Kindleberger once more, "Leadership to provide the public good of stability . . . seems a poor system, but like democracy, honesty, and stable marriages, is better than the available alternatives."[16]

The best-known example offered to illustrate the value of hegemony concerns world monetary stability during the interwar period.[17] Kindleberger argued that at this point Great Britain had already lost its hegemonic status, but its position had not yet been filled by the United States. During the period leading up to the Great Depression, many nations were faced with domestic pressure to raise tariff barriers, devalue their currency, and take other shortsighted actions that seemed likely to protect their national interests. If some strong nation had been willing and able to assert financial leadership by adopting farsighted monetary and trade policy, it could have stabilized the situation. Instead, all pursued short-term advantage, and the results were catastrophic.

There are some indications that American leadership in the post–Cold War period should be treated as a public good. Consider the complaints of European nations when they feel that the United States is not fulfilling its appropriate leadership role. In May 1993, to take one example, Under Secretary of State Peter Tarnoff announced that the Clinton administration's reluctance to get involved in the Bosnian conflict demonstrated a generally diminished willingness to intervene in trouble spots around the world. The Swedish foreign minister, Marghareta Af Ugglas, complained in response, "It is really tragic to give a signal to the world that you are not prepared to pursue your leadership. What does that tell the future dictators of the world?"[18] And as Flora Lewis described one recent economic summit, "There is a sense of helpless, fearful drift among the nations so sure of themselves not long ago, and a nostalgia for the days when America could be counted on to command, enabling everybody else to indulge in carping. The pleasure of America-bashing has vanished."[19]

It is easy to think of other international situations that might fit this paradigm.[20] Even if all states would like an agreement not to build nuclear weapons, there are formidable practical problems with constructing a compliance regime because enforcement is costly and few states are willing to contribute to the cost. The hegemon has more to lose from violations than smaller states (both because it is large and because it is more subject to nuclear threat). Its existence makes a nonproliferation regime possible, because smaller states would not get enough benefit to make it worthwhile to enforce the regimes themselves. Enforcement of nonproliferation treaties by the United States is a public good; for when states keep their promises to the United States, they are simultaneously keeping their promises to one another. The smaller states can all free-ride on the willingness of the United States to undertake the cost of enforcement, and in this way they benefit from American hegemony. As David Calleo put it, "Sustaining its world role in the present system costs the United States a great deal. To some extent, America's allies are free riders on the benefits of that American effort. In that respect, it is they who exploit the United States."[21]

In its strong form, hegemonic stability theory claims that hegemony is a necessary condition for solving collective action problems. "Without a stabilizer," writes Kindleberger, "the system in my judgment is unstable."[22] Some authors take a more optimistic view about the possibility of collective action in the absence of hegemony, particularly in posthegemonic periods where practices of cooperation developed earlier may persist through inertia.[23] It is agreed by many, though, that hegemony is beneficial in resolving problems about the provision of collective goods. Whether it is the only solution, or whether it simply is one element out of several, a world composed of a large number of roughly equal actors is generally thought to be more prone to suboptimal failures to act collectively. It is for this reason that some contemporary political scientists specifically praise the benefits of hegemony and characterize it as legitimate. The provision of public goods is the chief advantage of hegemony.

MARKET FAILURES

If hegemony is so generally desirable, though, why hasn't there been more widespread agreement to it? This is a standard problem for hypothetical-contract theory, for it is necessary to show why (if consent is such an important value) it does not matter that the supposedly beneficial arrangement was not voluntarily adopted. One of the possible explanations has to do with the high search and transaction costs of reaching agreement. Economists would describe the failure to make a mutually beneficial agreement because of such transaction costs as a "market failure."

The general argument can be illustrated in the analogous domestic context, by asking why domestic governments are not explicitly consented to. Failure of explicit consent is the chief reason that some philosophers have either been driven to inferring consent from such dubious indicators as remaining in the country, or have chosen to move to a theory of hypothetical consent. Governments seem to have many advantages; yet there is little evidence of actual agreement by most of the population. Why don't more citizens consent? There are three related parts to an explanation based on transaction costs: communications difficulties, information inadequacy, and strategic behavior.

COMMUNICATIONS, INFORMATION, & STRATEGIC BEHAVIOR

The communications difficulties impeding agreement on a scheme of government are enormous and probably insurmountable. It is not possible to gather together everyone that is to be bound by institutions, to ask their approval before the institutions are created. The potential citizens are too numerous and too spread out geographically; and of course, some of them have not even been born. In addition, some governments grew up gradually, through a very diffuse process that did not afford a general opportunity for participation in the government's formation. It is not clear at what point the government was "formed," so that it was appropriate to seek consent. Would consent have to be sought at every point that the state's political institutions started to take shape or changed direction?

Even for those governments that actually came into existence through explicit consent (such as the American federal government), the consent realistically can only cover a subset of existing individuals and cannot attempt to cover future generations. Perhaps a new constitutional convention could be held every few years, although this solution would still present questions of why citizens entering the polity in the interim should be bound. But, more to the point, this is obviously impractical, and not only because of the costs of holding such a convention. One must also consider the costs of redesigning legal and political institutions from the ground up when one of the very reasons for having a government is to provide continuity for all of those institutions in society that depend on stable legal arrangements.

Even if those costs were to be borne, it seems unlikely that it would be possible to achieve unanimity. In addition to the communications costs, there are problems caused by inadequate information. If the parties have erroneous or incomplete information about each other's preferences, they may mistakenly hold out for greater concessions, to the point that others are simply unwilling to go along. It is not enough to have good information about one's own preferences, because one's bargaining position will be affected by what one thinks the others are likely to agree to. Such information is hard to come by, and mistakes can stand in the way of consensus.

And in the unlikely event that there is effective communication and good information, there would still be problems of strategic behavior.[24] The strategic difficulties of reaching agreement are probably greatest when the process is spread out over time. If some citizens enter the picture after the remainder have already agreed, it may be virtually impossible to get them to go along. Why should they? The latecomers get all the advantages of the public goods that governments create even if they do not specifically agree, because the others are already bound. This does not mean that they actually disapprove of the government, or that they would not specifically assent if they were part of the group considering the matter at the outset. It simply stands to reason that they have nothing to gain by undertaking political obligations, because most or all of the benefits will be forthcoming regardless. One need not be a latecomer to take advantage of others this way; if one is strategically skillful, one may simply pretend not to be willing to go along in the hopes that the others will find it desirable to agree anyway.

It is, therefore, extraordinarily difficult to get unanimous agreement even to a scheme that is actually advantageous to everyone. Because of the problem of market failure, it can be claimed, nothing should be inferred from the fact that agreement was not arrived at. It therefore makes sense to ask, instead, what would have been agreed to if transaction costs were not so high, and if all the parties could somehow simultaneously be given the chance to bargain in a situation of perfect information. In such an ideal posture for negotiations, the hypothetical-contract argument would run, the parties would unanimously consent. The result would be a domestic government.

The same argument about hypothetical consent in the domestic case can be made in the international context. Indeed, some of the transactions costs would be even higher in the international than in the domestic context.[25] Particularly in earlier times, when methods of transportation and communication were more primitive, it would have been exceedingly difficult to reach actual agreement. Large portions of the world were effectively isolated from one another; the fact that Southeast Asian nations (for instance) did not explicitly consent to international understandings about free passage over the high seas or protection of diplomats does not mean that they would not have agreed if they could have been consulted.

Even under modern conditions, the sheer practical difficulties in getting multilateral discussions organized can be prohibitive. Treaty negotiations absorb enormous amounts of time, energy, and money. Trying to anticipate all the problems a treaty might have to address, and to draft accordingly, is a complicated process. The costs are worth bearing only when the likely gains are substantial. Strategic behavior or inadequate information can create an impasse because even if an agreement is beneficial, one or more of the negotiating parties may decide to hold out for more. If one state believes that the agreement is unduly advantageous to another, it may demand concessions in order to obtain for itself a larger part of the mutual gains.

As in the domestic context, an added layer of complexity arises from the fact that new states can enter the picture at any time. It is not enough to get agreement from all states that exist at some particular historical juncture. Either the states originally negotiating a treaty must successfully anticipate what later states will be willing to agree to, or they must be prepared to renegotiate when latecomers enter the picture. In addition, new states have little incentive to agree to arrangements that other states are already bound to follow anyway. By failing to agree, they can hope to capture the benefits of the existing world order without undertaking the costs. When new states enter a preexisting order, it therefore seems reasonable to ask simply whether they would hypothetically have been willing to agree to the existing institutional arrangements if they had been in existence at the time the arrangements were entered into. The market-failure explanation suggests that their failure actually to consent to particular norms of international behavior should not be a bar.

Similarly, market failure may explain why there has not been more agreement to international hegemony in general. For the same reasons that domestic governance would be hypothetically agreed to, international hegemony would be hypothetically approved, and the failure actually to consent should not stand in the way. Instead of inferring lack of consent from the fact that states did not explicitly agree, then, we should simply recognize that transaction costs are prohibitive and that the failure explicitly to agree is understandable under the circumstances.

Before continuing to identify some of the problems with the market-failure justification for hegemony, we should note how the economic theory of collective action appears twice in this argument, first as part of the claim that international hegemony is beneficial, and second as part of the explanation for the fact that it is not affirmatively agreed to. Hegemony is desirable, according to hegemonic stability theory, because without it public goods will not be produced. But if we ask why hegemony is not itself consented to, much of this answer also turns on arguments about collective behavior. The claim that other states will not approve hegemony because they can obtain the benefits without incurring the costs is, in essence, an argument that these states are free-riders. There are collective action problems with getting other states to consent to international hegemony.

The fact that the collective action argument does double duty should not be surprising. Hegemony is desirable because it facilitates the production of public goods. But hegemony is itself, according to the same logic, a public good; indeed, it is the ultimate public good, the one which makes possible the provision of all other public goods. It is an institution that provides benefits to the world at large, whose cost is borne largely by the hegemon, but whose benefits cannot be withheld from those who do not contribute. The very things that make hegemony desirable suggest that it cannot be achieved through explicit state agreement; if it were possible to produce international governance through explicit agreement, it would be possible to produce other collective goods this way also, and governance would not be so crucial. The hegemon therefore cannot expect to be authorized by other states to perform its functions; it must simply step up and assume the natural responsibilities of the strong. As Kindleberger says, "My Presbyterian mother-in-law used to put it simply: 'You have it to do.'. . . A leader, one who is responsible or responds to need, who is answerable or answers the demands of others, is forced to 'do it' by ethical training and by the circumstances of position."[26] The argument for the substantive desirability of hegemony and the claim that explicit agreement cannot produce it in this way fit together into a coherent whole.

THE FAILINGS OF MARKET FAILURE   Coherent, yes; but convincing? That is less clear. The chief problem with the market-failure formulation of hypothetical contract is that it seems only to supply a default rule. The market-failure approach to hypothetical consent specifies, essentially, that there are some circumstances where it is not possible for practical reasons to reach an agreement; in such circumstances, the fact that a particular arrangement was not adopted says nothing about whether it was desirable. Because the parties did not have a preference against the agreement, however, it does not violate their autonomy for the agreement to be imposed. Therefore, where it is possible to identify arrangements that would be beneficial to all, the fact that they were not agreed to is not a bar. Hegemony (or other institutional arrangements justified on market-failure terms) will, according to this line of reasoning, be Pareto-superior to world circumstances without it.[27] That is, hegemony must make one or more parties better off without making anyone worse off, because if it made any party worse off, that party would not agree.[28]

This is a default rule because it only aims to facilitate agreements that the parties actually want to have. Where the parties' actual preferences are unclear, it justifies arrangements that might reasonably be thought to be to the parties' advantage. But it does not provide a reason for overriding the actual preferences that the parties have, where those preferences can be ascertained. The fact that some hypothetical rational individuals would agree to a regime is not important, under the approach described above, where the parties themselves have different preferences. The contracting process is hypothetical, but the contracting parties and their preferences are real.

The basic problem with the market-failure approach to hypothetical contract is that the challenge to either domestic governance or international hegemony typically arises at a point at which it is relatively easy to determine what the parties want, because they are confronting one another in a concrete disagreement. At that point, pure transaction-cost reasoning that amounts to no more than a default rule is not of much use. A default rule only specifies what to do when the parties' preferences are unknown, and once a challenge arises, the parties' preferences are known. Either the party accepts the particular norm or hegemony in general, or it does not. To put it another way, if hypothetical contract only justifies agreements that are Pareto-superior, it isn't very helpful once one knows what the parties want, and that they do not want the agreement in question. Later in this chapter I will explain why the common assumption that public goods make hegemony Pareto-superior is mistaken. What matters for present purposes is simply that hypothetical-contract theory of the market-failure variety does not justify imposing an arrangement on parties who are known not to want it.

Here we must consider one important argument that could in theory resurrect the market-failure explanation. Admittedly, it is possible that the parties' rejection of some norm or of hegemony in general is influenced by the fact that they find themselves in the middle of a dispute. At that point, it is clear whom the norm will benefit and whom it will hurt, so that the chance is fairly high that one or the other of them will reject it.[29] It might be thought, therefore, that the objection could be circumvented if we gauged "hypothetical agreement" at some earlier point. True, at the point where the hegemon's legitimacy becomes an issue, the objecting state might not in fact consent. But what if it could be argued that the state would have agreed at some earlier time, before the current dispute arose? It didn't actually consent then, but the reason may be that the costs of communication, information, and so on made actual agreement unattainable at that point. It would have agreed then if there had been no market failure (the argument goes), and for this reason it ought to be bound now.

But it is not immediately clear why agreement should be measured at one point rather than another, and in particular why it is better to measure agreement earlier rather than later.[30] The most persuasive reason has to do with bias. There are some decisions that ought to be made impartially, and as to these, it is better to make decisions earlier, when the parties have less information about where their interests lie.[31] At this earlier point, they will not know what position they will ultimately come to occupy, and so if the arrangement is in general a good one, they will support it. For these reasons, it might seem that the best time to measure hypothetical agreement is ex ante. Buchanan and Tullock, for example, take exactly this approach in asking whether parties to a domestic constitutional system would have agreed at the time the system was established.[32] They argue that if one measures attitudes when the constitutional arrangement was chosen, the parties will be ignorant about whether particular arrangements will work out to their advantage. For this reason they will support institutions that are desirable as a general matter; altruism will merge with self-interest.

Note, however, that there is at most a contingent connection between the time at which decisions are made and the amount of information that is available to the decision makers. Typically, people have less information about their self-interest at an earlier point than at a later point; but this need not be true. There are some respects in which one's self-interest is knowable in advance and unlikely to change. Smart people, strong people, well-educated people, those who come from rich families, white people, and men can all pretty well guess that certain rules are going to work to their advantage (as can the weak, the poor, and so forth). Maritime nations have different interests than landlocked nations, and low-lying nations have different interests in a global warming treaty than nations that need to burn coal or cut their forests in order to develop. They should not be expected to "hypothetically" consent to institutional arrangements that do not protect their interests, simply because consent is sought before the fact.[33] Large, well-endowed nations, similarly, should be expected to be able to predict which institutional arrangements will work in their favor; hegemony, it might reasonably be thought, would be one of them.

What the hypothetical-contract theorists are really after, then, is not simply that the agreement be made at a different time but that it be based on a smaller set of information, one which does not include knowledge about one's self-interest. What is really at stake is not when the decision is made but how much the parties know when they make it, and these two are only contingently connected. This point about the value of ignorance is rather different from the market-failure explanation we have been considering, for the market-failure formulation is more likely to treat the *absence*, not the *existence*, of information as the problem. So long as the parties know what their self-interests are, according to this new argument, there is no reason to assume that they will agree to all arrangements that are collectively valuable. They will only agree to ones that appear Pareto-superior when a dispute arises, and this is a hard criterion to satisfy. For most interesting disputes about legitimacy concern institutional arrangements (such as hegemony) that are genuinely controversial and often contrary to particular states' interests.

But to guarantee this sort of ignorance, we need to move to a different sort of explanation for why desirable arrangements (as hegemony is alleged to be) are not agreed to. The market-failure explanation will not be sufficient because reducing transaction costs alone will not facilitate arrangements that conflict with some states' views of their self-interest. If we want to make the hypothetical-contract argument work, we should not go about it by trying to specify some particular time at which to measure agreement, but by directly specifying the amount of information that should be available to the parties. This leads to a second sort of explanation for why desirable arrangements are not adopted: partiality.

PARTIALITY

A more ambitious formulation of hypothetical-consent theory is possible. Under this view, it is not the practical problems of negotiating that get in the way of agreement, but the fact that the agreement in question would actually not be in one or more of the parties' interests. The argument for eliminating self-interest from consideration is that it is not reasonable to be partial.[34] Hypothetical reasonable people would agree to certain arrangements even if, as things worked out, the arrangements turned out not to be beneficial to them. Hypothetical-contract theory justifies imposition of such arrangements on the grounds that they would be assented to by persons who were ignorant about their eventual position in the scheme. Information about their ultimate gains and losses should be withheld, because hypothetical contract asks what reasonable and fair-minded people would agree to rather than what is in their self-interests. Partiality can be as much of an impediment to reaching fair agreements as practical difficulties in negotiation.

Unlike the transaction-cost argument, the partiality argument is not a default rule. It does not try merely to approximate what the actors would actually want, ever ready to reconsider when better information about their actual preferences becomes available. This solution, then, is potentially coercive in a way that the market-failure solution is not. It imposes upon states arrangements that they do not actually want and that do not work out in their favor. It does so on the grounds that some theoretically reconstructed actors—with different information from the actual actors—would have agreed, when the actual actors would not. This is the sense in which it is a more ambitious approach to hypothetical contract than the market-failure argument. The negotiating actors are hypothetical, as well as the process of negotiating.

This different approach calls to mind, obviously, John Rawls's *A Theory of Justice*.[35] Rawls argues that institutions are fair if they would be chosen behind a "veil of ignorance," for the parties act most fairly in a setting where they do not know their eventual position in society. In this setting, they do not know whether they will turn out to be talented or dull, rich or poor, physically well endowed or less fortunate. The hypothetical contract that interests Rawls is the one that would be arrived at by parties in this setting. But Rawls is not the only writer who has argued for decision in a situation of ignorance; so did John Harsanyi,[36] and Buchanan and Tullock, as we just saw, argued that constitutional principles should be chosen so far back in time that the parties do not know what impact the principles will have on interests. Many others have since taken up the theme of hypothetical contract.

What principles emerge once partiality is suppressed, and why should they be considered superior? Self-interest, speaking generally, discourages consideration of the interests of other members of society, with which one's own interests may conflict. If individuals are prevented from knowing what their interests will turn out to be, their ignorance will result in a greater level of altruism than they would otherwise show. But there are at least two different ways that one might be impartial; indeed, Rawls pursues a very different notion of what would happen behind the veil of ignorance than Buchanan and Tullock. One form of impartiality that might emerge, the one that Buchanan and Tullock and Harsanyi predict, is that individuals behind the veil of ignorance will maximize the total good to society and thus the expected value for each individual. The second, which more nearly corresponds to Rawls's notion, is that individuals will choose to maximize the situation of the person occupying the least advantageous position in society. Both must be examined before we can assess the plausibility of the hypothetical-contract argument for hegemony.

EXPECTED VALUE VERSUS MAXIMIN We will start with the claim that actors ignorant of their eventual position would choose to maximize the total benefit and thus each one's expected value. To say that hypothetical contract would further the total good of the group as a whole is not necessarily to assign entity status or personality to the group. The community need not assume existence apart from the individuals that compose it; indeed, liberals would be hesitant to grant the community such independent moral recognition. Instead, liberals might simply sum up the merits and demerits of different institutional arrangements to the individuals involved and choose the set of institutions that maximizes overall advantage. Taking this path leads to a roughly utilitarian hypothetical-contract theory, and to maximization of the expected value to each individual member.

Hypothetical-contract theory could lead to utilitarianism in the following way.[37] Persons who did not know what position they were eventually to occupy in society might reason that their prospects overall were improved by institutions that maximized overall advantage.[38] An institution that maximizes overall advantage also maximizes average advantage; and individuals who do not know what position they are likely to find themselves in would define their expectations in terms of the average. This is, essentially, Buchanan and Tullock's argument. The expected value of some particular institutional arrangement would equal the total benefit to society divided by the number of individuals.[39] In a situation where one has no information with which to differentiate oneself from the others, it is arguably reasonable to maximize the expected value and thus the total value to society.

Economists might describe the difference between the market-failure approach to hypothetical contract and the expected-value argument in terms of the difference between Pareto superiority and Kaldor-Hicks efficiency. The market-failure model requires Pareto superiority because states will not agree to an arrangement such as international hegemony unless it is advantageous to each of them. The market-failure model attempts to anticipate what states would actually agree to, and so it does not justify institutional arrangements where some states end up worse off even if other states' gains more than offset the loss. This is precisely the definition of Pareto superiority; a state of affairs is Pareto-superior to the status quo if every actor is at least as well off under the new scheme, and some are better off. Kaldor-Hicks efficiency is a less restrictive condition because the new state of affairs must only display enough gains over the status quo that it would in theory be possible to compensate the losers. Compensation need not actually be made. The Kaldor-Hicks criterion measures, essentially, the overall benefit to society of different schemes.[40]

The expected-value argument, unlike the market-failure argument, is insensitive to distributional concerns. The market-failure argument is sensitive to distribution in that no party can be made worse off under the new arrangement than it was under the old.[41] But under the expected-value argument the only thing that matters is the total good, not how it is distributed. This is no surprise, for it is commonly recognized that utilitarianism (which is linked to Kaldor-Hicks efficiency) is not concerned with how gains and losses are distributed over the population, so long as the net gain is as large as possible. It is this feature of utilitarianism that accounts for Rawls's observation that utilitarianism fails to take seriously the difference between persons.[42] The expected-value criterion is more morally attractive in the sense that it is impartial, but it has the normatively undesirable feature of not concerning itself with whether the distribution of benefits is excessively lopsided.

The principle that rational actors would chose to maximize expected value behind the veil of ignorance, however, is only one of the two ways to be impartial. The second is the maximin principle. For if one of the dangers of self-interest is that it will encourage the veto of arrangements that are beneficial to the group as a whole, surely another is that it will encourage the vetoing of arrangements that are beneficial to the poor and weak. If an individual is genuinely concerned about the position of the poor and weak, or is concerned about how he or she would fare on coming to occupy that position, a different response to ignorance of his or her eventual situation would be to guarantee the poor and weak the best position possible.

This observation leads to Rawls's well-known maximin argument. Rawls expected that individuals acting behind a veil of ignorance would choose arrangements that maximized the position of the worst off in society. The Rawlsian proposal does not guarantee that social benefit overall will be maximized. But it encourages impartiality, unlike the Pareto principle, and compared to the expected-value principle it is relatively egalitarian.

There has been dispute in philosophical circles over whether Rawls's reasoning really applies to the international context. In *A Theory of Justice*, Rawls specifically concluded that the maximin principle was not appropriate to international relations, although other authors have disagreed and attempted despite his objections to carry his reasoning over to create a theory of international wealth redistribution.[43] In a more recent work, Rawls has remained committed to some process of hypothetical contract in identifying principles of the law of peoples.[44] Again, though, he did not conclude that what he takes to be the usual domestic principles of justice would apply in the international setting.

We will not attempt here to engage in a finely tuned analysis of whether Rawls's precise methodology and conclusions apply. Neither will we attempt to settle the much disputed question whether the maximin or expected-value formulation is the more plausible approach to hypothetical-contract theory. Instead, we will simply ask whether either a rough maximin formulation, an expected-value approach, or a market-failure approach would justify international hegemony. Surely at least one of these must be satisfied if the hypothetical-consent argument is to work. Can hegemony, as a general matter, be justified in terms of promoting the good of world society as a whole, and the expected value of states? Can it be justified by what it does to improve the lot of the worst off? Does it advance the interests of every state in international society? If the answers to all of these questions are no, then it seems hard to argue that hegemony would be hypothetically agreed to.

HEGEMONY AND HYPOTHETICAL CONTRACT: THE ASPIRATION
Which, if any, of these formulations of the hypothetical-contract analysis are satisfied depends in large part on distributional concerns. How are the supposed benefits of hegemony distributed between states in the international community? The expected-value formulation demands only that the total benefit be maximized. But the market-failure formulation requires that hegemony be Pareto-superior; every state, that is, must be benefited. And the maximin formulation focuses attention on the benefit to the least advantaged in the world community.[45]

If we adopt the most benign account of international hegemony, we might conclude that all of these formulations are satisfied. The basic collective action argument about provision of public goods suggests that without hegemony they will not be produced. Hegemony may not result in production of the optimal amount of public goods, but at least the amount will be larger. This line of reasoning suggests that hegemony increases the total benefit to the world community, although it leaves open the possibility that some other scheme (world government, perhaps?) would be even more efficient. Hegemony, according to this argument, thus passes the test of increasing expected value.

Again on an optimistic view, some proponents of hegemonic stability theory would also conclude that hegemony passes the test of Pareto superiority. As Duncan Snidal describes it, "[The theory] claims that the presence of a single, strongly dominant actor in international politics leads to collectively desirable outcomes for *all* states in the international system."[46] Isabelle Grunberg, likewise, notes that the most prevalent version of hegemonic stability theory assumes that hegemony "creates a condition of Pareto optimality for all economic actors."[47] The conclusion of Pareto superiority follows from the definition of collective goods as ones from which noncontributing actors cannot be excluded. Everyone, therefore, shares in the benefit when public goods are produced.

Even more optimistically, the rhetoric of hegemonic stability theory supports the conclusion that hegemony satisfies the maximin criterion. The reason lies in the assumption that large states will bear the cost of providing public goods, while smaller states will ride for free. There is, therefore, a sense in which hegemony necessarily works to the advantage of the weakest and poorest states. As Snidal puts it, this claim that the weak are able to exploit the strong is what accounts for the "distinctive bite" of the theory: "After all, there is little new in the claim that a dominant state will enforce a stable global order for its own benefit: it is much more novel to claim that domination will benefit all and especially the weaker members of the international system. This," he concludes, "is no trivial difference," citing its "appealing normative implications."[48]

Some "casual empirical" support can be cited in favor of this somewhat surprising proposition, which, as Snidal observes, turns the traditional view of hegemony in the international system on its head.[49] It has been claimed, for example, that the states that benefit most from the existing principles of territorial stability and state sovereignty are the weakest ones. Legal recognition of the integrity of states is of great value to vulnerable states, which in previous times would have been annexed or conquered for colonies.[50] (The invasion of Kuwait, perhaps, illustrates the point.) Stronger states are able to defend themselves and do not need legal protection. The legal regime of respect for territorial boundaries might be depicted as a public good, for once the norm becomes ingrained it benefits all, and strong states will be willing to invest resources in getting the norm established.

A similar point can be made in the context of economic, as opposed to military, affairs: it may very well be that economic stability is most crucial to weak states, who are least well equipped to ride out financial storms. International fiscal instability, prolonged recession or depression, vicious trade wars, and wild fluctuations in commodity prices are quite arguably most damaging to the weak and impoverished. The aphorism that "when the elephants fight, the grass dies" applies in economic as well as military affairs. It is certainly plausible that during periods of economic instability, it is the better off who are best able to pull up the trade drawbridges and retreat into financial isolation.

There are two other respects in which hegemonic stability theory seems to support the conclusion that hegemony is most advantageous to weak states. The first is the claim that public goods will not be supplied without a hegemon. This claim is relevant because the maximin criterion requires not just that the least advantaged be made better off, but that they be made as well off as possible. It is not enough, therefore, simply to show that hegemony is better for weak states than anarchy; hegemony must be the best of all. By arguing that public goods will not be supplied without a hegemon, hegemonic stability theory supports the claim that hegemonic regimes, ceteris paribus, are always preferable to systems where no powerful actor dominates.

There may be some plausibility to the claim. In domestic society, the solution that all but anarchists accept for collective goods problems is governance, including coercive political institutions. We do not attempt to control crime, support a public highway system, or compensate for accidents without some governmental mechanism. Voluntary coordination and cooperation, it is assumed, are not enough; centralization of power is required. To the extent that the list of desirable international public goods is extensive or ambitious, then, one might tend to think that some analogous international institution is necessary.

Second, some versions of hegemonic stability theory underscore the advantage to the weak states by emphasizing the costs of hegemony to the more powerful. These costs result in a progressive weakening of the hegemon, and thus in a relative improvement in position of the weaker. Such predictions are the basis of declinist analyses of America's position in the world.[51] None of these points proves conclusively that the benefits of hegemony to weaker nations cannot be surpassed by other types of international arrangements. But the theory's rhetorical solicitude for the less well endowed is unmistakable. The boast that hegemonic leadership satisfies the maximin criterion is well within the theory's aspirations.

HEGEMONY AND HYPOTHETICAL CONTRACT: THE CRITIQUE

But this, as I said, is the optimistic version of the theory, the one which takes the most benign view of hegemony. There are reasons to doubt it, and in particular to doubt whether it satisfies either Pareto optimality or the maximin formulation. Suspicions arise, initially, around the fact that there is no explicit effort to calculate the possible *costs* of hegemony to the international community. (We will return shortly to the question of who receives the benefits.) Even if hegemony facilitates the provisions of public goods, it would surely be important to ask at what cost these goods are provided and who bears these costs. "Cost-benefit" arguments for hegemony must rest on estimates of both sides of the equation.

Several other possible problems with the hegemonic stability argument have been well explored in the political science literature, although typically not with the purpose of testing hypothetical-contract theory, or indeed any other normative theory.[52] The first is one that we have already alluded to: substantial doubt has been expressed over the claim that public goods cannot be provided in the absence of hegemony. Keohane and Snidal both deny that hegemony is the only solution, suggesting that cooperation can be achieved in other ways. "Rationality," argues Snidal, "does not prevent states from cooperating when that is in their best interest. . . . Nothing in realism's assumptions about states would rule out collective action."[53] The incentives for collective action, obviously, are there; for if states do not cooperate in the absence of hegemony, the goods may not be produced at all. Both Keohane and Snidal emphasize, further, that cooperative behavior (including production of public goods) can continue after the hegemon declines. This, of course, is a main thesis of Keohane's *After Hegemony*, and Snidal concurs.[54]

For many purposes, it may not matter much whether hegemony is the only way that public goods can be produced, or only one way. It would be interesting enough simply to learn that hegemony is one solution to collective action problems. But for normative purposes uniqueness matters, for whatever costs might arise from international dominance would be more defensible if hegemony were the only solution. In particular, if the critics are correct that public goods can be produced in other ways, then the case that hegemony satisfies the maximin criterion is seriously undercut, for the other ways of providing public goods may be even more advantageous to the least well off.

A second problem is probably common to all formal models: once an interesting model is constructed, there is a temptation to claim more territory for it than it can reasonably aspire to occupy. Hegemonic stability theory deals with the provision of public goods, but not all benefits that the world community desires are public goods. The technical requirement of excludability is very likely not satisfied even with regard to some of the most frequently used examples, such as free trade and stable peace. Several writers have pointed out that it is possible to exclude noncooperating nations from a free-trade regime; all that is required is to insist on reciprocity.[55]

World peace, in addition, can be extended to some areas of the world while being denied to others. Bruce Russett points out, for instance, that the "stable peace" that has resulted from American hegemony encompasses mainly the Western nations; the Third World has hardly been conflict-free.[56] Indeed, it can easily be argued that conflict has simply been exported to the Third World, where developing nations (and subgroups of their populations) fight one another as proxies for developed states. Similarly, it is possible to have norms of territorial integrity but to treat violations of them with much greater seriousness if they occur in some parts of the world than in others (Kuwait versus Tibet or East Timor, for instance). As with the point about alternative methods of producing public goods, this problem may be more serious for normative purposes than it usually is in the standard political science context, for the costs of hegemony are more defensible if there are lots of public goods to be procured and then distributed.

In fact, what the hegemon produces may not even be perceived as "goods" by developing nations, let alone public goods. "Smaller states," Grunberg points out, "may not perceive hegemon-led growth and its implications as desirable and may be reluctant to open trade and specialize for political reasons or out of concern for domestic stability."[57] It is clear, after all, that resistance to hegemonic plans is not unusual; this suggests that smaller states are not always overwhelmed by the hegemon's acts of purported generosity. As Grunberg points out, the radical literature takes a rather different view of hegemony than mainstream international relations theory does, and much of the reason is concern for less developed nations. Proponents of hegemony have not tried to take into account the actual distaste and distrust that smaller and weaker nations seem to have toward hegemons.

The collective action literature provides one explanation for the failure to go along with what the hegemon prescribes: it is strategic behavior, free-riding. But there is a problem with dismissing states' rejection of institutional arrangements this way. Why should failure to go along be characterized automatically as strategic rather than genuine? What looks to a political scientist like a case of widely beneficial hegemony may look to a state leader like subordination, whose symbolic, economic, and political costs are not outweighed by the supposed practical benefits.

The strategic-behavior characterization, in other words, involves second-guessing expressed state preferences. Liberals should be quite wary of dismissing the preferences that states claim to have. Indeed, doing so runs some of the same risks as labeling expressed state preferences "false consciousness," which is surely an illiberal move.[58] Both labels allow one to dismiss all inconvenient indications that states do not have the preferences one thinks that they ought to; both tend to make theories empirically incontrovertible. Before the excuse may be employed that some expressed preference is merely strategic, more evidence must be given than the simple fact that the preference is an embarrassment to collective action theory. The burden of proof should be on those who claim that the state secretly prefers or would benefit from something else.

A third set of problems, however, is probably the most pervasive and potentially troubling. Hegemonic stability theory is driven by an analogy to domestic collective action that is flatly inappropriate. Most domestic collective action problems take place within a structure of basic law and order; actors, even large actors, are constrained in the methods they use to pressure others. Hence the larger actors' frustration in their efforts to obtain contributions, and the smaller actors' ability to free-ride. If the larger ones were not limited by domestic legal constraints, they could simply force smaller states to contribute.

Thus, as Gilpin points out, because the hegemon is stronger, it may be able to extract revenue from weaker states in exchange for providing them with public goods.[59] The weaker states lose their ability to "exploit" the hegemon, as collective action theory predicts. Even if the collective action logic does demonstrate that the existence of hegemony is utility-enhancing, its assumptions about how the gains will be distributed are unwarranted in situations where the hegemon can simply rearrange the resulting gains as it chooses. This possibility of "coercive hegemony," as Snidal puts it, therefore undercuts the claim that hegemony is especially beneficial to weak states;[60] whatever benefits they receive may be offset by the donations they are forced to make. At this juncture, the argument that hegemony satisfies the maximin criterion goes completely out the window, or at least it should.

Some will undoubtedly find such "taxes" perfectly fair, indeed, positively desirable, even if they require abandoning the maximin principle completely. The reason would be that smaller nations should simply not be allowed to free-ride or otherwise behave "exploitatively."[61] The very use of the word *exploitation* makes the disapproval obvious. But why the pejorative connotations? Why shouldn't the small be able to "exploit" the large? Taking advantage of the fact that you are a small, weak state is no more unfair than taking advantage of the fact that you are a big, strong state. And that is something that committed market theorists seem to have no problem with so long as the exploitation is accomplished through voluntary transactions—as it is in the international "free-rider" context. Collective action theory predicts that small states will free-ride, but it does not claim that the hegemon does not get a net benefit out of providing the public good.[62]

The use of the loaded term *exploitation* presumes that some proper division of costs and benefits exists, aside from simply requiring that all interaction be voluntary and thus, presumably, to the benefit of all. The argument about exploitation seems to be based on a notion that the free-riders get more than their fair share of the benefit of the arrangement; their net benefit is larger than it should be. But how, aside from the market, do they claim to be deciding what is a fair share to contribute? Market theorists sneer at such claims when they are made by Third World nations, who cry "exploitation" when they feel that Western nations appropriate "too much" of the surplus value created by market arrangements that Third World nations enter into voluntarily. In such circumstances, market theorists are prone to claim a lack of objective standards for dividing gains from trade.

Here perhaps the answer is that the best division of contributions is the one that makes possible the optimal provision of public goods. The problem with free-riders is that when small states are allowed to free-ride, the end result is that less is produced than when all states are required to contribute. Initially, though, it is not clear why the extra contribution should come from smaller states. If we can solve the problem of providing the optimal amount of public good by simply forcing states to contribute, then we could equally well require that these contributions be made by the larger states (or by the mid-sized states, or by something in between).

Most fundamentally, moreover, the very fact that the hegemon is able to force other states to contribute undercuts our confidence that it is genuinely utility-enhancing to provide the good at all, or to provide it in given quantities. The international hegemon's ability to use force, in other words, destroys the collective action logic in two ways. I have already pointed out that that ability undercuts the logic's assumption about how gains from cooperation will be distributed, for the hegemon can simply rearrange the costs and benefits at will. But it also undercuts the presumption that gains exist at all. It can no longer be assumed that a hegemonic arrangement must be either generally beneficial, or a technical "public good," on the grounds that otherwise the weaker states would not have cooperated.[63] Once the possibility of coercive hegemony enters the picture, it becomes impossible to make assumptions that the public good in question is actually utility-enhancing; the hegemon may in fact be requiring small states to contribute to some enterprise that is not, overall, successful from a cost-benefit standpoint, but that happens to provide the hegemon with something that it craves. Not all lighthouses are cost-effective, after all.

Finally, and most important, once the possibility of coercive hegemony is introduced, there is not even any reason to assume that the hegemon will limit its use of coercive power to compelling contributions toward the production of public goods (even inefficient ones). As Stephen Krasner argues, the hegemon is equally likely to use its power simply to further its interests at the expense of other states.[64] Hegemons do not, for example, always support free-trade regimes; sometimes they are protectionist.[65] "Somehow," writes Grunberg, "hegemons are credited with a generosity that is not required by the original public goods theory."[66] No reason is given for assuming that the hegemon will limit itself to civic-minded acts of generalized benevolence.

Because of the possibility for predatory behavior, it simply cannot be assumed that hegemony will work to the good of the least advantaged in international society. It may; but then again it may not. As Keohane concludes, it cannot be said "that hegemony in general benefits small or weak countries. There certainly is no assurance that this will be the case. Hegemons may prevent middle-sized states from exploiting small ones and may construct a structure of order conducive to world economic growth; but they may also exploit smaller states economically or distort their patterns of autonomous development through economic, political, or military intervention. The issue of whether hegemony helps poor countries cannot be answered unconditionally, because too many other factors intervene. . . . It remains an empirically open question."[67]

The maximin test will therefore not be satisfied. But neither can it be assumed that hegemony will be utility-enhancing, because the hegemon may simply be requiring states to contribute to projects that benefit the hegemon while imposing even larger costs on the others. For the same reasons, hegemony cannot be assumed to be Pareto-superior; for once some states are required to contribute, there is no guarantee that the benefits they receive as a consequence will outweigh their costs. As Snidal concludes, the general question of how much asymmetry is beneficial to whom has no single neat answer, and a general presumption that hegemony is widely beneficial is unwarranted.[68]

The collective action argument is most persuasive where there are guarantees that states act voluntarily—as in the protected environment that most domestic legal systems attempt to provide.[69] In a world where formal equality is protected by overarching legal and political institutions, and where autonomy enjoys legal safeguards, the collective action logic seems appealing. The model of domestic economic markets provides one such example. As I noted in chapter 2, international relations theory is oddly taken with a view of the world in which formal equality is the norm. The uncritical employment of collective action models may be yet another example of the implicit acceptance of a formal model with great conceptual appeal but little empirical accuracy. A different way of looking at the world, however, leaves greater room for attending to the power inequalities that exist in fact. Instead of relying on the market model, we might rely on a model of domestic governance. The two are rather different.

The market model assumes a world of formal equals, with formally equal powers; it is just that some actors happen to be larger than others. Because they are larger, they receive larger total benefits from collective goods, and smaller states rely on this fact by allowing large states to do most of the work. The central difficulty, under such models, is how to ensure provision of the optimal amount of collective goods. The governance model (whether domestic or international) is more complicated. True, it recognizes that political leadership has the advantage of creating the potential for provision of public goods that would otherwise not be provided. But the "up side" of potential provision of public goods must be balanced against the "down side" that once coercive power comes into existence, there is no guarantee that it will be used in ways that are either utility-enhancing or distributionally fair. The key problem with hegemony, especially in the eyes of the weakest, is that it is something of a Frankenstein monster.

This fact is recognized even by proponents of hegemony. Thus, Kindleberger writes, "Leadership may be based on domination; it is sometimes called 'hegemonial.' But legitimacy of leadership can only come from persuasion. Leadership may also be lost if it becomes exploitive and illegitimate; if the leader, for example, mixes up the public good of maintaining the stability of the system, with the private good of buying up foreign firms or foreign resources."[70] This conclusion should be unsurprising (and incontrovertible) if one keeps in mind the similarities between hegemony and domestic governance. Governments are not simply large private actors; they possess unusual capacities to exercise coercive power, and they are not constrained by some overriding scheme of law and order enforced by a superior power. This is precisely the feature on which the normative concerns of government legitimacy focus. When one actor becomes by far the strongest, and virtually immune to pressure, this does not merely give rise to a better way to create public goods; it also gives rise to the potential for abuse. When we ask whether a government is legitimate, it is not an answer that governments make possible the creation of public goods. They also make possible a lot of other things, many of which are not desirable at all. The same is true for international hegemony.

If one asks whether it is generally true that domestic government benefits the least advantaged (or is Pareto-optimal, or enhances overall utility) the answer seems to be clear that no such generalization is warranted. Swedish social democracy is a very different case from Haitian military dictatorship or a British hereditary monarchy. Some governments, in some circumstances, satisfy these criteria; but it would be absurd to say that government generally is justified because it meets these criteria. As with hegemony, it is precisely because of the existence of coercive power and the possibility for its abuse that generalizations fail. Power can be used for good purposes or for bad. All that the public goods argument shows is that hegemony is not necessarily bad.

Once we turn away from grand claims that hegemony, per se, is beneficial, what are we left with? The claim that hegemony creates the potential for public goods still stands, but each case of international hegemony must be examined on its individual merits to determine whether that potential has been realized. Particular international norms, and particular actions by the system's strongest powers, may be justifiable on the grounds that they would be generally agreed to. The presumption of legitimacy, however, is gone; and much hard work remains to determine whether legitimacy exists in the particular case. The empirical questions on which this determination rests are structured by the particular form of hypothetical-contract theory that one espouses. To those who favor a maximin approach, the relevant question is whether hegemony benefits the least well off states in the system. Expected-value theories require instead that hegemony maximize the total benefit overall. Pareto superiority demands that each state derive benefit from the fact of hegemony. None of these questions is easy to answer; but each is more defensible than the superficially attractive shortcut of simply presuming that hegemony satisfies these tests by facilitating the provision of public goods.

SUBSTANTIVE VALUES AND HYPOTHETICAL CONTRACT

We should consider briefly a final possible approach to hypothetical contract, suggested by Rawls's discussion of international justice in a recent lecture. He argues that many of the basic principles of the laws of nations—territorial sovereignty, respect for human rights, adherence to treaties—would be agreed to behind the veil of ignorance even by states that were not themselves liberal states. In making his argument, Rawls considers the choices that would be made by what he calls "well-ordered states"; those that are not well ordered are outlaw states, that need not be consulted in making institutional arrangements.[71]

What is of primary interest here is this process of disqualifying certain states from consideration in the original contract formation. Rawls's argument is that a certain subset of states—those with the desirable characteristic of being "well ordered"—would hypothetically agree to certain norms. "Well-orderedness," under the Rawlsian view, requires satisfaction of some rather substantive criteria, such as respect for basic human rights and a commitment to nonexpansionist means. This approach suggests a third interpretation of what hypothetical contract is all about. Under that interpretation, one might ask what a hypothetical group of people with a certain set of substantive commitments might agree to. The hypothetical negotiation process would focus on what "reasonable" actors would agree to, but reasonableness would consist of acceptance of certain substantive values (such as the principles of well-orderedness) rather than merely ignorance of their own ultimate self-interest. This approach to hypothetical contract incorporates clearly substantive commitments into the original decision process.

Now, there is a sense in which all of hypothetical-contract theory is about substantive norms, because it is substantive norms that the hypothetical-contract device is employed to create. But that does not mean that hypothetical contract theory is indistinguishable from theories of justification that rely on substantive norms directly. First, hypothetical-contract arguments are designed to keep reliance on substantive norms to a minimum; the process is supposed to be neutral as among differing substantive premises. The substantive norms, in other words, are supposed to be the product of the argument, not its premises. Second, there are many sorts of arguments that rely on substantive norms without relying on the hypothetical-contract device at all. If one bases political theory on a commitment to human rights, one need not justify this commitment by reference to what the parties would have agreed to. This sort of theory, in fact, will be explored in the following chapter. Thus, Rawls's reliance on substantive commitments—his presumption that only the preferences of well-ordered states should matter—is a striking feature of his international hypothetical-contract analysis.

Of course, it has been suggested by Michael Sandel that even Rawls's original version of hypothetical contract behind the veil of ignorance incorporates controversial assumptions that shape the resulting theory of justice.[72] Whether or not this is true, note how much more substantive is a process that explicitly disqualifies actors that do not share a particular moral perspective. If one were inclined to justify a Roman Catholic state, one could set up the contractual process so that it inquired only into the arrangements that reasonable Roman Catholics would make; to generate a Marxist or monarchist state, one might define the set of original participants accordingly.[73]

Because this version of hypothetical contract quickly becomes tightly entangled with substantive commitments, it is impossible to distinguish it completely from arguments that are based directly on substantive principles. But then some (such as Ronald Dworkin) have argued that it is not clear what exactly the device of hypothetical contract adds to one's substantive notions of fairness anyway.[74] The common import of both the Sandel and Dworkin objections is that much of the philosophical work of the hypothetical-contract device is being performed by other, unexpressed premises; the device by itself is not what is producing the results.

The critics of hypothetical-contract theory may or may not be correct that even in the usual domestic setting the theory tends to sneak its philosophical premises in through the back door. It is nonetheless clear that substantive premises can infect certain versions of hypothetical-contract theory, such as Rawls's approach to international relations. In addition, once one starts to rely on substantive arguments of this sort, they may have direct implications, without the intermediation of hypothetical-contract theory. For this reason, it makes sense to turn at this point to the issue of whether American hegemony might justifiably be based on premises of substantive morality.

7

SUBSTANTIVE

MORALITY

In the spring of 1993 the Western world was transfixed by the unfolding horror in the former Yugoslavia. Serbians, Croatians, and Bosnian Muslims fought ferociously and bitterly to obtain territorial control over parcels of land in Bosnia-Herzegovina. The United Nations brokered one cease-fire after another, virtually all of which were violated within hours of their effective dates. Word leaked out of truly heartbreaking atrocities: mass murder of civilians, gang rapes, torture, mutilation, and virtually every other cruelty that the human mind can imagine. Tens of thousands of innocent people were driven from their homes under a program of what came to be known by the chilling phrase "ethnic cleansing." Large numbers of refugees were trapped in cities utterly lacking even the most minimal facilities to care for them, and were dying in large numbers from shelling and sniper fire. Overworked doctors operated on the injured in futile efforts to save those they could, performing amputations without anesthetics or proper surgical equipment.

Perhaps worst of all, the devastation appeared to be a deliberate policy of political and military leaders. U.N. relief convoys were repeatedly refused admission to cities filled with refugees as thousands were on the brink of death from cold and starvation. War crimes violations such as murder of civilians and rape were not merely the sporadic abuses that are the unfortunate companion of almost any war, but part of what seemed to be a genocidal plan to crush resistance

and drive opposing groups from the lands that they had inhabited for generations. While it was apparent from the outset that there were abuses on all sides, it
was also clear (and it become increasingly so as time went on) that the most fla-
grant perpetrators were the Bosnian Serbs, backed by the Serbian government of
Slobodan Milosevic. When both the Bosnian Muslims and the Croatians signed a
peace agreement brokered by U.N. representatives Cyrus Vance and David Owen,
the Bosnian Serbs rejected the plan and fought on. Some of the Serbian leaders
later accepted the agreement at a meeting in Athens, but a referendum of the
Bosnian Serbs held in mid-May 1993 overwhelmingly rejected the settlement.

What were the people of the world to do? The French and British opposed
taking military action to protect civilians, to roll back Serbian territorial gains, or
to deliver relief supplies. The reason, at least in part, was that French and British
troops were on the ground in Bosnia, and the countries' leaders feared for the
troops' safety. The Russians also opposed taking action. Russia had traditionally
viewed Serbia as a compatriot and ally; and Boris Yeltsin's political position was so
weak as to make him reluctant to provide his nationalistic opponents with ammunition. China has traditionally been reluctant to support intervention in the
"domestic" affairs of other nations. Radical action by the Security Council, then,
seemed quite unlikely.

President Bill Clinton had campaigned on a promise to do more to stop the
slaughter in Bosnia; on taking office, however, he came to see things differently.
For many months he held at bay those of his advisors and the segments of the
American public who felt that stronger action should be taken. The economic
boycotts earlier adopted had clearly weakened Serbia but had not slowed the
Bosnian Serb attacks. By late April important officials in the State Department
were urging publicly that something be done, arguing that the United States had a
"moral obligation" to save the Bosnian Muslims from genocide.[1] "In effect,"
their letter read, "the result of this course has been Western capitulation to
Serbian aggression." The American ambassador to the United Nations agreed that
more forceful action was necessary.

Few missed the parallel to the Holocaust, the historical event that virtually
defines the concept of genocide. The very day that the State Department letter was
made public, President Clinton spoke at the opening of the Holocaust Memorial
in Washington, D.C. Both he and Elie Wiesel (who also spoke) alluded to the
parallels.[2] It was not simply the fact of genocide that made the comparison apt; in
context, what was perhaps more striking was that the rest of the world, on both
occasions, allowed the killing to continue.[3] Observers wondered, have we learned
anything? Fifty years from now, will our grandchildren look back in shame,

wondering how our generation could have knowingly let this happen but absurdly confident (just as we were until recently) that they would act differently if they were ever placed in such a situation, and that a holocaust would never be allowed to happen again?

The argument for intervening in Bosnia is that simple morality permits—or indeed requires—stronger nations to stop mass killings if they are able. Substantive morality itself, according to this position, justifies intervention even when other nations have not consented. There are many different sorts of situations in which, it could be argued, substantive morality bestows a right of intervention. The strongest case may be the prevention of genocide. Overthrow of truly vicious dictatorships and the establishment of democracy may be another, or prevention of mass starvation (as our intervention in Somalia suggests).

There are as many different means of intervention as there are goals. Direct military intervention is one; but it may also be possible to act through local intermediaries (by assisting "freedom fighters"), to take covert action, or to offer states benefits (such as trade liberalization or foreign aid) if they comply with human rights norms.[4] One thinks of Vietnam, the Bay of Pigs, Allende's Chile, or the invasion of Panama; but also of the pressure to democratize in the Philippines (in the 1950s and then during the Aquino revolution), the support for a right of Jewish emigration from the Soviet Union, or the pressure to release political prisoners in post-Tiananmen China.

The first purpose of this chapter is to evaluate the argument that substantive morality directly, without the intervention of positive norms established by state consent, is an adequate basis for intervention by strong states in the internal or external affairs of the weaker.[5] The second is to ask whether substantive morality might also give rise to a duty to intervene.

SUBSTANTIVE MORALITY AND CONSENT

Some, but not all, international responses to egregious violations of substantive morality can be justified by state consent. We noted earlier that justification based on ex ante consent requires both that the substantive norms being enforced be grounded in consent and that the processes used to enforce them be consensual. If either the norm or the enforcement process has not been accepted, then another justification must be found. Yet it is easy to think of moral norms that do not rest on state consent, and even easier to think of cases in which their enforcement would not have been consensual.

It would be futile, for example, to try to use ex ante consent to explain why the Allies should have intervened to prevent the Holocaust. Some of the substantive norms the Nazis violated were not sufficiently well developed or widely adopted during World War II to ground a claim that Nazi Germany had consented to them. That is the reason for concern over whether the Nuremberg Trials after the end of the war unfairly imposed a retroactive obligation on the conquered Germans.[6] A fortiori, Germany had not agreed in advance to any enforcement mechanism for prevention or punishment of these violations.

There are, similarly, problems with defending intervention in Bosnia on a theory of ex ante consent. True, we now have in place human rights norms that clearly prohibit the sorts of atrocities being committed there.[7] But have the Bosnian Serbs consented to them? Here we face a rather murky set of issues about who must have consented, given the degeneration of the former Yugoslavia into civil chaos. The same problem must be solved with regard to whether they have consented to U.N. enforcement procedures. And even after assuming that the Bosnian Serbs are legitimate successors to a state that was bound by human rights norms and by U.N. procedures, the fact remains that thus far the Security Council has not authorized military intervention. Consent to U.N. procedures is irrelevant if what is at issue is unauthorized action by the United States and its allies. Intervention in Bosnia would clearly be much harder to defend on a theory of ex ante consent than, for example, the U.N.-sponsored actions during the Persian Gulf war or the Korean War.

If ex ante consent would not justify forcible intervention, contemporaneous consent is even further from the mark. It would not be possible to argue that the Bosnian Serbs somehow consented to forcible intervention given that they definitively rejected the favored world design for peace—the Vance-Owen plan—at the polls. Certain remedies, such as trade embargoes, might be defended on contemporaneous consent grounds because they are not coercive. The nations that refuse to trade with Serbia or with the Bosnian Serbs are only withholding what the Serbs are not entitled to anyway, since no state has a right to trade with any other.[8] But these remedies have not, so far, been effective in preventing or reversing the abuses; additional and more forceful action may have to be employed (and, therefore, justified) if the world community is to achieve its goal. And it is this intervention that cannot be justified without direct reliance on substantive morality.

Perhaps one might ask whether the Bosnian Serbs might have consented in some hypothetical ideal bargaining position. But even John Rawls seems to acknowledge that outlaw states would not necessarily agree to all human rights norms, and Serbia (with its expansionist vision of its own historical destiny) would probably fit into his category of outlaw states.[9] More to the point, though, there is something deeply troubling about phrasing the whole issue in terms of Serbian consent.[10] The Serbs, and the Bosnian Serbs, are the perpetrators of human rights abuses. Why should we expect them to consent? Why should they have to consent before action is taken? Isn't there something wrong with placing the decision in Serbian hands? After all, the Bosnian Muslims did not consent to be murdered, raped, or driven from their homes. Why must the world community obtain Serbian consent before stopping their crimes? Did the lack of Nazi consent justify the rest of the world's inaction in the face of Nazi genocide?

The issue of proceeding without state consent and solely on the basis of substantive morality is most likely to arise when the moral norms at issue are norms of international human rights. This is not to say that only human rights norms have the potential for justifying intervention without consent; there are other principles of international substantive morality that might, in the right circumstances, directly justify intervention. For example, under the international moral principle of territorial integrity, territorial aggression against an innocent state could justify intervention by stronger powers even without consent to the norm. But it is more likely in such circumstances that ex ante consent would be available as a justification, so that resort to substantive morality would be unnecessary. The reason is that where the interests of states are at stake, rather than the interests of individuals, there is a greater likelihood that states would have already reached agreement about standards of conduct. States have incentives to develop rules regulating their conduct vis-à-vis one another; they have fewer incentives to develop rules to protect individuals at the expense of state power. Thus, for example, states have generally failed to codify a human right to democracy—a right which would, of course, typically come at the expense of states.[11]

Even more than with the recognition of substantive norms of human rights, states have been quite reluctant to create or recognize international institutions dedicated to human rights enforcement. Even when standards of conduct have been agreed to, there has rarely been agreement to procedures for their protection. For this reason, consent is unlikely to provide a justification for intervention to protect human rights. Jealous of their sovereignty, states have made it clear that outside intervention in their "internal affairs" (a domain which most states understand to include many if not most human rights abuses) is prohibited.[12] Security Council action, moreover, to which there is general advance agreement, is not appropriate under the charter unless there is some sort of international breach of the peace, and many gross violations of human rights do not meet this standard.

Consent is not, for this reason, adequate to deal with such problems. It protects only against abuses by nations that have been high-minded enough to agree to human rights enforcement in the first place, and leaves truly outrageous violators free to do as they like. If we believe in inalienable human rights, then surely they must be protected from abuses even when the violators have been consistent in refusing to recognize them or provide for their enforcement. While it is no doubt advantageous as a matter of practical politics to gain the consent of states to human rights norms and to their enforcement mechanisms, as a matter of principle it seems clear that the very concept of human rights does not square well with the requirement that states can only be bound by their consent.

In keeping with this intuition, international law has recognized a category of norms that are jus cogens; they are binding despite lack of recognition or even rejection by individual states. Thus, a treaty to deny human rights or to support apartheid or the slave trade is considered null and void; state consent is not enough to make it valid.[13] The law of jus cogens demonstrates awareness that state consent is not the only source of international law. Some international norms are so deeply rooted that they cannot be pushed aside by contrary state agreement. The existence of a category of jus cogens acknowledges a hierarchy of international norms, with some entrenched beyond removal and founded, ultimately, on a natural law of international relations.[14] As put by the Mexican delegate to the U.N. Conference on the Law of Treaties, "The rules of jus cogens [are] those rules which derive from principles that the legal conscience of mankind deem[s] absolutely essential to coexistence in the international community."[15]

How does this substantive morality that transcends consent fit within a general liberal framework? We have been exploring the possibility of a liberal justification for international hegemony, and to this point the justifications we have considered have been based to a greater or lesser degree on autonomous consent, an obvious liberal value. Certainly, recognizing a category of norms that overrides state preferences impinges on the autonomy of states. But the protection of human rights from state oppression is no more a violation of liberal principles internationally than it is a violation of liberal principles domestically. Liberal democrats expect that some norms will be entrenched against interference by democratic processes; because they are central liberal values, however, this does not offend liberal politics. It is true that in some cases the entrenchment of human rights can be explained by prior consent; the American Bill of Rights, for example, was ratified in accordance with democratic constitutional processes. Yet other nations, such as Great Britain, recognize comparable rights without a written constitution. And in American history, after all, there is a tradition of natural law recognition for individual rights, honored by the Declaration of Independence, among other things. Even in the liberal tradition, then, consent is not an absolute prerequisite to the recognition of individual rights.

STANDARDS OF CONDUCT AND THE RIGHT TO ENFORCE THEM

Even if some international norms are beyond state consent, this does not mean that state consent is irrelevant as a general matter, or that all desirable rules of conduct must be grounded in universal moral principle. State consent is important in adding to fundamental moral principle, filling in blank areas or developing ways to implement basic morality. The rules of nuclear nonproliferation may be highly desirable, but it is hard to argue that they derive, in all their detail, from substantive morality.[16] Most people would leave international protection for endangered species to state consent, let alone the more technical rules protecting intellectual property rights in international markets. As to such matters, state agreement continues to be relevant; they are subject to positive lawmaking. It is only as to a limited number of compelling universal norms that hegemonic intervention is justified absent state consent.

Saying that substantive morality justifies a particular intervention requires two things. First, the norm that is being enforced must be morally compelling, in the same sort of way that the prohibition on genocide is. Second, it must be morally correct for the hegemon to enforce it.[17] We saw this dichotomy—between substantive norms and enforcement power—earlier, in the discussion of consent. Just as both the norms and the enforcement power must be agreed to for consent theory to take hold, both the standards of conduct and the right to enforce them must be entrenched by universal principle for morality to provide a justification.

Intuitively, both of these claims seem strong in those cases, such as the Holocaust, that cry out for intervention. It seems clear both that Nazi Germany violated fundamental moral principles and that the Allies had a right to intervene to stop the violations. But the Holocaust, of course, is a special case in many respects. Not only was the scope of the horror almost unprecedented, but the Allies' claim to intervene was reinforced by the fact that Nazi Germany had initiated an aggressive war, so that military response was already appropriate on other grounds. Absent such special circumstances, both claims potentially present problems. The chief issue with the first is likely to be whether a particular norm is really universally applicable, or whether it is merely a product of some particular culture. This is the problem of cultural relativism. The chief difficulty with the second concerns whether even an admitted violation gives outside nations a right to intervene. This is an issue of communal integrity.

CULTURAL RELATIVISM   The main objection to the claim that human rights norms are morally compelling is that they are culturally relative; that the hegemon's morality may be fine as applied to its own actions and its own people, but that it cannot legitimately be applied to other groups. Such accusations are often made by states resisting pressure to conform to human rights norms. African nations have sometimes claimed, for instance, that certain Western freedoms such as the right to speak and to form political parties are not appropriate for African society.[18] Similarly, China has argued that Western multiparty democracy is not appropriate to its circumstances, and Islamic countries have denied the general relevance of Western notions of the equality of women.

There is no denying that some moral norms vary from one culture to another. Certain societies ban marriage to second cousins, the consumption of alcohol, or the use of mind-altering drugs; others encourage them. The cultural relativity argument is hard to rebut directly. Rebutting it seems to require establishing the existence of objective moral truth, and objective moral truth is notoriously difficult to establish. But there are ways to undercut the cultural relativism argument that cast sufficient doubt on it to blunt its thrust enough for present purposes. The philosophical power of the argument has been vastly overrated.

First, it is often not clear whether the cultural relativism argument is sincere. Some states that defend their practices from what they deem "cultural imperialism" themselves have universalistic moralities, such as Islam or Marxism, and for this reason can hardly take a position of pure cultural relativism.[19] The states that criticize the West for cultural imperialism undercut their own criticisms when they criticize the West on moral grounds, for instance for its unwillingness to redistribute wealth to poorer nations. If they are correct that different moral principles apply to wealthy northern and Western nations than to less developed southern ones, then the south has no basis for criticizing the north. Conversely, if they are correct that their own moral principles apply to powerful nations, they cannot be true cultural relativists.

Second, many of the international outrages that we see are not defensible on grounds of cultural relativism even if one accepts the general relativist claim. For relativism to be an objection, it is not enough that morality may in theory differ from culture to culture; morality must in fact differ. Perhaps it is only contingently true (as the relativist would claim) that two societies happen to agree on some particular moral principle; whatever overlap exists may be entirely coincidental. But that coincidence provides enough of a foundation for one culture to criticize the other. Even if the overlap is only coincidental, it exists as a matter of fact; and the shared norm provides a basis for criticism and for pressure to comply.

Many accusations of human rights violations fall squarely into normative areas where there is substantial overlap. This chapter opened with the case of former Yugoslavia. If the United States were to intervene, its actions could hardly be criticized on cultural relativism grounds. For it would be hard to argue that murder of civilians, gang rape, and deliberate starvation are considered innocent activities in the Balkans. The accused perpetrators, of course, do not claim that they are; instead, they argue that they are wrongly accused by an ignorant and biased world community, or that their enemies are committing abuses that are even worse. Any person, Serb, Croatian, or Bosnian Muslim, who was subjected to these gross abuses would feel with certainty (and with justice) that he or she had been wronged. Most human rights abuses involve the perpetration of harms that are undeniably wrong in the eyes of all parties to the dispute.

Third, many international violations are themselves cross-cultural. The oppression of Tibetans by Chinese, the invasion of Kuwait by Iraq, and the murder of Bosnian Muslims by Bosnian Serbs (and vice versa) involve disputes between cultural groups, not within cultural groups. The violators cannot use cultural relativism as a basis for criticizing outsiders for intervening when they themselves are outside intervenors subject to the same charge. Once a state assumes the right to take action against another nation or cultural group, it has no principled basis for objecting to a stronger power taking action, in turn, against itself.

COMMUNAL INTEGRITY Assume then that a violation of basic human rights has been shown. What should the remedy be? This really is a separate question, for it is possible to argue that even genuine violations do not give other states a right to become involved. This distinction (between the existence of a wrong and the right to become involved in remedying it) is one that we make all the time, as for instance where feminists argue that whether or not abortion is morally wrong, no one should interfere with a woman's right to make the decision; or where a religious observer declines to compel others to be more observant even though he or she believes that it is morally correct to be devout. Such respect for another's choice to do "the wrong thing" is premised upon the other's autonomy. It is possible that all that international morality requires of states is that they themselves observe human rights norms; that it neither requires nor permits them to enforce those norms against other nations. Other nations' choices to do "the wrong thing" may be a protected part of their communal integrity.

Indeed, this seems to be the point that states accused of human rights violations are typically making when they insist that other states have no right even to inquire about possible violations. Even if there were some violation, the argument seems to go, the stronger states would have no valid claim to get involved. Unwillingness even to allow collection of human rights data reflects a belief that there are no circumstances under which such information might be put to any legitimate use. If the existence of a violation is irrelevant, because it does not provide a basis for other states' action, then such a posture is perfectly understandable. Put bluntly, the claim is that even demonstrable violations are none of the other states' business.

Michael Walzer offers an intriguing hypothetical example which seems to support such a claim.[20] Imagine, he says, that a country called Algeria is dominated by a fundamentally illiberal culture that violates the rights of women and religious minorities and infringes the rights of free speech and political association. Now imagine that you have a magical potion that, if put into the water supply, would fundamentally change the culture and political beliefs of all Algerians so that they would all turn into perfect Swedish social democrats. The potion, he asks us to imagine, would do no physical harm of any sort and the Algerians would not remember that they had ever been any different (and would therefore harbor no resentment). Nonetheless, concludes Walzer, one should not administer the potion. It would be wrong for an outsider to Algerian culture to transform it completely in this way.

Walzer's example may seem fanciful; philosophers' examples sometimes do. But an interesting analog exists in international experience, where the potion (in effect) was given and had the desired effect. That example concerned the transformation of the Japanese political system after the Second World War. The occupying Allies completely restructured Japan, changing it from a militaristic monarchy to a liberal parliamentary democracy.[21] The restructuring was highly intrusive into Japanese culture, political values, and economic practices. Of course, Japanese culture is highly resilient, and even after all of these changes, it remains distinctly Japanese. But the impact on Japanese society is apparent if one compares its present practices to those before the war.

One might regret the damage to Japanese culture and even conclude that it outweighed the advantages of the ultimately successful introduction of liberal democracy. Given Walzer's analysis of the hypothetical, it seems likely that he would. But there are at least two respects in which his hypothetical example may be misleading and in which the communal integrity argument is unpersuasive. First, it is possible that his conclusion may be influenced by the fact that the violations in his hypothetical example are not truly compelling. If we were to ask ourselves the same question about present-day Yugoslavia, it seems fairly likely that most of us would come out the other way. Imagine that you have a potion that would turn the members of all of the different ethnic and religious groups— Croat, Serb, and Muslim—into pacifistic, international–law-abiding cosmopolitans with no trace of any ethnic or religious animosity. Most of us would not hesitate for a moment on the grounds that administering the potion would destroy the atavistic, vengeful culture that currently dominates the region.[22] Similarly, it seems unlikely that many of us would hesitate to use the potion on Nazi Germany.

On this precise point it seems likely that Walzer agrees. Walzer himself, at other places in his argument, recognizes that some offenses are simply so heinous that they warrant intervention of a sort that would normally not be appropriate.[23] The second point is one that he probably would not acknowledge, though. The other misleading aspect of the hypothetical is that it seems to suggest that the most important fact is the *outsider status* of the person who would be administering the potion.[24] Cultures can be destroyed from within as well as from without, and the loss is equally great.[25] Walzer imagines the difficult position of the Westerner poised to deliver the elixir; but the same quandary would exist if the elixir were in the hands of an Algerian dissident. Should one individual play God? How can one foretell the consequences of a radical change in society? How does one count into the balance the value of an indigenous and historically grounded but morally flawed culture, with its own distinctive literature, customs, and traditions? These questions are not unique to changes from the outside; changes from within can be as radical, destructive, and motivated by alien moral conviction. The outsider status of the intervenor is a red herring.[26]

Of course, as Walzer argues, it is possible that outsiders will know less about local conditions than insiders, and for this reason they may misunderstand or overestimate the severity of the violations or underestimate the difficulties in remedying them.[27] There are pragmatic reasons that it would be better for insiders than outsiders to take action.[28] But these pragmatic concerns do not give rise to a categorical bar to outside intervention. At most they suggest that outsiders must be extremely careful when they decide to intervene and when they choose their methods; outsiders should know their facts. Such pragmatic concerns do not support a general conclusion that other states may not intervene to enforce human rights norms.[29] In addition, it is legitimate to be concerned that strong states might sometimes use human rights violations as a pretext for intervention that is really motivated by selfish concerns.[30] But this possibility does not mean that intervention is never justified; it simply means that intervention for selfish motivations is not appropriate.

The fact that insiders are justified in resisting human rights abuses is the key to understanding why other states also should be permitted to intervene. Few doubt that the victims themselves have a right of resistance to crimes perpetrated against them.[31] Few doubt, in addition, that other groups in the same society have a good claim (if not in fact an obligation) to come to the aid of the victims; this is why we so admire the courage of those in Nazi occupied Europe who risked their lives to try to save the targets of Nazi genocide. But if victims within states, and locals who would assist them, have a right of resistance, then it is hard to understand why they should not be able to summon outside help. The right of other states to enforce human rights norms, in other words, is derivative of the right of the victims themselves (and their local allies) to resist.

Viewing the rights of other states to become involved as derivative of the rights of insiders allays in two ways some genuine and legitimate fears about outside intervention. First, because the right to intervene is derivative, other states have no greater right to act, and no greater range of remedies, than the victims themselves would. This point is sometimes obscured in discussions of whether intervention from abroad is appropriate. Where the subject is intervention from abroad, the discussion almost invariably turns to military intervention, for the simple reason that this may be the only strategy that seems likely to be effective. If all human rights violations justified intervention by other states, it might be feared, then every repression of free speech or every unjust imprisonment would bring the armies of stronger nations rushing in to right the wrong.

But domestic victims (and their local allies) would in many circumstances themselves not be entitled to use the sort of large-scale violent means that are the closest direct analog of outside military intervention. Even as a domestic matter, some violations would not warrant risking violent loss of life. The simple fact of a violation of human rights does not make any response, of any type or magnitude, appropriate; that is one reason that terrorism is widely condemned. Full-scale armed revolt is not an appropriate remedy for minor violations of free speech. The only violations that would justify military intervention are those that would justify armed rebellion and potential loss of innocent life within the country. As Charles Beitz puts it, the problem with military intervention is not that it is intervention, but that it is military.[32]

The second reason it is important that the right to intervene is derivative is that other states do not have a right to enforce human rights norms if the victims themselves would prefer that outside intervention not occur. This "waiver" argument reflects the simple liberal disinclination to paternalistically second-guess those whose interests are more directly at stake. If the claims of other states to intervene are derived from the right of victims to resist, and if victims can choose not to exercise their own rights to resist, then they can also waive their right that others become involved. The reason that this matters is that the victims themselves may be opposed to outside intervention. Indeed, nationalism being the emotional force that it is, it should not be surprising if many victims of human rights abuses would prefer to suffer rather than to seek assistance from outside.[33] This unwillingness to ask for outside help even when one's own internal efforts to resist have been unsuccessful should be respected.[34]

HEGEMONIC INTERVENTION

There is a large literature on the moral arguments for and against humanitarian intervention, with certain authors generally very skeptical and others generally less so.[35] By and large, however, one factor that has remained somewhat in the background has been the identity of the state initiating intervention. Nothing in the discussion above specifically turns on whether intervention occurs at the initiation of the stronger states. While it is, for obvious reasons, typically the strongest states in the international system that seek to intervene on grounds of substantive morality, this is not invariably the case; in both Liberia and Uganda, for example, interventions were initiated by nearby African nations, not by superpowers.[36] Issues of cultural relativism, the rights of outsiders to become involved, and so forth are as germane to interventions in these circumstances as they are to hegemonic interventions. While there may be a general recognition that intervention by hegemons, specifically, presents the greatest potential for abuse, most arguments about intervention have been framed in terms that would apply across the board. It is worth pausing to consider the specific ways and reasons that hegemonic intervention poses special problems. In what respects should the Tanzanian intervention in Uganda be evaluated by different standards than (say) a potential American intervention in Bosnia?

There are two ways that the legitimacy of intervention on the basis of substantive morality may be influenced by the fact that it was initiated by the hegemon. The first is that recognizing the legitimacy of intervention in such instances widens the power disparity between the weak and the strong, especially given that strong powers are likely sometimes to intervene in circumstances where intervention is not really justified. The second is that strong states are more likely to have intervened in other cases in the past; thus, with strong states there is an issue of whether the overall pattern of intervention is justified. We will consider here the effect that recognizing intervention based on substantive morality has on the distribution of power; the following section addresses the problem of selective intervention.

Weaker states that are compelled by stronger ones to adhere to what the strong term international morality will certainly be convinced that this is simply another case of the powerful imposing their views on those unable to resist. It takes no imagination to envision the horrible consequences that can follow from self-righteous hegemonic intervention. One need only recall some of the many historical excesses: the U.S. intervention in Vietnam, the Soviet invasion of Afghanistan, and even the Nazi conquest of much of Europe illustrate the damage that can be done by powerful nations convinced that they are in the right. With strength, often, goes righteousness; and with righteousness, arrogance and then abuse. Righteous excess, of course, is not limited to the international setting. Comparable domestic examples would also be easy to list; the Cultural Revolution in China, Pol Pot's rule over Cambodia, or the mass collectivization of Soviet farming during the Stalin era. Whenever one powerful central authority possesses the strength to impose its views of justice on the weaker, and to override their resistance, the potential exists for tyranny and for disaster.

Cut off from the requirement that weaker states must consent, hegemony, in short, threatens to grow into world dictatorship. While the hegemon may be motivated by a vision of a better world, the vision it furthers is undeniably its own vision. Perhaps a world dominated by a righteous hegemon is preferable to a world dominated by a grasping, self-interested one; but there is certainly an argument to be made that the opposite is true. Probably more lives have been lost to ethnic, religious, or ideological crusades than to simple greed. There are several threads to the argument that strong states must pursue their moral objectives with restraint, self-doubt, and some humility.

LOSS OF AUTONOMY   The first thread is implicit in what has just been said. Allowing powerful states to intervene for reasons of international morality effectively shifts the balance of power further away from equality of power to domination by the stronger. It is the stronger states that are likely to be able to exercise the power, as just noted, and in this respect the right to intervene is the right of the strong. Michael Walzer makes a similar point when he says, "Rights are in an important sense distributive principles. They distribute decision-making authority."[37] Walzer is concerned that the right to intervene gives authority to foreigners, in contrast to a right of communal integrity, which preserves decision-making authority for the community itself. Giving the right to foreigners, of course, means giving it to those foreigners powerful enough to exercise it.

Now the same can be said for intervention based on contemporaneous or prior state consent; this argument about redistributing power does not single out intervention to enforce human rights or other principles of international morality as uniquely threatening to the autonomy of weaker states. However, the argument has particular force when the claim to intervene is based on natural law and not consent. The reason is the negligible role reserved for state will when the hegemon's justification rests on morality.

Norms based on consent depend on the will of the coerced state, while substantive morality does not. The four theories of justification that we have examined follow in progression; each values the will of the weaker states less than the previous one. Contemporaneous consent is more respectful of the autonomy of weaker states than ex ante consent, which is in turn more respectful of state autonomy than hypothetical consent, which in turn is more respectful than substantive morality. Substantive morality accords state will no particular importance at all, because universal standards of moral conduct do not depend on state agreement; indeed, they are intended not to.

Actual contemporaneous consent is the most consent-oriented because it depends solely on what the involved states want at the time that the hegemon's action is taken. The weaker state's will is never overborne by the will of the stronger under this theory, for no action can be taken unless the weaker state agrees. Actual ex ante consent is also highly dependent on consent because the existence of norms depends on prior agreement by the states. It is slightly less deferential to the autonomy of weak states because they are bound by a preexisting norm that commitments must be respected, so that weaker states can in some circumstances be forced to obey.[38] The power of the stronger state is somewhat enhanced because it is authorized to compel weaker states to carry out their commitments.

Hypothetical consent also makes concessions to what states want, but the concessions are far less substantial. The theory still has aspirations to respect for state autonomy, because it founds norms on what states would supposedly want. But the norms are not based on what actual states actually want; instead, the norms rest on what reasonable states in their position would hypothetically want. Even this limited amount of deference to state autonomy, however, exceeds the negligible deference offered by a justification based on substantive morality. Substantive morality, as a standard, makes no concessions whatsoever to what states want. What matters is moral correctness, not state will. If contemporaneous consent is one end of the spectrum, then, substantive morality is the other.

It is clear that the degree of control that weak states have over their own destinies decreases as one moves to theories that require a lesser degree of state consent. Respect for autonomy works in the favor of weaker states. If their autonomy is protected, then they cannot be coerced or commanded against their will. From the point of view of weaker states, then, the degree to which hegemony is objectionable increases as one moves from contemporaneous consent, to ex ante consent, to hypothetical consent, and then to substantive morality. Each is more "dictatorial" than the last. For the weaker states' chance to protest some particular hegemonic action simply by virtue of the fact that they do not want it diminishes at each step.

Now it could be pointed out that the hegemon's power decreases as well. For as we move from a system in which legitimacy depends solely on what states agree to, to one where it depends solely on moral correctness, the hegemon's will is also increasingly restrained. Morality is no more supposed to be based on what strong states want than on what weak states want; the preferences of both are equally irrelevant. The hegemon is not supposed to be enforcing its own will when it compels other states to behave according to international morality; and so it might seem that the overall balance of power has not shifted, since the power of both diminishes correspondingly. It could be said, then, that the weaker states' discretion to act is admittedly lessened, but only to the same degree as the stronger's. The reason that things do not work out this way in practice is the possibility of error, and the asymmetry that this creates.

THE CHANCE OF ERROR There are innumerable historical cases where powerful states convinced themselves that morality required some particular course of action but sounder minds in later times concluded just the opposite. "Lesser" peoples were once though to benefit from colonialism; all developing nations were thought to need undiluted capitalism (or socialism); and the obvious correctness of one's own religion made it seem imperative to save other people's souls through the use of force.

Sometimes the problem is that strong states confuse moral principle with self-interest; it is only to be expected that this will sometimes happen. On other occasions they confuse the moral principles peculiar to their own particular culture with universal moral truth. They then feel entitled (if not obliged) to impose this view on other cultures. The fact that some moral principles are universal does not mean that all are; but it is to be expected that norms indigenous to one culture may be perceived within that culture as supplying the only just or rational way to do things.

The chance of error is greater when international action is based on substantive morality than when it is based on state consent. Of course, it is possible that a strong state may err even if the standard of justification is the weaker states' agreement, because there may be doubt over whether the weaker state actually did consent, or what it actually consented to. No matter what the standard of justification, there are likely to be unclear or borderline cases, and where there are difficult cases there are bound to be errors. For this reason, any principle that legitimizes compulsion by strong states will give them power at the expense of the weak, who never have the option of imposing their mistaken judgments on others.

The problem is greater, though, when the standard is consistency with substantive morality. Consent is easier to determine objectively than substantive morality, even if there is no litmus test that guarantees that mistakes will not be made. Consent leaves tangible traces; determining whether some state consented to a norm (however difficult that may be) is likely to be easier than deciding whether the norm is part of universal moral law. In addition, where positive norms are at stake, the international community may have established effective decision processes to determine disputed questions. Consent to these international institutions validates the decisions the institutions reach.

The U.N. Security Council, for example, is empowered to act only where a threat to international peace and security exists.[39] Since there is no other authoritative body that has been designated to decide this issue, the council itself must resolve to its own satisfaction the question of its own jurisdiction before it acts. Of course, there is always a possibility that one of its decisions might be a mistake. But the very fact that a decision process exists seems to suggest that the resulting decision is authoritative so long as the proper process was followed. Errors are validated so long as they are made in the appropriate way, and it is usually easier to determine whether processes were followed than whether the decision itself was correct on its merits.

Moving to a standard based on substantive morality introduces many uncertainties that increase the risk of error. There is no authoritative process for determining what international morality requires; for this reason there will be sincere differences of opinion and the weak will always resent the fact that the stronger states' version of international morality wins the day. To the extent that the hegemon acts on self-interest or on its own erroneous view of what morality requires, weaker states are correct in complaining that their legitimate prerogatives have been diminished while the power of the hegemon has been increased. At a minimum, weak states will genuinely *believe* that this is what is happening. Sometimes they will be right.

MORAL LUCK   There is a third factor in the claim that hegemonic intervention must be taken very seriously and undertaken very cautiously. The intervention will likely be judged on the basis of consequences that are virtually impossible to predict. A conscientious national leader trying to do the right thing in a difficult situation will be painfully aware that the potential for miscalculation is unavoidable and that whatever error history exposes will be squarely on his or her shoulders. Where the hegemon's action is based on the consensus of many states—or even more, where its actions are also based on the consent of the state the hegemon seeks to influence—the burden is not so great. If there is a mistake, at least it is a shared mistake. The hegemon has no such guarantees when it acts alone, as hegemons are able to. Clearly, some world leaders waste little energy worrying about whether their actions will be thought moral many decades hence. There are other leaders, though, about whom this cannot be said, leaders that genuinely seek to do the right thing in times of doubt and crisis.

The judgment of history tends toward strict liability. Future generations will not be concerned primarily with whether it seemed reasonable at the time for the hegemon to act as it did, but with whether it was right. Often decisions must be made on wildly inadequate information. Bernard Williams characterizes the analogous issue in personal morality as "moral luck."[40] He uses the example of an artist, such as Gaugin, who ignores his moral responsibilities and sets off for a life of solitary dedication to his art. As Williams describes the situation, if the artist's work turns out to be brilliant, we will think that his neglect of his other moral responsibilities was justified; but if it turns out to be mediocre, we will blame him for abandoning those to whom he had a moral obligation. Yet the eventual quality of his work is not something that can be known with certainty at the time the artists acts. The judgment of moral worthiness can only be made retroactively.

In the same way, the morality of a hegemon's decision to intervene may turn on whether it is a long-run success or a failure at furthering human rights and international morality, even though this is simply unknowable in advance. This is a staggering responsibility for a statesman or stateswoman. The fact that it must sometimes be borne alone can only make things worse. If things go well, one is hailed as a prophet, acclaimed for one's willingness to act on principle when others held back timidly. If things go poorly, one is criticized for one's unwillingness to listen to what others had to say, and the decision is added to a long list of historical examples of the arrogance of power.

Earlier I mentioned the American restructuring of Japan at the end of the Second World War. This act of American hegemony is a hard one to judge, because in most circumstances we would not approve military occupation to change a country's political system. The case may be sui generis in that the military occupation was already in place for another reason—Japan had lost an aggressive war it had initiated—and because one rationale for the political restructuring was to prevent future international aggression. The primary factor that counts in favor of the intervention, however, is that it worked out relatively well in the long run.[41] How would we judge American efforts to democratize Japan if they had turned out as badly as our efforts in Vietnam? But this, surely, is an example of "moral luck"; the United States could have been no more confident about the success of Western liberal democracy in Japan than about other cases where it attempted, much less successfully, to promote similar institutions.[42] The awareness that so much turns on factors that are ultimately unforeseeable gives cause for caution.

THE OBLIGATION TO INTERVENE

To this point, we have considered only the first half of the equation: recognizing a right of moral intervention by the strongest powers tends to exacerbate the imbalance of power, because the version of morality that is imposed is the hegemon's version, complete with all the hegemon's mistaken judgments. Even if one assumes, however, that the hegemon's decisions are unfailingly accurate, a substantial problem remains. Weak states generally can engage only in single, isolated instances of intervention; strong states generate a pattern of interventionist activity. The hegemon's actions must be evaluated as a whole, and this includes its choice of cases not to intervene as well as choice of situations to become involved. The question so far has been whether stronger states have a right to intervene to enforce international morality. But there is equally an issue whether there exists an obligation.

Much of the debate over the role of the United States in stepping in to prevent the killing in Bosnia has concerned the obligation, not the right, to intervene. A *New York Times* article in early May 1993 quoted ordinary Americans interviewed about the conflict in the Balkans; they dealt with the issue in terms of whether the United State had a responsibility. One said, "It's absurd. Why are we forever being dragged into these things?" "It should be stopped," said another, " but we shouldn't try to stop it on our own, not with American boys. Terrible as it is, it's basically Europe's problem." What the *Times* described as "a small handful" expressed the opposite view. "Since others won't stop it, we have to step out front and do it," one woman argued. "They're killing children over there in cold blood. This isn't something you argue about. You just grit your teeth and do it because doing something is the right and moral thing to do."[43]

This framing of the question, with its focus on the obligation to intervene, is perhaps a testament to the ease with which most people thought the issue of permissibility resolvable. It seemed to them only too obvious that the right to intervene existed; if so, then the real issue was whether there was a moral responsibility. One way to argue that a moral responsibility exists is to draw an analogy to personal responsibility. Some philosophers argue that each of us has a moral responsibility to help prevent human suffering when it is possible to do so at a reasonable cost.[44] If I were to see a small child drowning in a shallow pool, I would jump in to save her; if thousands of innocent civilians are being murdered, starved, or raped in Bosnia, the United States has an obligation to do what it can. This seems to be the reasoning of the woman who said that we should grit our teeth and "do it" because it is the right thing to do.

The problem with making this argument in the international setting is that many people would not accept it even in the analogous domestic setting. People resist the notion that they have positive responsibilities to help others, preferring to couch the issue in terms of charity. Helping out is morally admirable, not the fulfillment of a duty. Such people are unlikely to accept the argument that the United States should make sacrifices simply "because it is the right and moral thing to do." From this perspective, there is no reason a strong state should not, if it chooses, simply lapse into autarchy. Isolationism is, from this point of view, morally defensible.

But the isolationist position is somewhat beside the point when it is the *hegemon* that is seeking reasons not to become involved in some particular issue of international morality. The reason is that a hegemon is already deeply involved in world events. The question raised by the hegemon's disinclination to become involved is not whether some strong power might choose autarchy, but whether a strong state that already dominates international relations might pick and choose among the various issues in which to intervene. The issue is one of selective involvement.[45] If the question is, "Why are we forever being dragged into these things?" the answer is, "Because we want cheap oil, access to other states' economic markets, secure defense, and all the other benefits of international involvement, and because we have gotten involved in the past whenever we thought that involvement promoted these interests." The United States is not dragged in. It jumps in, with both feet. And the real question is whether it should be able to have the benefits of international hegemony without the costs. After acting as the world's policeman when that suits its fancy, can the United States then retreat into the role of private citizen when that role seems more appealing?

We have already dealt briefly with the question of selective involvement, for selectivity is also an issue when the basis for hegemonic intervention is the enforcement of international norms established by either prior state consent or hypothetical consent. The issues are roughly parallel, for in all three cases the problem with selectivity is that it threatens the very basis for enforcement in the first place. All three of these approaches ground international action, in different ways, on the authority of norms—whether norms that are founded on state consent, norms that would be hypothetically agreed to, or norms of universal morality. Selective intervention undercuts the claim that the basis for intervention is the norm rather than state interest, the desire to help out an ally, or some other motivation for which the norm merely supplies a pretext.

The basis for choosing which cases are worthy of intervention, in other words, must be consistent with the foundation for intervention in the first place.[46] Justification for international hegemony involves more than an ad hoc reference to one theory or another that might happen to justify the action in the particular case. It also requires justification of the entire pattern of interventions, so that a decision not to intervene when doing so doesn't further the state interests undercuts the hegemon's legitimacy in those cases where the hegemon does initiate action. Hegemony involves more than one act or another in isolation; hegemony is a pattern of behavior, because it is the fact that the hegemon systematically gets its way that distinguishes its actions from those of powers that happen to get what they want once in a while.

Here, the basis for intervention that we are exploring is substantive morality. Consistent with this philosophical foundation, the test for when the norms must be enforced should also rest on substantive moral principles. Selectivity is prima facie morally suspect. This is not to say that there can never be good reasons to refuse to intervene, however. As a moral matter, there can well be circumstances where enforcement is not required. In domestic society, of course, some norms go unenforced or underenforced; and while this is sometimes clearly wrong (as where crimes against women or racial minorities are treated less seriously than crimes against propertied white males), there are also situations where it is defensible. Three sorts of reasons for nonenforcement must be considered: doubt about what is the right thing to do, inability to achieve results at a reasonable cost, and conflicting moral priorities.

UNCERTAINTY All of the reasons that it is appropriate for a strong state to show caution and exercise self-restraint before intervening serve to justify the decision not to intervene. Intervention comes at the expense of weaker states; it can be based on mistaken moral judgments; and its consequences are difficult or impossible to predict. These are reasons that a strong state should be quite certain that it is doing the right thing before it imposes its view of morality on other states. In this respect, the question of *permissibility* of intervention is linked to the question of *obligation*, for doubt about the first issue is relevant to resolution of the second. Where there is substantial uncertainty about whether intervention is permissible, intervention cannot be obligatory.

Doubts arise from at least three different sources and have both normative and empirical dimensions. What is the moral standard of conduct? What does it mean when applied to the particular case? And what sort of response is justified? The first consideration involves the difficult determination whether one's own moral beliefs are really universal norms, or whether they are particular to one's own culture. The second involves both interpreting those norms and determining disputed facts: which side committed violations, how serious were they, and were there any extenuating facts? The third asks what remedy is appropriate and likely to be effective for a violation of this sort: economic isolation, military intervention, diplomatic pressure, and so forth. All three issues can be very difficult to resolve, and it is reasonable that a state left with uncertainty about them should be disinclined to intervene. The burden of proof, in other words, is on the party seeking intervention.

INEFFECTIVENESS The second principled basis for refusing to intervene is that it is not possible to resolve the problem at any reasonable cost. This, obviously, has been a main concern about intervention in Bosnia. Because the war in Bosnia is a civil war, the response is not as straightforward as simply retaking territory by driving back a group of invaders. So long as Serbs, Croats, and Muslims live in close proximity (one of the goals of the intervention being to put an end to the drive toward ethnic segregation), it will be virtually impossible to stop the bloodshed. The United States and its allies are fearful that their intervention would need to be massive and longstanding, an economic and military drain. Peacekeepers would be subject to conflicting demands from the three sides to the dispute and would make none of them happy. In the long run, it is feared, all parties to the dispute would turn on the troops that were sent to end the fighting. If the interventionist forces then left, the fighting would resume where it had left off. These problems have led some to conclude that the problems of the Balkans are hopeless. Similar considerations dominate discussion about whether the United States should stay involved in Somalia.

In deciding what counts as "reasonable" cost, the severity of the violation and the costs of nonintervention must be kept in mind. Most important, it is not enough merely to add up the costs to the stronger state to determine whether they pass some threshold that defines "too much." The problem with the U.S. response in Bosnia is that its talk about "effectiveness" seems to mask an unwillingness to extend itself when U.S. interests do not seem to be at stake. In the context of international intervention, the price of inaction must also be taken into account when determining whether the costs of achieving just results are "reasonable." This is true even though the costs of inaction are being borne by foreign victims.

CONFLICTING MORAL PRIORITIES One of the most important costs of intervention that must be kept in mind is the opportunity costs it imposes. If a state—even a very powerful one—occupies its energies resolving one problem, this limits its abilities to deal with crises in other areas. Once opportunity costs are taken into account, there may be good reason not to intervene even though the act seems justified from an isolated cost-benefit perspective. In the domestic context, governments set priorities about which problems to attack and how energetically to attack them. Priorities come into conflict in the international setting as well, for even a hegemon has limited resources. The United States may have to decide between promoting democracy in Russia by not pressing Boris Yeltsin just before an important referendum or promoting peace and stopping human right violations in the Balkans by urging Russia to put pressure on the Serbs.[47] Although it is morally tragic, there may be times that inaction is required by the very fact that it is not possible to do everything at once.

How should these three considerations be combined to factor into the decision whether intervention is obligatory? And how do they fit with the claim that while a state may choose not to become involved in international interventions as a general matter, once a hegemon has chosen to become involved, it must base its decisions on principle, not favoring its allies or choosing to protect only those substantive norms it finds convenient? There are two important points. First, the level of international involvement is a question of the hegemon's self-interest; it involves an allocation of resources to international enforcement of substantive morality. Second, though, the precise question of whether to intervene in a particular case must rest on principle; it involves determining which cases are the strongest ones for hegemonic intervention. Briefly put, the hegemon determines how much to commit; allocation of the committed resources then depends on the morally cognizable needs of the international system.

The hegemon chooses the level of commitment because no state has an obligation to act as hegemon if it chooses not to. A wealthy and potentially powerful state might decide to avoid international entanglements altogether, and in particular to avoid asserting any pressure and influence on other states. That is the course of action, we all know, that was urged upon the United States by George Washington in his Farewell Address in 1796, although it was not the path ultimately chosen. To the extent that it chooses not to use its wealth and power to alter what other states do, a powerful state is not acting hegemonically. Autarchy is a legitimate choice; in domestic government, the closest analog perhaps is abdication.

What triggers the obligation to act on principle is the choice to become involved, and in particular to become involved in pressuring other states to do what they would otherwise choose not to. It is coercion that must be justified; and we have explored various possibilities for its legitimation. Selective intervention violates the principles that underlie these possibilities. As with domestic political leaders, there may be no obligation to rule; but if one accepts the mantle, one must then rule justly. Although the level of international involvement depends on a powerful state's self-interested decision, once the level of commitment is set, the decision how to allocate those resources must be made impartially and with regard to the principles justifying involvement in the first place.

At this point, what matters is the priorities of the international community. When the basis for intervention is substantive morality, these are moral priorities.[48] What is the best use of limited resources, given the suffering that exists around the globe? Within the level of commitment already established, allocation of resources must be based on a moral cost-benefit calculation that takes into account the likely moral benefits of intervention, as well as the likely moral costs, including the opportunity costs of the likely resulting inability to deal with violations elsewhere. This means that intervention is never appropriate (even if it would be justifiable when viewed in isolation) when a more morally compelling call for intervention goes unanswered. Urgent moral needs deserve the first response.

The establishment of moral priorities will never be an easy matter, any more than setting priorities for the rationing of other goods, such as health care or educational resources. The factors that must be addressed include the seriousness of the human rights claims raised and the likelihood that an adequate remedy can be found, as compared to competing commitments. Into this equation must be factored any moral doubt (such as over whether the norm in question is really universal or whether it properly applies in the present case), as well as empirical uncertainty about the consequences of action and inaction. To claim that a cost-benefit calculation is required is not to proceed under false pretenses of scientific precision, nor to deny the tragedy of trade-offs. Simply put, there is no other way to decide than setting priorities for which situations need the most immediate attention. Where resources are scarce, this means balancing the costs and benefits of logistical support for U.N.-supported elections in Cambodia or Angola against the gains of taking forceful action to restore the democratically elected government of Haiti. It requires comparing the commitment of troops to feed the people of Somalia against the considerable investment in the international order's rules against territorial aggression represented by the allied war against Iraq.

The record of the United States on the question of selective intervention has not been a reassuring one. There are some cases in which the decision not to intervene, while quite an uncomfortable one, can be defended. Bosnia arguably presents a case where it may be virtually impossible to effect a long-term solution at any cost that could reasonably be borne; but can the same be said of the U.S. posture toward Haiti after the September 30, 1991, military coup?[49] The United States, of course, has been willing to intervene to "promote democracy" on many occasions in the Caribbean and in Latin America. The invasions of Panama and Grenada are only the most recent examples. It hardly needs pointing out that the United States has selected its opportunities to intervene on criteria such as national interest or protecting governments with friendly ties to Washington. When the United States chooses to intervene on this basis, it undercuts its claim that other interventions are based on substantive morality.

CONCLUSION

It is not surprising that there are certain principles which international law protects even from explicit state agreement. The category of jus cogens contains norms such as prohibitions on genocide that are not subject to alteration by treaty. The category contains the most basic and fundamental principles of international society, which are not open to continuing renegotiation. Despite talk of the cultural relativism of substantive morality, it provides no basis for rejecting claims of universal norms, only the grounding for a healthy respect for the need to think carefully about whether one's own norms fit that category.

It may seem philosophically naive simply to say that states may intervene when necessary to compel obedience to important principles of substantive morality. What makes that conclusion hard to avoid, despite its philosophical unsophistication, is that there are cases in which intervention seems quite clearly to be called for but where consent—of any form—won't give the explanation. I have not attempted to say much about what precise results this commitment to substantive morality produces, any more than I have been specific about the substantive results produced by relying on contemporaneous, ex ante, or hypothetical consent. I have focused instead on principles that drive the methodologies; on the reasons for relying on actual or hypothetical consent, on the weaknesses of a theory measuring consent contemporaneously or before the fact; on objections to dispensing completely with the notion of consent; and so on. To further specify what substantive positions these approaches require would be an enormous task. Instead, we will briefly examine how these four methods fit together, before moving on to some of the issues that lie beyond the reach of liberalism.

8

GLOBAL

LIBERALISM

AND THE ''NEW

WORLD ORDER''

Around the time of the Persian Gulf war, President George Bush proclaimed: "Now, we can see a new world coming into view. A world in which there is the very real prospect of a new world order. In the words of Winston Churchill, a world order in which 'the principles of justice and fair play protect the weak against the strong . . . .' A world where the United Nations—freed from cold war stalemate—is poised to fulfill the historic vision of its founders. A world in which freedom and respect for human rights find a home among all nations. The Gulf war put this new world to its first test. And, my fellow Americans, we passed that test."[1] Of course, political rhetoric is often adopted for purely political purposes; its employment often demonstrates little more than the fact that some politician thinks it will sell. But there is typically an interesting story behind the fact that some politician thinks the rhetoric will sell. Bush seized on the rhetoric of "new world order" because it presented a vision that he expected to be attractive to the American people.

What did he hope that the American people would find attractive about it? The phrase has a high-minded air; it projects a sense of principle, and also optimism. It alludes to one of the great occurrences of the Bush presidency, the end of the Cold War, for it was the disappearance of the threat of the old Soviet Union that made this "new" world order possible. The wording also alluded, somewhat more subtly, to the responsibilities the United States was undertaking to bring the new order into existence. With the Soviet Union out of the picture, the duty was the United States' to create order from anarchy and lawlessness. In context, it was clear that the order would come into being with the United States at the helm.

Bush's New World world order, in short, contemplated American hegemony, but hegemony of a principled sort. Bush anticipated American dominance that would be both legitimate and, to some extent, welcomed by the global community (or, at least, by its right-thinking members; he did not expect an enthusiastic reception from the Saddam Husseins of the world). The ideal of principled hegemony that Bush projected with this phrase is precisely the ideal that we have been attempting to explore in the last four chapters. Whether Bush himself sincerely shared this vision of principled hegemony or not, it was a vision he expected the American people to understand.

What are the elements of this vision, and how do they connect to the theories of hegemony that we have been investigating? Bush never really disentangled the various threads in the skein, philosophical niceties hardly being essential to his purposes. Roughly, they included a commitment to international law and multilateral institutions; American leadership guided by American benevolence; peace and stability in relations between nations; and respect for democracy and human rights. The justifications we have considered for American hegemony touch on all these themes.

First, consider contemporaneous consent, which is basically a theory of leadership. The relevance of this justification for American hegemony lies in the hope that American leadership can be exercised through example and persuasion. American authority, it was hoped, would not emanate "from the barrel of a gun";[2] it was to follow at least in part from our special position as leader of what we once called the "free world." As Bush put it,

> For two centuries, America has served the world as an inspiring example of freedom and democracy. For generations, America has led the struggle to preserve and extend the blessings of liberty. And today, in a rapidly changing world, American leadership is indispensable. . . . As Americans, we know that there are times when we must step forward and accept our responsibility to lead the world away from the dark chaos of dictators, toward the brighter promise of a better day. . . . Among the nations of the world, only the United States of American has both the moral standing and the means to back it up. . . . This is the burden of leadership and the strength that has made America the beacon of freedom in a searching world.[3]

The new world order's paradigmatic example of contemporaneous consent was the way that Bush had convinced our allies to join together in the fight against Iraq. With the hostile Soviet Union out of the picture, it was hoped, the United States would continue to lead the world through diplomacy.

The relevance of the second theory—ex ante consent—is even clearer. A keystone of the new world order was supposed to be adherence to international law. The paradigm example, again, was provided by the Gulf war, although here the relevant aspect of the war was the punishment of Iraq for its violation of Kuwait's internationally guaranteed sovereign borders. International law, as we saw earlier, is grounded primarily in the prior consent of the members of the world community; the role of the United States as enforcer of international law thus rests, ultimately, upon the consent of states. Recognition of the importance of working through the United Nations—another key feature of the "new world order" vision—is in keeping with both international law and prior state agreement, for it could not be unfair to hold Iraq to procedures provided by the U.N. Charter, a document to which it was a signatory. Thus Bush remarked, during the buildup of forces in the Gulf, "These goals are not ours alone. They've been endorsed by the United Nations Security Council five times in as many weeks. . . . We can now point to five United Nations Security Council resolutions that condemn Iraq's aggression."[4]

The new world order connects to the third theory, hypothetical consent, through the concept of public goods. The advantage of hegemony lies in its ability to provide international peace and stability. America's self-image conforms neatly to the picture of the large and powerful state, surrounded by ungrateful free-riders. It is for the rest of the world's benefit that the United States fills the role of world's policeman. Although the United States initially bore the bulk of the costs of the Gulf war, for example, it expected the rest of the world to contribute, on the grounds that the war was waged for their benefit as well as for ours. "At home," Bush said, "the material cost of our leadership can be steep. That's why Secretary of State Baker and Treasury Secretary Brady have met with many world leaders to underscore that the burden of this collective effort must be shared. We are prepared to do our share and more to help carry that load; we insist that others do their share as well."[5] It is also reasonable, according to this view, for us to pressure other states in other respects, such as trade policy; for as world leader, we have kept our markets open while other, free-riding states take advantage of American generosity.

The connection between Bush's vision of the new world order and the fourth theory is almost too obvious to need restatement. The motivating force behind American hegemony is supposed to be the spread of human rights values—the

American version of them, that is—to the rest of the world. Thus we use American power to promote democracy, human rights, and freedom (including economic freedom) in nations that are less fortunate. We are motivated by a moral vision, the vision of the founders of this country, and it is the morality of our purpose that justifies our international actions.

Bush's grand and happy vision of the new world order, then, taps all of the rationalizations we have given above for the legitimacy of American dominance. Once one wipes away the sticky stream of American exceptionalism, lurking underneath one finds the very themes we have discussed in the last four chapters. The four rationales have not, of course, been disentangled in quite this way. But then they need not be. The rationales themselves are overlapping and fit together harmoniously into a coherent whole.

This is true in three respects. First, the four rationales demonstrate a continuity of theme. We have already noted the progression: from the first to the fourth, there is increasing attention to moral norms and decreasing attention to the positive preference of states. Yet precisely because these four are points on a spectrum, there is continuity. Each demonstrates the tension in political life between political preference and moral correctness, between positive and natural law; the four theories simply balance the two and resolve the tension between these competing values at different points.

Second, the four are overlapping in what they justify. There will be many actions which could be explained in terms of more than one of the rationales. This is not surprising, given the commonality of the themes underlying them. If an institutional arrangement is something that hypothetical rational individuals would have agreed to, it should not be too surprising when actual individuals (some of whom are probably rational) have agreed to it. It should not be surprising if those things that rational people would agree to are also attractive moral principles, or things that states agree to contemporaneously. Because these four theories overlap, in many cases the legitimacy of an action will be strengthened by the existence of alternative justifications. One need not, therefore, specify one's philosophical foundations too precisely, and the multiplicity of possible justifications means that the action can be made morally palatable to a larger spectrum of public opinion.

Third, there is an understandable preference to justify action, where possible, with the theory that gives the greatest deference to weak states' wills. Where both ex ante consent and substantive morality would justify the same action, for example, it is reassuring to be able to explain the action in terms of what the weaker state has previously agreed to. This is because we are always insecure having to explain things in terms of a substantive morality whose existence we cannot objectively demonstrate to others. The more determinate the theory, and the less dependent on what may be seen as the subjective preferences of the strong, the more satisfying the explanation. Given two possible explanations, then, there is a tendency to rely on the one more dependent on actual consent.

In practice there are no incentives to disentangle the liberal justifications for hegemony; it is actually rather attractive simply to treat the liberal defense of hegemony as something of a composite picture, with elements selected opportunistically to suit the political purposes at hand. While less than philosophically fastidious, the tendency to pick and choose does not offend the basic liberal orientation. It should be kept in mind that domestic government is also difficult to justify completely under a single one of these four rationalizations. The explanations we have surveyed in the international arena have been less than entirely successful in the domestic arena as well. None has achieved universal acceptance among philosophers, even among liberal philosophers, for much the same reasons that the theories are less than completely convincing internationally.

The philosophical sloppiness characterizing the new world order is something, then, that we can live with. What is troubling is another sort of tendency to "pick and choose"—unbridled discretion to decide whether to raise the flag of principle at all. The Bush administration was as content explaining the Gulf war in terms of domestic jobs and oil prices as it was describing the war as a consequence of the new world order.[6] The suggestion that American jobs depended on a cheap and steady supply of Middle Eastern oil led quite predictably to the comparative judgment, a short while later, that the United States had no security interest in Bosnia.[7] This was selective intervention with a vengeance; and it was right in line with President Clinton's later hands-off approach to both Bosnia and Haiti.

The moral difficulties with such role reversal can be best appreciated by imagining how it would seem for a domestic government to declare that it had no interest in enforcing legal norms where its political supporters had not been among the victims. There may be some theories of politics that would not flinch at such a position, but they would not be liberal ones. For this reason, we have emphasized on several occasions the need for consistency and the prohibition on selective intervention. Perhaps the single phrase that best sums up the problem with selective intervention from the liberal perspective is "rule of law." The President hammered home this concept time and again in selling his vision of a new world order; for the new world would be one where "the rule of law supplants the rule of the jungle."[8] The liberal rule of law contemplates a government that enforces norms, not the political preferences of those in power; that is neutral between favored and disfavored groups in society; and that places the rights of the individual over the interests of the state. Selective intervention favors the allies of important powers, elevates the interests of the hegemon over the needs of weaker states for protection, and discriminates between comparable factual situations based on the identity, and the political power, of the complainant. The President's endorsement of the rule of law recognized the importance of principle to the process of public justification. Unfortunately, this endorsement was all too sporadic and not especially convincing.

It seems, then, that all the philosophical arguments explored above reside already in our public discourse. Consent, international law, consistency and the avoidance of selectivity, substantive moral values—all of these themes have been sounded in the discussions of the appropriate uses of American power after the end of the Cold War. The last four chapters, then, have simply tried to give more analytical structure to a set of beliefs that are already prevalent in American culture, to give a somewhat more clear-headed exposition to intuitions that we already have about the political morality of international relations. I have deliberately delayed a full-scale challenge to those intuitions, preferring first to develop their positive aspects by putting them in a somewhat more intellectually rigorous form. If the last four chapters have been successful, then, their success lies in their having shown that a surprisingly coherent philosophical point of view underlies existing forms of justification.

But we can no longer postpone the head-on challenge. Not everyone, it must be admitted, favors the sort of liberal approach to international relations that I have been developing. Some of the critics come from the realist camp, which we have already addressed in length in chapter 2, accusing the new world order rhetoric of "rigid legalism."[9] Others attack from the left. Liberalism has, of course, been vigorously attacked in recent writings on domestic political philosophy. There is no reason to think that it should be immune to such attacks in the international context.

While the major project here has been to sketch a basic liberal picture of international governance, the critics of liberalism have had much of value to say in identifying where domestic liberalism is weakest. Some international relations theorists have recognized the importance of these critiques of domestic liberalism to international affairs. The concluding chapters of this book will attempt to develop some of the ways that these criticisms are important to the liberal themes that we have already identified, and to an assessment of the legitimacy of international hegemony. The topics of the two following chapters are state identity and state consent.

PART THREE

A CRITICAL

RESPONSE

9

STATISM

It is time to take a more critical look at the liberal theory of international hegemony developed in chapters 4–7.[1] To this point, the goal has been an explanation for American hegemony that rests on liberal values of autonomy, substantive rights, and state consent; to that end, the previous chapters have examined the various types of agreement that states might be said to have given to U.S. actions, and in particular to U.S. enforcement of international legal norms. But the underlying assumption that hegemony would be justified if states consented to it has gone largely unchallenged. This and the following chapter take a closer look at that assumption.

A central issue concerns an argument that has become familiar in contemporary domestic political theory: that it is mistaken to focus exclusively on the autonomy of the individual actors in a system, because the actors are in significant ways themselves constituted by the system. In domestic political theory this argument is often associated with Michael Sandel, whose *Liberalism and the Limits of Justice* criticized John Rawls's liberalism for its purportedly excessive individualism.[2] Liberalism, some critics claim, unrealistically divorces the individual from the social forces that shape his or her identity.

Similar complaints have made their mark in international relations theory. Various communitarian and critical schools of thought have taken issue with the assumption, said to be common to mainstream international relations theory, that the identities and preferences of states can be treated as exogenous "givens." Critical scholars—feminist, structuralist, constructivist, reflectivist, postmodernist, and otherwise—argue that states and their "interests" can be as much a product of the international system as the international system is a product of their interests. If this is the case, then the supposed consent of states may be illusory, because states do not arrive at their preferences autonomously but through a process of socialization by the international political order. An international version of the communitarian/critical argument is, in this way, applied to the relations between states.

But the original domestic version of the communitarian and critical argument is, in fact, equally relevant to questions of international relations. There are two important issues of how communities relate to individual actors; for not only must we investigate the relationship between individual states and the international system, but we must also keep in mind the relationship between individual human beings and the states they inhabit. This latter question cannot simply be bracketed as a problem of domestic politics, although it is of course an important question for domestic theorists as well. For it is also a question for international relations scholars; on its answer depends one's position on whether, or why, the international system should take states as opposed to individual human beings as the relevant actors.

The liberal theory of international hegemony that we have developed is oddly compatible with communitarian and critical arguments on this second issue of the relationship between states and individuals.[3] It seems to accept the domestic part of the communitarian argument; the claim that the identities of individual human beings derive at least in part from the communities that they belong to. For the actors that it examines are states, not human beings; and these, in true communitarian spirit, are groups rather than individuals. Only once attention is shifted to the international arena does individualism set in, and resistance to communitarian logic grow. At that point, the theory insists on the independence of the state from the larger community that it, in turn, inhabits. International politics, as we have described it, takes place in a community of communities.[4] The liberal theory we have developed, however, does not seem to recognize that the same processes of communal identity formation that account for the normative significance of states might also create a higher identity, at the international level.

There are, for this reason, two sides to the criticism of state consent as a basis for international norms generally, and as a basis for international hegemony in particular. The first concerns the respective roles of states and of the world community at large; the liberal argument we have developed vests power to consent or to reject community political arrangements with individual states belonging to the international community. But there is also a question of the respective roles of states and their individual citizens, and here it is the more inclusive unit, rather than its constituent members, that is privileged. States are empowered at the expense of the community as a whole (they are granted autonomy either to consent to community arrangements or not to), but they are also empowered at the expense of their individual citizens, since it is *states* that must consent to community political arrangements, not individuals.

A theory of international hegemony that rests on state consent, for this reason, must be able to defend itself on two fronts simultaneously. On the one hand, it must justify its own statism—its elevation of state power at the expense of the individual. On the other, it must show why the world community as a whole does not sit in the same relationship to states as states do to their own people. This chapter deals with the problem of statism; of why international hegemony should be founded on *state* consent. Chapter 10 deals with the communitarian/ critical argument against state autonomy; asking why, in other words, international hegemony should be founded on state *consent*. The former is a question about what are the appropriate sorts of entities whose interests should be considered in world politics. The latter is a question about what norms properly regulate those actors' relationships with one another.

The feature of statism at issue here is the privileging of state actors over their competitors—individuals, multinational corporations, or nongovernmental organizations—as the relevant actors in the world political systems. As such, statism is surely a serious challenge to liberal theory, for liberal theory is typically thought to be grounded in the special normative qualities of individual human beings, in particular their capacity for autonomy and free agency. While the tension between liberal individualism and statism is recognized in certain philosophical circles, its seriousness has not generally been fully appreciated.[5] There is reason to doubt whether any theory sufficiently statist to accommodate the consent-based approach to international hegemony explored in chapters 4–7 can truly reconcile itself with liberalism's emphasis on individuals.

Whether one prefers to treat this incompatibility as a defect of liberalism or as a defect of statism is, of course, a matter of opinion. Those of a sufficiently cosmopolitan and liberal persuasion might be entirely willing to abandon the notion that world politics should be conducted primarily by states. As a matter of ideal theory, this is of course one possibility. But statism is sufficiently firmly rooted in international practice and common intuitions that liberalism's inability to explain it must count as problematic at least. For present purposes, moreover, statism seems a necessary fact of life. Our goal is a better understanding of the normative foundations of the current institution of international hegemony. If liberalism is inconsistent with statism, it seems unlikely that there could be a liberal justification of international hegemony as it exists today. Perhaps the ultimate conclusion will be that hegemony and liberalism are mutually exclusive. Before arriving at that conclusion, though, we should consider carefully all possible avenues for reconciling liberalism with statism.

THE TENSION BETWEEN LIBERALISM AND STATISM The liberal argument for international hegemony that we explored above rests on a qualified form of statism. The argument is *statist* because three of the four rationales that we considered were based on the rights of states; these were contemporaneous consent, ex ante consent, and hypothetical consent. Each of these rationales was designed to protect the autonomy of states by holding that states can only be bound by their own voluntary choices. The liberal argument was nonetheless a *qualified* form of statism because the fourth rationale—protection of substantive moral rights—recognized individuals as the primary rights bearers in some circumstances, namely, where human rights are at stake. This last rationale limited the extent to which states might do as they please at the expense of individual citizens.

This qualification should not obscure, however, the generally statist character of the arguments. With regard to certain specific individual rights, state interests were subordinated, it is true. But these qualifications leave the bulk of international decisions to the states' consent. Most international actions do not violate human rights; there are few human rights constraints on most economic, social, and military decisions. Outside the ambit of human rights norms, the liberal model that I have described leaves it to the states to agree on norms and political institutions one way or the other, as they see fit.

There is a prima facie tension between liberalism and statism, even qualified statism. Statism seems more compatible with communitarian premises than with liberal ones.[6] Statism assumes that the citizenry can be dealt with as a single entity speaking with a single voice, the voice of the nation as a whole. The individual's position in world politics is derived from the position of his or her state. From the outsider's point of view, no attention need be paid to differences of opinion within the state itself. Even if one does not in fact believe that no differences of opinion exist, differences of opinion are treated as irrelevant to outsiders. There is something seemingly illiberal, though, in assigning to each individual the position of the group as a whole. The individual's personal views and perspectives are reduced to the group median; the individual is dealt with solely qua member of the group.

Viewed from the outside, in a statist system, the individual state is opaque.[7] The outsider does not try to lift the veil that shields the state's inner workings from outside scrutiny, because what matters is the decision of the group acting as a community, not how individuals differ from one another. The outsider deals with the group as a single entity, with a particular center of gravity and all of its mass, so to speak, concentrated at that point. The metaphor that is sometimes used in international relations is the metaphor of the state as billiard ball. One characteristic of billiard balls that the metaphor conjures up is that they are rigid on impact; billiard balls bounce off one another without affecting one another's internal workings. But another relevant characteristic is their opacity. One does not inquire into the inner workings of a billiard ball. They are black boxes; the output is all that matters, the process generating it inscrutable but also irrelevant.

There are two ways that the traditional liberal emphasis on individual human beings conflicts with statism. The more obvious one is that there may be cases in which the rights of states and the rights of individuals compete. The intensity of competition varies along a spectrum from manifest and critical to indirect and mild. At the more intense end of the spectrum are cases where one state claims that other states have no right to become involved in its domestic human rights violations because the autonomy—the sovereignty—of each state over its domestic affairs must be inviolate. Here the underlying tension between liberal individualism and statism blossoms into full-fledged conflict. At the less intense end of the spectrum are cases in which the incompatibility of state and individual rights is likelier to evade attention. Where the world community recognizes the foreign policy decisions of a dictatorial regime instead of the foreign policy preferences of its people, this recognition elevates the state at the expense of individuals. The choice of the dictator is respected, rather than the policy favored by the state's citizens.

Whether the conflict between states and individuals is muted or intense, all such situations require a choice between competing interests. There is also, however, a subtler source of tension between statism and liberalism. Even where the two do not directly compete for primacy, recognizing states as rights bearers dilutes the special status liberalism accords to human beings. Where individuals are treated as the only sorts of entities entitled to protection for their autonomy, it seems appropriate to attribute that protection to something special about the nature of individuals. Where other sorts of entities are accorded comparable protection, then the reason cannot be some characteristic that only human beings have. The addition of states to the list of protected entities in this way subtly threatens to undermine the rationale for protecting individuals. For it is then uncertain what the reason would be for guaranteeing individual autonomy; it seemingly would have to be some characteristic individuals share with nation states, but it is not clear what that characteristic is.

The consent-based model of international relations, as has often been noted, is based on an analogy between states and people.[8] Just as people are entitled to be bound only by norms and arrangements that they have consented to, so states should be free from imposition of nonconsensual political institutions. The autonomy claims of states, in this way, are parasitic upon the autonomy claims of individuals. But parasites characteristically weaken their hosts, and this parasite is no exception. Extending autonomy to states threatens to drain some of the force from the autonomy claims of individuals, by denying the relevance of the uniquely human attributes that seem to account for autonomy's persuasiveness.

The tension between liberal individualism and statism has not prevented certain liberal philosophers from taking an essentially statist view of international relations. John Rawls is perhaps the clearest example.[9] Rawls envisions international relations as a process of state agreement to international norms.[10] He sharply differentiates domestic from international politics, both in terms of the process of decision making and in terms of the decisions that he expects would result. The international norms that he imagines states agreeing to are quite different from the domestic norms that he thinks would be adopted within states. More important for present purposes, international decisions are made only after domestic political institutions have been formed; and the decision makers in international politics are representatives of states as a whole, not individual people.

Rawls's critics claim that he has no adequate justification for this two-step process. At one point Rawls seems to suggest that the different treatment is a result of the difference in circumstances; that nations are relatively disconnected from one another, while within domestic society individual interactions are more frequent and intense.[11] Domestic societies are portrayed as cooperative enterprises, while international society is an aggregation of relatively autonomous units. The result is a set of international moral norms that are strikingly libertarian, in contrast to the more generous norms of intragroup sharing that Rawls envisions for domestic politics.[12] But, as Charles Beitz has argued, it is not empirically appropriate to treat the two contexts as qualitatively different.[13] At one time it might have made sense to differentiate between the national community, which is arguably an essentially cooperative enterprise, and the international arena, where far less interaction takes place. But it is hard, Beitz claims, to justify this sharp dichotomy today. Thomas Pogge, likewise, demonstrates the artificiality of dividing into two parts the process of establishing political institutions, with the governments of states established first and the norms that apply to international affairs established thereafter by the states' own representatives.[14]

Beitz's own arguments suggest what seems a potentially more suitable way to reconcile liberalism with statism.[15] A more promising approach would treat the deference due to states as only presumptive and not conclusive. The problem in reconciling liberalism with statism is that there are two competing sets of primitive concepts, states and individuals. Statism elevates the state above the individual (for international purposes, at any rate).[16] Liberalism seems to do the opposite. But if we treat the state's power as at most presumptive, then liberals might be able to have their individualistic cake and eat it too. The state would have only *derivative* entity status; it would be entitled to moral standing only insofar as it acted on behalf of individuals. "A group right is derivative if it is delegated by one or more original holders of the rights. . . . To hold that a group right is derivative, and most particularly to hold that it is derived from individuals, is compatible with liberal individualistic theory, for the group right is then reducible to an individual right."[17] When its interests came into conflict with the rights of persons, liberals could resolve the conflict in favor of the rights of the individual. Granting entity status to states, under this view, would not dilute the special moral status of individuals because the rights of states would be explicable in terms of the rights of individuals.

DERIVATIVE STATISM The liberal explanation for statism, then, might go as follows: States can, under the right circumstances, actually act so as to promote individual autonomy. Liberal states—those that are democratic and respect human rights—help individuals to achieve their goals by providing political institutions for making cooperative interaction possible. Greater individual security is possible in a state; states provide personal physical safety, as well as safety for one's property, so that one can adopt a life plan and build toward one's goals. States provide a way for individuals to band together to share the uncertainties and risks they face in daily life, so that individuals who wish to cooperate will have a way to do so and those who tend toward predatory behavior can be kept in check.

Just as it is desirable that there be states, it is also desirable that there be a diversity of states in the world, rather than a single universal state. People have varied preferences and beliefs, and the chance that one's state will be responsive depends in part on how large a state it is. A larger number of smaller states creates greater choice and greater responsiveness, whether choice is understood primarily in terms of "exit" (leaving for another state with views more to one's liking) or "voice" (using one's influence to change policies that one does not like).[18] It also creates the potential for social experimentation, so that many different ideas can be tested and their consequences compared and evaluated.

Although it is often possible for a single state to satisfy widely different preferences, there are some differences about quality of life that are hard to accommodate within a single state. Some people want to live in a rural atmosphere with a deep commitment to preserving the environment in a pristine fashion; others prefer the busy cosmopolitan lifestyle of a densely settled city. Some people would dedicate a high percentage of public money to the arts; others might want to promote sports or casual amusements. Some crave a cradle-to-grave safety net; others prefer a less paternalistic system that leaves individuals to make their own insurance arrangements. A single world government would level all of these differences, having no way to respond differently to the different preferences and beliefs that different groups of people have. To promote diversity and responsiveness, it is better to have a large number of states that are truly independent of one another. This, at any rate, might be the liberal argument.

There are, for this reason, plausible liberal reasons to have states and to grant them substantial independence. What matters for present purposes is that, under this view, states are merely a means to the end of promoting liberal goals. As soon as states stop promoting diversity, autonomy, security, and so forth, the justification fails. The key value is the promotion of the interests of individuals; states play only a secondary role, by providing individuals with the means to fulfill their life plans.

One can easily imagine a world that would suit this liberal vision of derivative states. In that hypothetical world, every state would be a liberal democracy, and each state's international actions would reflect the wishes of its people. These states would adopt international agreements through the process of consent; and because the states themselves consented to international norms and procedures, and the people themselves consented to the states, there would be effective agreement by the citizenry to the international norms. The state would act as the agent for its citizens. What matters, in this vision, is the liberal rights of individuals, but so long as states protect those rights and respect democratic processes, statism is consistent with the individuals' ultimate normative importance.

It is no surprise, for this reason, that authors such as Charles Beitz do not object to the existence of states per se. They have no problem with statism so long as the state respects the human rights of its citizens. What concerns Beitz (and others, such as David Luban) is the possibility that statism will be used as a barrier to humanitarian intervention by outsiders who want to put an end to domestic injustice. "Unjust institutions do not enjoy the same prima facie protection against external interference as do just institutions, and in fact, other things being equal, interference with unjust institutions might be justified when it has a high probability of promoting domestic social justice."[19] It is not statism per se that creates problems, however, but the sort of hard-core statism that treats the state, rather than the individual, as the ultimate rights holder. Derivative statism is not objectionable.

Beitz and other likeminded philosophers recognize that this is a rather utopian vision. In today's world there is tremendous hue and cry over "state sovereignty" every time that outsiders seek to use their influence to put an end to torture, political persecution, racial and sexual discrimination, and the like. Their object, though, is not to validate existing practice; to the contrary, their object is to criticize it. While such philosophers recognize the divergence between today's world and what they recommend, they find the difference to the world's discredit, not their theory's. On the other hand, this vision is at least compatible with a certain degree of statism; and as noted earlier, this fact may be essential to any chance for general acceptance. This argument for derivative statism seems to mesh perfectly with the liberal theory set out in chapters 4–7. As noted earlier, while the liberal argument is a statist one, its statism is qualified by the fact that it treats individual rights as preeminent when state sovereignty and universal human rights conflict. While liberalism recognizes an important role for state consent, it also recognizes the importance of universal moral norms. As to these, the liberal theory holds, there is a justification for action that does not rely on state consent: moral correctness. So we seem to have combined the best of both worlds, in a theory that captures the realities of world politics to a certain degree but that nonetheless packs a genuine critical punch.

DERIVATIVE VERSUS QUALIFIED STATISM There are obvious problems with this notion of derivative statism, however. On the one hand, it may give states too much authority at the expense of individuals. While we assumed that states promoted the good of individuals by making possible political diversity and free choice, it must realistically be acknowledged that people actually have very little freedom of movement. The right to choose one's political community is largely illusory; political communities are assigned to individuals primarily through the accident of where they are born. The argument also overlooks the fact that the more states exist, the more potential exists for externalities, that is, for one state's policies having effects within the territory of another. The peaceful residents of rural Walden may be subjected to noxious fumes produced by upwind Gotham. So long as state independence is preserved, there is no way for the Walden voters to control their own destiny because they do not vote in the Gotham elections.

On the other hand, the liberal vision of derivative statism fails to recognize the tremendous moral significance of national membership in many people's lives. By treating states as simply a means to the end of individual fulfillment, it misses the real significance of state affiliation, replacing it with a thin and watery liberal facsimile of what is in actuality a potent moral force. If liberalism views the options for dissatisfied citizens in terms of exit and voice, a communitarian might respond that the third alternative is loyalty. The loyalty option suggests that individuals might be better off changing their lives so as to fall in step with their environments, rather than fickly changing their environments to suit their preferences. Ties to one's community are not so easily picked up or put aside, like a change of clothing.

These are serious questions, and it is not clear whether this utopian liberal vision can really capture either the appeal or the danger of national commitment. Liberals and their communitarian critics are likely to weigh these considerations differently and come to different conclusions. These considerations are less important, though, for present purposes, than the inability of derivative statism to explain the precise phenomenon under investigation: the relevance of state consent to international norms generally and to international hegemony in particular. The problem with derivative statism is that if its premises are taken seriously, they diverge much more widely from current practice than at first appears, and in ways that are not necessarily very attractive. Derivative statism cannot account for the normative value we attach to the consent of undemocratic states.

In the international context, derivative statism means that requiring a state to abide by a norm is legitimate only so long as the state consented to the norm and the people consented to the state. Derivative statism holds that state autonomy not be respected where the state's decision was not approved by democratic domestic processes. The problem with using this criterion to select which international norms and institutions are worthy of respect is simply that there are too many international norms and institutions which violate this criterion, because the states that agreed to them are not democracies. Many of these norms and institutions, furthermore, do not violate human rights; indeed, many are substantively attractive even to liberals. It is tempting to work backward; to infer that because most human rights abuses are committed in violation of liberal political standards requiring democratic consent, their invalidity is *due to the fact* that they were committed in violation of liberal political standards requiring democratic consent. But there are many other norms that are also generated in violation of liberal democratic norms; and if the derivative statism argument is sound, all of these would have to be invalidated, as well.

Consider, for example, the treaty obligations of a nondemocratic nation such as Syria. Syria does not have a liberal democratic political regime; from this it follows (if derivative statism is correct) that if Syria violates basic human rights norms, such violations cannot be cloaked with the mantle of state sovereignty. So far, so good. But if one is concerned that liberal democratic process values are offended when human rights are violated, one should also be concerned about Syrian decisions to join the United Nations, to sign a nuclear nonproliferation treaty, to adopt a human rights convention, or to enter into peace negotiations with Israel. These decisions are not made in a democratic fashion either. Once it has been announced that the Syrian government is not an agent for its people, this fact invalidates all of the decisions—good or bad—that the Syrian government makes, not just the ones that violate human rights or that are undesirable for some other reason. The same process that resulted in the human rights violations is responsible for the decision to enter the United Nations or sign the nonproliferation agreement; the process defect infects all of these decisions equally.

But if we wipe from the books all international commitments entered into by nondemocratic states, very few international norms will be left standing. At present most of the world's countries are not liberal democracies; over the course of history, even a smaller percentage of regimes have been. Virtually any rule that dates to premodern times is the product almost entirely of states that were not electoral democracies of the sort that liberals would approve. Ironically, the derivative statism argument would tend selectively to invalidate many of the most desirable international commitments, in that some nondemocratic regimes are particularly belligerent and especially in need of the restraint that international agreements can provide.[20] If the derivative statism argument were correct, then there would be no reason that Iraq should not be able to wage wars of territorial aggression, or that North Korea should have to refrain from building nuclear weapons. Liberal democracies, however, would have to honor such international agreements.

Derivative statism is different from the theory of qualified statism that we investigated in earlier chapters. Qualified statism imposes substantive limits on what states may do; so long as they remain within those substantive limits, states may consent or withhold consent as they please. Derivative statism, in contrast, is a more thoroughgoing rejection of state autonomy, and a more thoroughgoing commitment to individual autonomy. Its limits apply even when substantive requirements such as human rights norms have been met. Qualified statism is adequate to protect individual human rights not to be tortured, discriminated against, and so forth. But it does not go far enough to protect individual autonomy; for that, one needs a radically individualist theory like derivative statism which invalidates all agreements made without electoral approval.

QUALIFIED STATISM AND INDIVIDUAL AUTONOMY   If it goes too far to invalidate all international agreements made by undemocratic regimes, then the question must be whether deference to the more desirable international commitments of dictators can be justified in liberal terms. Can qualified, as opposed to derivative, statism be squared with a commitment to individual autonomy?

The best chance for reconciliation lies in the fact that honoring the treaty commitments of dictators is not the same as condoning their political methods. Disapproval of dictatorship does not necessarily lead to the conclusion that all of a dictator's commitments should be treated as null and void. Even though the process is flawed, this does not necessarily require rejecting its outcome; once a decision has been made, perhaps it deserves to be treated as final. The proper remedy, according to this argument, is to try to change the process by which decisions are made—to promote democratic regimes around the world. In particular, no one has claimed that individuals should in any way be inhibited from local political action to replace the dictatorship with a democracy. But as to decisions that have already been made, perhaps the process point should be treated as moot.

This possibility illustrates a characteristic of statism that I pointed out earlier: opacity. The argument just made, essentially, is that for purposes of international politics states should be treated as opaque. It is not that outsiders necessarily believe that states' internal workings are perfect from the point of view of liberal democratic theory; the point is, rather, that their imperfections are not the business of the outside world. Once a decision has been made, it is to be treated as conclusive, allowing no room for second-guessing of the state's domestic politics. This is the state as "black box." Questions of internal decision-making practices are to be bracketed off.

But the question is, why? The opacity argument does nothing more than re-
state the conclusion, which is that the internal failings of the state are irrelevant to
the authoritativeness of its decisions. This is simply another way of saying that the
autonomy of the state should be respected, even at the expense of the autonomy
rights of individuals to be governed in a democratic fashion.[21] The argument
merely reiterates the importance of the line dividing the inside of the state from
the outside. Once a decision issues forth into the outside world, questions about
its pedigree are foreclosed. This is one powerful way to state the claim that the
relevant entity is the state; decisions are effectively and authoritatively "made" at
the point that the state considers the resolution final. But it is a restatement of the
statist position, not a justification for it, and in particular not a justification that
squares it with liberal individualism.

Walzer actually makes a somewhat similar claim when he argues that intervention in the affairs of other states is typically unjustified, even when the point of
the intervention is to reform the other state's political inadequacies. The similarity lies in the fact that limiting outside intervention does not inhibit local
political agitation to replace the dictatorship with a democratic regime. The
argument sharply distinguishes local remedies (which are considered appropriate) from externally initiated efforts to right local wrongs. Walzer has a plausible
argument for this distinction; he notes that a state's citizens, typically, will fight
against outside military intervention, so that outside intervention puts the lives of
local citizens at risk.[22] But note that this argument is only available in the precise
context to which he addresses himself, humanitarian intervention by military
means.[23] No local person's life would be put at risk by the unenforceability of the
treaty commitments of unelected regimes.

If one wanted to try to generalize Walzer's argument to give it application in
the present context, then one might say that what matters is that in some circumstances local people would want the outside world to recognize the authority of
their government, even though it is not elected. Here it might be pointed out that
the ability to sign treaties is a source of strength for a state, and depriving a state of
its power to do so diminishes the state's political influence, perhaps at the expense
of the very people whom liberal theory sets out to protect.[24] People may cherish
their own state's sovereign capacity to do so even if their state is not democratic,
and even if they would ideally prefer that their state be democratic. Depriving a
state of its ability to function in world politics may only add insult to injury from
the point of view of those who care about the international stature of their state,
however imperfect it may be as a matter of domestic arrangements.

The main problem with this claim is that it does not seem to present a blanket justification for enforcing dictators' treaty obligations generally. There may be some treaty obligations of nondemocratic states that can be justified in such a fashion, but this argument is likely to be exceedingly inapt as a warrant for international hegemony, or, for that matter, for any other commitment that seriously impinges on the freedom of action of states. In the eyes of individuals that would maximize the international stature of their state (even if it is undemocratic), consent to international hegemony would be an unattractive vehicle. While Walzer may be correct that citizens want their states to be free from outside military intervention and will fight to preserve that freedom, citizens rarely fight for the right of their state to subordinate itself to an international hegemon.

There is something rather flat about the claim that a state's subordinate status can be justified on the grounds that the ability to commit to subordinate status can be a source of power of which we would not want to deprive the state's citizens. Did the Filipinos want the Marcos government to have the power to provide the United States with territory for U.S. naval bases? Were the people of Eastern European nations pleased that their governments possessed sufficient sovereignty to invite the Soviet Union to invade? Was the cost in lives and property of Iraqi civilians during the Gulf war justified by the fact that they wanted their state to have the power to make a binding commitment to enter the United Nations and submit itself to Security Council enforcement procedures?[25] Where questions of international hegemony are at stake, such inferences about popular opinion are considerably less plausible than they are in the sort of circumstances concerning Walzer.

A slightly different point would be that the agreements themselves (as opposed to possession of the power to make agreements) are in the interests of the people of the state. There are at least three problems with basing the nonelected regime's authority to make international commitments on the fact that they are beneficial to the people of the state. The first is that the international system does not limit enforcement to treaty commitments that are in the best interests of the state and its people; indeed, asking about the best interests of the state's people is not even on the agenda. It is a sufficient condition for enforcement that the treaty was agreed to. A treaty commitment may later be recognized as a bad bargain for the state's people; but this alone is not a basis for nonenforcement, even for nondemocratic states. Russia may have made a mistake when it sold Alaska to the United States, and the people of czarist Russia certainly had no veto over the deal; but a bargain's a bargain, nonetheless.

Second, if substantive desirability is enough—if it is enough, in other words, that the agreement is in the best interests of the citizens—then it is not clear why consent of the state should be a *necessary* condition for enforcement. If enforceabil-ity can rest on substantive desirability alone, it is hard to understand why we should attach any importance at all to the fact that a nondemocratic regime agreed. Why not require dictatorships to adhere to nonproliferation treaties even if they have not consented? Yet no one seems to be suggesting that consent is flatly irrelevant; it seems that there is a better case for enforcing norms that non-democratic states agree to than norms that nondemocratic states did not agree to. What liberalism seems hard pressed to explain is why the consent of the *state* does matter when the consent of the state's *people* does not.

Third, and most important, an argument that rests on the belief that some treaty is in the best interests of a state and its people simply does not take very seriously the notion of autonomy. The argument seems to suggest that the inter-national community (or, perhaps more realistically, the most powerful states in the international community) has the capacity to decide what is best for the citizens of weaker states. Once a dictator signs an agreement, the international community is empowered to decide whether there was a conflict of interest between a dictatorship and its people—a decision that requires powerful states to determine what the local people's best interests are. This notion denies those people the right to determine their interests for themselves, a right which can be exercised in unpredictable and idiosyncratic ways.

This entire line of reasoning seems, in fact, to contain within it the seeds of a justification for benevolent dictatorship. One of the important aspects of a com-mitment to individual autonomy is the belief that individuals themselves are best equipped to determine their own best interests, and that it is not possible or permissible simply to figure out what is in their best interests and then impose it on them. If we really take seriously the commitment to individual autonomy, then we must be prepared to respect even those preferences that strike us as irrational.

Thus, we must be prepared to respect the possibility that the people of North Korea might prefer that their state not be party to nonproliferation treaties, or that the people of Iraq might choose not to relinquish the option of waging war on innocent (and wealthy) nearby nations. It cannot simply be assumed that since the powerful states of the world community think these norms to be self-evi-dently good ones, and in weaker nations' own self-interest, that it is permissible simply to impose these norms on them. Respect for individual choice means respect for the individual's right to choose either way. To the extent that we would not respect the choice not to be a part of the United Nations, or the choice to retain the right to build nuclear weapons or wage aggressive war, then the opposite decisions are not really respected as genuine choices either. We cannot claim that the reason that a commitment to U.N. norms, to nonproliferation, or to respect for other states' territorial integrity is respected is that it was voluntary.

Unfortunately, there simply isn't any way to determine the actual wishes of the people involved. A nondemocratic regime is not about to allow foreign observers to submit proposed international treaties to a referendum. It is unlikely that there will be many cases in which popular opinion is so clear and so public that it is possible to state with any accuracy that the people actually and definitely want—or don't want—the treaty in question. The democratic avenue for making decisions is closed off, at least for the time being. Given this fact, it doesn't seem a very attractive solution simply to enshrine the choices of the very individual or group that has made democratic determination impossible. Honoring the treaty commitments of dictators, however, does exactly that.

The recognition of treaty obligations incurred by nondemocratic regimes is, purely and simply, an acknowledgment that the regime in question is the de facto political power in the state in question. It is a pragmatic concession to the fact that, if nondemocratic regimes cannot consent on behalf of the people of Syria or Vietnam, then no one can. Too much of the smooth functioning of the international system is at stake to disallow the consent of nondemocratic regimes. There is no point attempting to cloak this pragmatic reality in liberal principle of the consent of individuals; for the consent of states is ultimately prior to the obligations of individuals when one considers the mechanics of the international system.

INDIVIDUAL RIGHTS AS DERIVATIVE Given that, as things are currently done, the democratic nature of the state is irrelevant to whether its commitments are considered binding, it makes more sense to say that an individual's international rights and responsibilities are derivative of his or her state's rights and responsibilities than the other way around. Aside from individual rights that arise directly from universal human rights norms, the international rights and responsibilities of a Syrian, Burmese, or Saudi Arabian come by and large from commitments made by regimes that they have not elected. By agreeing to a treaty, states acquire both a responsibility to adhere to it and the right to enforce it against other states. This gives the citizens of those states responsibilities and rights as well; they are only held to the costs and promised the benefits of those agreements that their states enter into. The rights of individuals stem from the fact that their states have obtained rights of enforcement.

Just as a citizen's international rights and obligations are initially acquired through membership in a particular state, so also are they altered through a change in political affiliation. When an individual moves and takes up citizenship in another country that has not signed a particular agreement, he or she loses both the costs and the benefits of that particular treaty. If a state forfeits its rights under a treaty (perhaps by failing to comply with its terms), then its citizens forfeit their rights as well. To some degree, in fact, individuals have not been legally permitted to initiate their own actions to protect their rights; they have been required to wait and hope that their states will take action on their behalf.[26] This is true regardless of whether the states in question are democracies or dictatorships.

The fact that individual rights and obligations are to such a degree derivative of the rights and obligations of their states is hard to square with liberal assumptions. This is particularly so given the fact that citizenship is itself an arbitrary assignment, from a liberal point of view. One typically acquires one's citizenship by being born in a certain location or to a certain set of parents; citizenship is largely ascriptive.[27] One's citizenship is, further, a consequence of the fact that some particular state has territorial sovereignty over some particular piece of land; my having been born in New York City only makes me an American citizen because at some earlier time control of that piece of land was wrested first from indigenous peoples, then from the Dutch, and then from Great Britain.[28] Territorial borders frequently are nothing more than a historical consequence of state military power. One does not consent to being born in a certain place, nor to the fact that some particular geographical location is within the borders of one state rather than another.

Liberalism seems to have no good explanation for why this should be the case; communitarian logic, in contrast, accepts as inevitable the fact that we are born, arbitrarily, into particular communities and over time become products of those communities—with or without our consent. The communitarian has no particular hesitation about envisioning the relevant actor as the group rather than the individual, or about seeing the individual primarily through the prism of his or her group identification. Statism is hard to square with liberalism but an easy fit with theories of community.

Statism thus seems a distinctly communitarian notion that international liberalism seeks to embed, inexplicably, in an otherwise liberal matrix of international relationships. The aspirations to liberalism of the theory I have been describing in chapters 4–7 lie in the claim that the norms they propose for governing state political interaction are modeled on liberal norms, norms that require an actor's consent before it can be bound. Their liberalism rests on the fact that international politics and international hegemony are supposed to be grounded on the consent of states; international liberalism seems much harder, in contrast, to square with the fact that international arrangements are founded on the consent of *states*. We now turn to the question of why, even if states are thought to be the relevant actors, the operative norm should be consent.

10

BEYOND

CONSENT

The reason for basing international hegemony on state consent is the protection of the autonomy of weaker states from imposition at the hands of the stronger. So long as political arrangements are based on state consent, political authority seems to be voluntary and therefore legitimate. But this argument assumes that autonomy, and volition, are meaningful. If the decisions that states make merely reflect the practices of the international community, there is no important reason for deferring to them. States would merely be automatons, not free agents; and their choices, which would be nothing more than a consequence of world community pressure, would not be worth protecting. Where volition is lacking, consent is not genuine; and such illusory choice is neither a necessary nor a sufficient condition for political legitimacy.

The accuracy of the assumption of individual autonomy is a recurrent question in modern domestic political theory. Critical theorists and communitarians object to what they see as a tendency of liberals to divorce individual actors from their social contexts, arguing that the appearance of consent that liberalism creates can be illusory. Consent theory, they argue, misleadingly posits arm's-length transactions in which individuals come together to establish social and political institutions; this picture is misleading because society creates individuals as much as individuals create society. People, it is argued, are as much a product of the social and political structures that they inhabit as those structures are a product of people. Autonomy, therefore, should not be the central value to promote, and consent is the wrong normative focus.

This critique of liberalism, having arisen originally in domestic political theory, has been brought to bear on international relations theory by critics who are sympathetic to the domestic argument. Robert Keohane describes the divide between mainstream "rationalists" and these critics, whom he calls "reflectivists," as central to international relations research, and in particular to the design of adequate research strategies.

> [Reflectivists] emphasize that individuals, local organizations, and even states develop within the context of more encompassing institutions. Institutions do not merely reflect the preferences and power of the units constituting them; the institutions themselves shape those preferences and that power. Institutions are therefore *constitutive* of actors as well as vice versa. It is therefore not sufficient in this view to treat the preferences of individuals as given exogenously; they are affected by institutional arrangements, by prevailing norms, and by historically contingent discourse among people seeking to pursue their purposes and solve their self-defined problems.[1]

Keohane recognizes that it is somewhat artificial to treat the holders of such views as members of a single school of thought. He lists such diverse scholars as John Ruggie, Robert Cox, Hayward Alker, Richard Ashley, Friedrich Kratochwil, and Alex Wendt as subscribing to something like this view; he could easily have added many more, including in particular R. B. J. Walker, Nicholas Onuf, and V. Spike Petersen.[2] The term *reflectivist* that he proposes has not won uniform acceptance; another term that has been used is *constructivist*, focusing on the fact that identity is socially constructed.[3] Some of these writers might be more comfortable calling themselves simply postmodernists, say, or feminists. But the title to be given liberalism's critics is of little importance to the present enterprise. For present purposes, what matters is the rejection of the simple liberal paradigm of state identity implicit in previous chapters. Despite the vast differences among scholars who reject mainstream international relations theory, they nonetheless share doubts about the autonomy of states.

The authors just listed are predominantly concerned with "descriptive" rather than "normative" international relations theory, although skepticism about the utility of the distinction is widespread and deep. But their rejection of state autonomy, whether specifically designed to or not, has important normative consequences for a justification of world political processes that purports to be founded on state agreement. For if state identity and preference are merely artefacts of world political processes, then it is not clear that consent is the right norm on which to ground international political arrangements. The reason is that preferences and choices do not really reflect the autonomous decisions of states.

Whatever one thinks of this argument as a matter of domestic political theory—applied, that is, to the relations between individual human beings and their governments—it is telling as applied to the relations between individual states and the world community. States are especially vulnerable to the charge that they are socially constituted and therefore not autonomous. Thus, even if one rejects the critics' domestic arguments, their international claims are cause for deep concern. The object of this chapter is to show why. There are, essentially, two reasons. First, more than individual human beings, states are social and conventional, and not biological, creatures. The conventions that create them come, in substantial part, from outside the individual states themselves—from the world community and not domestic politics. The second reason builds on the arguments of the previous chapter, for the problem is statism. Once statism moves us away from the assumption that smaller units of a system must always consent to political arrangements (by rejecting the claim that state power is conditional upon individual consent), then the bottom drops out of the argument that states must consent to the larger political system of which they, in turn, are part. States cannot reasonably demand greater freedom as against the international political order than they grant individuals citizens as against their own authority.

At stake is the question of whether to view world politics from the top looking down or from the bottom looking up. Does the system constitute the actors (and is this morally acceptable)? Or do the actors constitute the system (and is this the way things ought to be)? One way of stating the difficulty with the liberal theory of hegemony we have developed is that it is *top-down* when the question is the respective roles of the state and the individual, but *bottom-up* when the question is the respective roles of the state and the international political order. Somewhat inconsistently, then, this model protects the prerogatives of the state when it is a choice between the state and the world community, but also when there is a choice between the state and the individual. This "heads I win, tails you lose" approach, I will argue, is difficult to justify.

THE SOCIAL CONSTRUCTION OF STATES

Are individuals more vulnerable to the social forces of the world that they inhabit, or are states? There are arguments on both sides. It is possible, on the one hand, to argue that states may in fact be less open to the social construction of identity than individual people are, because individuals are more deeply embedded than states in the social networks they inhabit. While it is possible for a state to be relatively autarchic, it could be claimed, there are few opportunities for people to live as hermits. A larger proportion of an individual's attention is likely to be directed to interactions with others than the proportion of state attention devoted to international relations. Of course, the density of some particular actor's social interactions is an empirical question; the international relations of a small entity such as Switzerland or Hong Kong may be more important to the shaping of its identity than the interpersonal relations of an isolated hermit.[4] But it might be claimed that, on the average, social context is less important to state identity than to individual identity.

The important countervailing consideration, however, is that individuals are to some degree biologically determined, while states are purely conventional social constructs. One need not subscribe to sociobiological theories of individual personality to recognize some role for biological determination of identity. Only the most radical of postmodernists would deny the importance of the material reality of our bodies, which seemingly can be taken as givens. Although it can be claimed at the periphery that there are questions of biological identity only answerable through recourse to social convention (is a fetus part of a pregnant woman's body? whose body is a transplanted organ part of?), individuals are nonetheless different from states in the degree to which this sort of social construction is determinative. If everyone in the world woke up one morning believing that the Soviet Union did not exist (or that Palestine did exist), then "reality" would follow suit. The same could not be said about the existence of Saddam Hussein, although of course the meanings that we attach to the biological individual we identify as Saddam Hussein are highly social.

In addition to their more or less determinate biological existence, individual people also have the experience of free will. This is not the place for a digression into the philosophical subtleties of whether free will exists or whether all of our choices are really, instead, determined by prior influences. Regardless of philosophical subtleties, it remains the case that when we make choices, we frequently feel as though they are open choices—choices that can be made either way, as we decide. States do not seem to be the sort of entities that have free will—in fact, it is not even clear what the question of free will would mean in connection with state decision making. There is no state consciousness, no state mind, in which to locate the capacity to reflect and to choose.[5]

The importance of these two points lies in the need to locate a foundation for the emphasis on state autonomy. With individual people, it is easy enough to locate the appeal of autonomy; it lies in the sense of self and of free will that most of us (correctly or not) experience. Even if we are wrong about our autonomy as people, it seems at least to be an understandable mistake; but the claim for state autonomy is noticeably less intuitively attractive. This is one reason why, I would claim, even those who remain committed to individual autonomy might nonetheless concede the social construction of states. Perhaps it is not possible, overall, to prove that states are more socially constituted than people. Yet it is clear that there are some respects in which states are more vulnerable; and these differences make the claim to state autonomy more doubtful than the corresponding claim for human beings.

There are both descriptive and normative dimensions to this distinction between states and people.[6] The descriptive claim, to which we will turn directly, arises from the argument that states are not in fact autonomous; that they take their identities in important ways from the world political community. The normative claim, to which we will turn immediately thereafter, concerns the degree to which whatever independence exists is worth protecting. In both respects, states seem to have a weaker claim to autonomy than people do, and for this reason less of a claim that international political arrangement should be based on their consent. One example, admittedly an extreme one, should illustrate the general point.

Suppose that an overwhelmingly powerful nation installs a puppet government in a weaker neighboring state. The puppet government is able to come to power only with the assistance of this hegemon, and the hegemon's assistance is the only thing standing between it and downfall at the hands of mass local opposition. If the puppet government "consents" to a certain subservient relationship with the hegemon, in what sense should this arrangement be normatively privileged? As a descriptive matter, the decision to submit was determined by outside interests instead of domestic preferences. As normative matter, it is hard to see an argument for protecting a choice that was not authentically, indigenously, and freely made.

It is important to note, with regard to this example, that there is no obvious analogy to this problem in interpersonal relations. The problem arises because states are social organizations within which there are, potentially, severe problems of conflict of interest. Decisions are made by the state's leaders but are attributed to the states themselves. Biological individuals have a high degree of cohesion; it is harder to imagine decisions made by the individual, and on behalf of the individual, that are not the decisions of the individual.[7] From this difference follows the claim that, to a greater extent than with individuals, decisions made by state leaders on behalf of the state may be the product of external influences at least as much as of autonomous choice. For under certain circumstances state leaders may be more responsive to external than to domestic forces.

There are at least three ways that world political processes shape the identities of states. The first is suggested by the extreme example of the state that is literally a puppet of some nearby power: it is that the identity of the regime that makes choices on behalf of a state may be influenced by world politics. The second concerns the territorial boundaries of states. Unlike the corporeal limits of individuals, territorial boundaries are established in large part by social convention. Third, the very fact that the world community is structured as a system of states, rather than some other way, is a product of social practices. World political institutions to which no effective consent has or can be given thus determine that individuals are represented by states, that their states take the particular territorial shape that they do, and that these particular territorial states are represented by the regimes that they are.

THE IDENTITY OF PARTICULAR REGIMES   What a state consents to, obviously, is influenced by the identity of the regime that governs it. This is true in democracies; the election of Bill Clinton to the American presidency meant that the United States would sign the international biodiversity treaty, for example, when George Bush only the year before had announced that the United States would not.[8] It is even more the case with nonelected regimes, however. Democratic regimes are responsive to popular will; where popular opinion is relatively settled on a particular international agreement, it will not matter too much which party is in office. But nonelected regimes have much greater freedom to set foreign policy without consulting the preferences of the population, and so the preferences of the leaders themselves are key to whether consent will be given. As with democratic regimes, their chief constraint is that they act so as not to lose power; but their hold on power does not depend so directly on pleasing the populace.

Nonelected regimes are therefore more vulnerable than elected ones to the charge that their states are not autonomous, because they have greater freedom to respond to outside influences if state leaders choose to. We noted in the previous chapter that the nondemocratic nature of a regime undercuts its claim to exercise power on behalf of individual citizens; entity status as a state must therefore be justified in some other way. The related point here is that at the same time that it grounds the rights of the states on the rights of its people, responsiveness to popular will demonstrates independence from the world political community. To the degree that a nation's identity is shaped by domestic forces it is less open to pressures from the outside; conversely, to the degree that its identity is the product of external forces, it cannot be explained in terms of responsiveness to domestic political preference. Popular sovereignty in this way kills two liberal birds with the same stone, establishing a positive reason for deferring to state choice as well as helping to rebut the claim that choices are imposed from the outside.

If the identity of the regime is important to consent as a general matter, it is at least equally important when the question is consent specifically to institutions of international hegemony. Some regimes, notoriously, have been much more accommodating to U.S. interests than others; indeed, much U.S. Cold War–era foreign policy was oriented toward ensuring the continuance in power of the more accommodating ones. (The same was true of Soviet foreign policy.) To the extent that the legitimacy of international hegemony is claimed to be founded on state consent, U.S. hegemony is more likely to pass the test if the Somozas and Batistas of the world are in power than if the Ortegas and Castros are. The former are likely to support U.S. initiatives wherever possible; the latter will be obstructionist whenever the opportunity presents itself.

But surely consent obtained by subverting local political processes should not count as genuine consent. If, at one extreme, the hegemon has effectively selected the regimes that are then called on to supply consent, it does not seem that the hegemon would have a particularly strong claim to legitimacy. To the contrary, we would denounce the arrangement as imperialistic. The fact that colonial powers in some cases ruled indirectly, through the installation of domestic puppet regimes, did not make colonization morally acceptable. The Warsaw Pact nations "consented" to Soviet domination; so did the government of Afghanistan; and the Endara government in Panama has consented to the continuing U.S. military role.[9] State consent is not an adequate justification for hegemony where the selection of other state's leaders is strongly influenced by the hegemon.

It would be a mistake to think of this difficulty solely in terms of cases of outside military intervention. It is true, of course, that valid consent cannot be given by a regime that is forcefully installed by an outside power, such as the Soviet puppet government in Afghanistan, the Vietnamese-installed regime in Cambodia, or the Vichy government in France during World War II. If that were the sole problem, however, it might be solved without much ado simply by disregarding the consent of any regimes installed by force. Such a rule would be an obvious analog to rules regulating the consent of persons; if an individual is forced to agree to some arrangement at gunpoint, we do not treat the arrangement as consensual. Eliminating such instances of consent would not bring the international system crashing down around us, because there are not too many examples that are so blatant.

But there are numerous methods other than physical force for installing favorable governments or influencing the policies of governments that already exist, and if all of these were included, it *would* pose a threat to the world political system as we know it. In his article on the impact of international events on domestic politics, Peter Gourevitch lists some of these: "Of course, the clearest form of external influence on politics is outright invasion and occupation, though occupation can be complex, as it usually requires native collaborators. Less clear empirically but equally obvious conceptually is 'meddling': subsidies to newspapers or to fifth columns, spying, assassination, and so on."[10]

Gourevitch could have added many other examples, not quite as nasty as spying or assassination. When the United States gives economic aid to the Egyptian government, it helps an existing, relatively friendly, and secular government to stay in power despite challenges from Islamic militants. The United States sought to further similar objectives by refusing to become involved after Algeria nullified elections that Islamic militants seemed poised to win. When Clinton stood behind Boris Yeltsin in the face of domestic challenges to his authority in the spring of 1993, Clinton was hoping to influence the course of Russian politics so as to increase the likelihood of Yeltsin's continued control. Such examples cannot be as easily managed as cases of direct military intervention, where an exception fits neatly within the standard notion of consent theory.

The argument is also not limited to influence over a small group of political leaders of a country; domestic political processes can also be affected by influence over elite classes, more broadly defined. The actions of powerful nations can reinforce the elite status of such groups, helping to maintain them in power. Once this has taken place, it is not clear why the consent of such elites should have any normative weight. Compare the claim in the *dependencia* literature of the existence of a comprador class; an economic and social elite that is more in step with powerful outside interests than with the interests of the local masses, and that is kept in power in part by the favor of those outside interests.[11] In what sense is a decision to restructure the nation's economy, made under pressure from the International Monetary Fund or foreign banks, autonomous if only a small percentage of the population of a country wants to go along and if that small percentage is empowered to make decisions only by the very outside interests to which consent is supposedly given?

Sometimes the explanation offered is that elites have cynically sold out to outside interests; they understand their common interest with outsider groups and their lack of common interest with the local masses. But there also is a possibility that elites have simply been deluded into accepting outside values when these values are not actually to their benefit.

> Most observers would argue that the manipulation of *material incentives*—the use of threats and promises to alter the preferences of leaders in secondary nations—is the dominant form through which hegemonic power is exercised. . . . But there is also a more subtle component of hegemonic power, one that works at the level of *substantive beliefs* rather than material payoffs. Acquiescence is the result of the socialization of leaders in secondary nations. Elites in secondary states buy into and internalize norms that are articulated by the hegemon and therefore pursue policies consistent with the hegemon's notion of international order.[12]

This phenomenon can exist with local masses as well as local elites, for the populace at large might also come to internalize values that are imposed from without. Critical theorists would claim that these are not actually in the masses' interests, despite their popular acceptance.

Liberals, of course, are skeptical of such claims, preferring to describe the beliefs and preferences of those who experience socialization as having been voluntarily adopted. Their differences of opinion with critics and communitarians raise important issues, but those issues are not essentially different in the international context than in the domestic context; the debate is over the status of the beliefs of individual people who have been subjected to social pressure. This is not a debate that can be definitively settled here; critics will continue to be skeptical of individual autonomy, while liberals will continue to believe that individual choice exists. What matters here is that the inability to convince liberals on this point is not fatal to the critical case in the specifically international setting. While critics may find the argument convincing, and while it is an important argument, it is not a necessary one in the international context. There, the critics need not claim that socialized individuals are not necessarily acting in *their own* best interests; they need only claim that such individuals are not necessarily acting in *the state's* own best interests, and this is much easier to show. Where state consent is grounded on persuasion only of an elite kept in power by outside influence, even a liberal should not treat the state as a whole as having voluntarily adopted or ratified the external position, and the state cannot be said to have acted autonomously.

TERRITORIAL EXISTENCE   The second general way that the world community, and its powerful states, shape the identities and interests of its weaker members is by safeguarding or failing to safeguard their territorial existence. Regardless of which regime governs a state, its identity depends on the particular parcel of land with which it is associated. But territorial identity is, in turn, in large part a function of the norms and practices of the world community. There exists a potentially infinite number of different ways to draw the map of the world.[13] Which one will be recognized as authoritative? This depends in large part on the responses of other nations to attempts to alter existing borders. The world community regulates the birth, death, and succession of territorial states.

To a substantial degree, of course, the birth or death of a state has to do with its material capabilities as well as with the social reaction of the states around it. A state's military strength, its ability to successfully defend its borders from external attack, and its ability to maintain a functioning central government are to some degree a matter of material reality. But it is quite striking the extent to which the reactions of other states to these material facts can either enhance a would-be state's viability or undercut it. One need only compare the ease of entry into the world community of states whose existence was favored to the obstacles placed in the way of those whose existence was not.

Consider, for example, the favorable reception extended to the Baltic states when they broke away from the former Soviet Union. They were enthusiastically recognized and given seats in the United Nations, and Western nations pointedly signaled the Soviet Union that any Soviet change of heart threatening the new states' independence would be met with hostility. This favorable reception was motivated by a number of special circumstances concerning the Baltic states' history. They had been independent during the interwar period; the Soviet Union had annexed them illegitimately; and they had continued to protest their independence, with some support from other nations, during the entire effective period of their annexation.

The treatment of the Baltic states should be contrasted with the reception given the efforts of the various emerging republics of the former Yugoslavia. When Slovenia declared its independence, there was little problem. The emergence of Croatia and then, more importantly, of Bosnia clearly indicated the role of world opinion in state formation. The question in Bosnia has been whether there should be a single Bosnian state, composed of three different but interlocking communities (Muslim, Croatian, and Serb), or whether the territory should be divided along ethnic lines, with the Croatian and Serbian portions perhaps annexed to the larger nearby states of Croatia and Serbia. The world community—

particularly Europe, the United States, the Russian Slavs, and the nearby Muslim states—has watched closely, trying to steer the process in whatever direction thought to be the most favorable. As a general matter, there has been support for the independence of Bosnia but resistance to dividing Bosnia further into ethnic states at the expense of the Muslims. The world community, obviously, forms its own normative judgments about which territorial entities ought to be admitted into the company of states.

Compare, moreover, the birth of the state of Macedonia. One of the former republics of Yugoslavia, Macedonia provoked enormous resistance from Greece when it sought independence. The obstacle was its name; Greece claimed "Macedonia" for one of its own northern provinces, and argued that the new state's choice of a name reflected ambitions against Greek territory. The new state's recognition and entry into the United Nations were delayed for many months as a result.[14]

Another example of how politics influence the birth of states concerns the so-called homelands of South Africa. In its desire to promote and preserve apartheid, the government of South Africa set aside several parcels of land to create supposedly independent nations for several black African tribal groups. The goal was a more complete form of segregation, which would leave South Africa free to relinquish any responsibility for those living in the homelands while still taking advantage of their workforce, which continued to be employed at low-wage jobs in South Africa. These states have never been recognized as independent by any other nation; yet South Africa continued to maintain their boundaries as international borders.[15]

Death and succession of nations states is as much a product of world political processes as birth. One need only contrast the fates of East Timor, Tibet, and Goa with the efforts on behalf of Kuwait. East Timor and Goa were colonies, Tibet was at least semiautonomous from China but not recognized as an independent state for many international purposes, and Kuwait was a formally independent nation. Each of these entities was forcibly annexed by a militarily more powerful neighbor. Kuwait was rescued, of course, by an international coalition headed by the United States. The others received little international support, although some verbal objections to the annexations were registered.[16]

As with support for the birth of a nation, this selectivity illustrates general community norms. In the case of Goa, the international community to some degree quietly supported the annexation. The reason was primarily anticolonial sentiment; India's seizure of Goa militarily from its Portuguese colonial rulers was applauded by some former colonies. East Timor and Tibet undoubtedly suffered from the fact that they had never been recognized as formally independent and admitted into the official community of nations. Thus David Strang urges an "institutional perspective" highlighting the importance of the norms of state sovereignty and recognition: "The institutional perspective . . . suggests that stability will vary greatly with the sovereign status of a polity. Polities defined as sovereign should be stable. . . . Polities outside the network of mutual recognition should be much less stable. . . . Acts that would be treated as intolerable aggression when the injured party is a member of Western state society may be condoned or applauded when directed at polities outside the network of recognition."[17] Goa, East Timor, and Tibet were never beneficiaries of authoritative processes of world political protection. It was thus easy to acquiesce in conquests that India, Indonesia, and China, respectively, claimed as nothing more than reassertion of historically appropriate rule.

In the case of Kuwait, Iraq also made historical claims about sovereignty over the victim's territory. But Kuwait had for decades been recognized as formally independent; moreover, of course, it had powerful allies. Most significantly, geopolitical considerations made it imperative to many powerful nations that the Iraqi dictator not be allowed complete dominion over such a large portion of the world's oil wealth. No such strategic consideration compelled aid to East Timor or Tibet; and political considerations actually favored divesting Portugal of control over Goa, given the unpopularity of colonialism.

Succession, like death, is also governed by world community processes. Recent redrawings of territorial borders have raised question about the responsibility of new states for the acts of their predecessors. Most obviously, Russia is seen in many respects as the successor to the Soviet Union. It inherited the Soviet Union's seat on the Security Council and, to some degree, its role in world politics. Debts incurred by old states that have now divided (in the case of Czechoslovakia or Yugoslavia) or combined (in the case of Germany) must be allocated among the state or states that replace them.

The ability to determine which states exist gives a certain measure of control over the political predisposition of the states one must deal with. Powerful states are more likely to help friendly states come into existence and to preserve them intact when they are threatened. Kuwait's gratitude to the United States, of course, is likely to be exhibited in its future willingness to cooperate with American initiatives. In contrast, for years the United States kept the People's Republic of China out of the United Nations, and kept Nationalist China not only in the United Nations but on the Security Council as a permanent member. It did so through its enormous political influence over world political processes. In the long run, of course, its efforts were unsuccessful; it had to acquiesce in the existence of the People's Republic. World community processes do not have 100 percent control over the political life and death of states; the PRC ultimately could no longer be kept on the sidelines, and the sovereign state of Bosnia may perish despite the wishes of many other states. But in many other circumstances, and especially at the margin, community opinion (and the opinion of the world's strongest states, in particular) can be a life-or-death matter. Those states that are favored by the international community are more likely to survive and to thrive.

These problems of birth, death, and succession are reflected in the international norms concerning state recognition; for recognition amounts to formal entrance into the world community. The importance attached to the decision whether to recognize reflects the extent to which state identity is a matter of community acceptance, because recognition is treated by the world community as a very serious matter. There are two schools of thought on the subject. One holds that it is the act of recognition that in fact creates the state; this is referred to as the constitutive theory.[18] Thus, in a critical argument about the social identity of states, David Strang cites Oppenheim's statement that "through recognition only and exclusively a State becomes an International Person and a subject of International Law."[19] Strang concludes: "States are not individually empowered as sovereign actors . . . who then establish relations with each other. Rather, notions of sovereignty imply a state society founded on mutual recognition. The status of each state is thus tied up with that of the others in a continuing process of mutual legitimation."[20] Under the view of recognition that Strang cites, a state is a purely social creation because it comes into existence only by virtue of its treatment at the hands of other states.

There is another view of recognition, however, which is probably the dominant one today and which seems to grant states a more objective existence. The so-called declaratory theory holds that states exist independently of whether they have been recognized, and that all that the act of recognition does is to acknowledge a preexisting fact. While the influence of social conventions pursuant to this definition is less obvious, it is nonetheless substantial. For, as has been pointed out by international lawyers, this definition also rests on legal norms. "The declaratory theory assumes that territorial entities can be—by virtue of their mere existence—readily classified as having the one particular legal status, and thus, in a way, confuses 'fact' with 'law.' For, accepting that effectiveness is the dominant principle in this area, it must none the less be a *legal* principle. A State is not a fact in the sense that a chair is a fact; it is a fact in the sense in which it may be said a treaty is a fact; that is, a legal status attaching to a certain state of affairs by virtue of certain rules."[21] The standards by which a state is held to exist or not to exist are social and legal ones; they concern the extent to which a state must have effective control over a piece of territory, a population, and so forth.[22]

This view of recognition differs from the first in that states are not supposed to have the discretion to withhold recognition from states that already exist as a matter of "fact." This aspect of the definition has led to debates over whether there exists a "duty" to recognize, which would seem to attach in all situations where the norms in question are satisfied. What this view shares with the constitutive theory of recognition, however, is the extent to which recognition depends on other states' views about what counts as an appropriate state. Both theories treat recognition as a social conclusion, not an empirical fact. The difference is that in the latter case, those views are supposedly codified into general norms which must be applied evenhandedly to all cases, while in the former, other states are entitled to make the decision on an essentially ad hoc basis. The difference lies in whether recognition decisions are made, in essence, at the wholesale or the retail level. Regardless of what one thinks on that issue, recognition is a matter of community processes.

WHAT KIND OF ACTORS? In the liberal argument set out in earlier chapters, the actors that are empowered to consent are traditional territorial states. If a French Catholic prefers that she would rather be represented on the international scene by the Roman Catholic church, this preference will not be honored. A Palestinian living in the occupied West Bank might wish to be represented by the Palestinian Liberation Organization, but until recently much of the international community did not respect that preference.[23] The same is true for indigenous groups striving for recognition in the state community.[24] I might desire to participate in world politics simply as a feminist, a cosmopolitan, or an environmentalist, but such ideological groups lack authoritative status and voting rights in world decision-making bodies. My primary vehicle for expressing these points of view is political activism directed at influencing the world's traditional territorial states, which hold the vast bulk of world political power. I cannot simply say that I am not bound by the choices that the U.S. government makes on my behalf; as the world is presently constituted, the officially recognized actors are all states.

The limitation of full international status to territorial states has led to some dispute and doubt about the proper international role of certain sorts of borderline entities; the Holy See is an example. The See is the central administrative organ that governs the Catholic church; as a religious body it has not been recognized as a "state," even though the pope has long played an important role in world politics. The Holy See is, however, associated with the state of the City of the Vatican, which is a territorial body and has been recognized by many states. The precise connection between the Holy See and the City of the Vatican has given international lawyers opportunities for long and erudite discussion.[25] The United States did not fully recognize the Vatican until 1984, when it upgraded diplomatic relations to the level of an embassy.[26]

The critical literature has had much to say about the conventional nature of territorial states and about the commitment of the international political system to their sovereignty.[27]

> Reflective critics of the rationalist research program have emphasized the inadequacies of rationalism in analyzing the fundamental practice of sovereign statehood, which has been instituted not by agreement but as a result of the elaboration over time of the principle of sovereignty. Sovereignty seems to be prior to the kinds of calculations on which rationalistic theory focuses; governments' strategies assume the principle of sovereignty, and the practice of sovereign statehood, as givens. Indeed, according to some critics of rationalistic thinking, sovereignty is of even more far-reaching significance, since it defines the very nature of the actors in world politics.[28]

At issue are, among other things, the history of this particular form of social organization; the continued relevance of territorial states under contemporary conditions; whether territorial states are a progressive or reactionary influence; and the alternatives that exist today, that existed in previous times, and that may come into existence in the future. Some critical literature, it is true, continues onward in the state-centric tradition;[29] but this is not out of any lack of appreciation for the contingent nature of the territorial state system. What is clear is that the pressure to organize as states is a form of socialization which influences aspiring political actors to constitute themselves as certain sorts of political entities, rewarding those that are able to take the preferred political shape and disempowering those that are not.

I have already remarked, in the previous chapter, on the statist character of international political processes and the challenge it presents to liberalism. I noted that it undercuts the commitment to the individual as the central figure in liberal politics. The point here is a bit different, though perhaps related. It is not the *content* of the commitment to statism that is at issue, although the content of the commitment is indeed a challenge to the liberal view of things. Rather, the issue is the *source* of that commitment. What supports the statist system? Statism is a product of international political processes as a whole. I cannot, as an individual, simply decide that my assigned state will not represent me, and that I should instead be represented by the Roman Catholic church or the World Wildlife Fund. But neither can my state make that decision for me. Nor can a single state decide that it prefers to be a part of a world federation, with individual states relinquishing their sovereignty to a central government. It cannot decide to divide itself into two international legal entities, one composed of all of its Muslim inhabitants and the other of all of its Hindu inhabitants. It can accomplish this goal, as India more or less sought to at independence, only by dividing into two separate territorial states, one predominately Hindu and one predominately Muslim;[30] the same is true of Bosnia. The world political system requires that its important actors take a territorial form. As the resulting horrors of population transfer in such examples suggest, while there are evident attractions to organization along the lines of territorial states, the costs of requiring this form of political structure should not be underestimated.

THE ROLE OF INTERNATIONAL NORMS   To say that community practices shape state identity is not to say that decisions whether to recognize certain sorts of actors are necessarily either arbitrary or oppressive. Some of the examples that I have given suggest quite the contrary; often such decisions are the product of shared and substantively desirable normative commitments. For example, the fact that India was able to annex Goa with minimal protest in the United Nations was a consequence of the world community's opposition to Portuguese colonialism.[31] The fact that the Baltics were welcomed as independent states resulted from the widespread perceptions that their annexation was unjust and that their inhabitants had suffered repression under Soviet rule. Community practices are typically not ad hoc or arbitrary; they are governed by norms.

The problem is that liberal theory has no way of explaining where these norms come from and how they operate. It is the critical theorists who have been most attentive to the constitutive norms that influence the choice of actors to admit to world political processes.[32] Mainstream theory, the critics argue, is inattentive to such things, choosing instead to try to focus on the supposedly scientific empirical study of distribution of material capabilities among states. Such efforts serve only to disguise the relevance of normative structures in world politics, and in the process of disguising these normative structures to make them more difficult to criticize. Even those parts of mainstream theory that are somewhat more attentive to the role of norms (such as neoliberal institutionalism) take states, it is claimed, as the authoritative actors. The state-centric structure of most international relations theory is treated as a fundamental, irremediable "given" of international politics, which it would be as idle to criticize as the orbits of planets around the sun. The goal of the critics' focus on normative structures, then, is in large part to highlight them as a proper subject of normative attention, so that they can be properly evaluated and the decision whether or not to acquiesce in them will be treated as the normative decision that it is.

Even if mainstream theory were directly to focus on such issues, it does not seem that these norms can be justified in the way that liberals might find most comfortable, namely, in terms of state consent. Clearly the groups that are excluded from taking part in world political processes do not consent to their own exclusion. The norm of consent presupposes some prior notion of who it is that must consent; excluding some groups from political participation is then permissible because they are not among actors whose consent must be obtained. But the prior notion of whose consent must be obtained is not itself established by agreement. And it is just this prior notion that critics want to focus on and that liberals, they claim, prefer to ignore.

The lack of consent to community practices that identify the relevant actors has consequences for the legitimacy of the norms that those actors subsequently agree to. For the sorts of norms that are subsequently agreed to, clearly, are influenced by the sorts of political entities that agree to them. World political institutions might well look very different if they were generated by processes that treated as dispositive the preferences of economic interest groups, indigenous peoples, or religious communities—or if the relevant decision makers were individual human beings. The subsequent choice of norms is also influenced by the identity of the regimes that represent individual states, in that existing states (in particular, the most powerful ones) are likely selectively to favor regimes that share their ideological perspectives and interests. Thus it will not do to try to bracket the question of state identity, as though any problems on that score could safely be cordoned off. If there is a selection bias in the choice of actors, it will infect the decisions that they make and the international arrangements they consent to.

My purpose here is limited to showing how international "constitutive" structures cannot be explained in terms of the consent of states. They antedate the state, and explaining them in terms of state consent makes about as much sense as using "consent" to describe the infant's attitude toward the womb that gave it birth. To be fair, of course, liberals would probably not claim that states consent to the foundational principles that define which actors are to be empowered to consent. The circularity is just too obvious.[33] But what would they claim? This leaves us with no explanation of where the basic constitutive rules have come from, or at least no explanation comfortable to liberals. This puts the autonomy of states, and the moral necessity of state consent, at issue because states are as much a product of the international system as the system is a product of the preferences of states.

THE MORAL NECESSITY OF CONSENT

What are we to conclude from the fact that state identity is a product of socialization by the world community? The critical theorist sees this claim as somehow fatal to the liberal commitment to autonomy—the autonomy of states in the international sphere, and the autonomy of individuals in the analogous domestic setting. But is this so? Liberals don't seem to think so. Liberals are as aware as other people that preferences and beliefs are socially conditioned.[34] They understand that it is no coincidence that women in Saudi Arabia perceive their role in life differently from women in Scandinavia. They don't believe that the former have simply autonomously chosen to wear veils and not drive cars, while the latter have autonomously chosen to work outside the home and bear children outside of wedlock. Liberals are impatient with long-winded critical expositions of what the liberals see as obvious: that social environment influences personal identity.

The difference between liberals and their critics is not primarily a descriptive one concerning whence individuals obtain their preferences and beliefs. Nor does it seem to be over whether free choice is ever, in theory, possible. Critics seem largely agreed that free choice is a theoretical possibility—indeed, a goal of many critics is to further progress toward a truly emancipatory political system in which genuine choice is an option. A key difference, however, seems to be the question of *what to do* about the fact that many individual preferences and beliefs are the product of social conditioning. The liberal tendency is to respect individual preferences anyway, while the critics do not share that inclination.

Liberals are uncomfortable with the vanguardist notions of "false consciousness" that they find lurking in claims that individual preferences and beliefs need not be respected. Emphasis on the social sources of identity tends to reduce the individual to a puppet of social conditioning; by dissecting at length the sources of individual beliefs, critics are treating individuals as simply a passive channel for the larger forces in society. The vanguardist flavor of some of these analyses comes from the intimation that the individuals in question are unaware of their own passivity, and that the critics are the only ones with "real knowledge" of how the social processes operate. Particularly in some earlier Marxist attacks on liberalism, there was a sense that those who understood reality better were the chosen ones, fit to manipulate the untutored masses for their own eventual greater good. It is easy to understand liberal aversion to such claims, especially after seeing how such vanguardism translated into reality in various experiments around the world.

The liberal commitment to autonomy, from this perspective, is not so much a product of some set of empirical beliefs about what percentage of the decisions that people make are autonomous, as it is of the belief that people's choices should be respected even where we suspect they might be socially conditioned.[35] The Saudi Arabian woman's decision to wear a veil is honored not because the liberal thinks she came to it all on her own, but because it is a mark of disrespect for another person to dismiss the choice she has made as mindless, passive, or directed from the outside. In the same way that we are aware that people make factually mistaken choices, but respect them anyway, we are aware that people sometimes merely act as products of their social environment, but respect their choices nonetheless. This is part of according the appropriate dignity to other individuals.

In addition, the liberal commitment to autonomy reflects an attempt to provide greater future opportunities for genuine choice. Basing decision on individual consent helps to clear as much space as possible in which autonomy can operate. Making decisions for other people, paternalistically, does not encourage them to exercise their innate capacities for reflective choice; it creates a situation, instead, where the capacity for individual reflection atrophies. The liberal commitment to autonomy, then, is an aspiration as much as it is a conviction about how things currently operate. By acting "as if" individual choice were generally autonomous (even when we know that it is autonomous, at best, only part of the time), we both treat other people with the respect due to equals and support the exercise of independent judgment by providing an environment in which choice is ever more likely to flourish.

Critics are quick to point out that the effect of not challenging preferences formed by social conditioning is to allow social conditioning to continue, and to disguise the socialization that is really going on as individual choice. Logical argument and persuasion may not be enough to expose to the individual the extent to which his or her beliefs are merely the product of social pressures. The liberal solution, it is charged, effectively entrenches existing socially powerful forces which shape our beliefs and values and which we reproduce, accordingly, in the social conditions we create for future generations. Accepting the individual's preferences as they currently exist is deeply reactionary, it is claimed, and this is the danger of an otherwise attractive aspiration to accord each individual the respect that he or she deserves.

But the liberal (and here I must agree) sees at least as great a danger in the critical strategy. While the liberal strategy threatens to entrench the products of our social conditioning, the critical strategy threatens to entrench the process of social conditioning itself. The critical strategy acknowledges the "reality" of socialization, thereby accepting it as an unavoidable given, and simply seeks to harness it to promote a more attractive set of substantive beliefs. By seeking to harness a phenomenon that liberals consider unfortunate—sociopolitical influence over individual perception and conviction—it grants that phenomenon too much legitimacy. By granting it this recognition, it brings the process out in the open, where it is subject to criticism, it is true, but where it also has a chance to grow and flourish. Critical theorists, ironically, should be more sensitive than they are to the effect of official recognition on legitimation; for they have often pointed out the extent to which mainstream perceptions of "what is" shape mainstream perceptions of "what ought to be," and vice versa. They should therefore recognize the dangers in acknowledging social conditioning as a part of preference formation; recognizing that it exists slides inexorably into accepting it. Far better, a liberal might reasonably think, to fight socialization directly than to try to enlist it on the side of one's own substantive priorities.

It would be pointless here to try either to develop the subtleties of the contending positions or to assess their merits; it is enough to show the surface plausibility and intuitive appeal of both. For my object is to ask what the debate means for international relations theory, and for the consent of states. And on this score, the liberal emphasis on autonomy and consent has considerably less appeal than it does in the domestic sphere. Most obviously, to the extent that the liberal argument turns on the special respect due individual human beings, it simply has no application to the consent of states. It might be different, as we saw in the previous chapter, if the respect accorded states were justifiable in terms of their derivative status as agents of individual human beings. But if the consent of nondemocratic states is to be treated identically with the consent of democratic states, the reason must be the status of states in their own right, not state status as derived from the rights of their citizens.

A different moral basis, then, for state autonomy must be shown. Another possibility is simply that states are the constituent units from which international society is aggregated. There might be thought a benefit in decentralizing power, in locating it in the smaller units of which the international system is composed, rather than at the apex. While liberalism in large part concerns the special rights of individuals, it has, in addition, another theme: skepticism about power concentration. Decentralization and diversity per se are arguably good things from a liberal perspective, regardless of whether decentralization means placing power in the hands of individual human beings or placing power in the hands of states in the international system. What matters is to retain the power in the smaller units that count as individual actors in the system, by vesting these actors with the power to grant or withhold consent.

This is a plausible argument for requiring consent; for there is value in decentralization of power even if the recipients are conventional actors, such as states, rather than human beings. The problem with making the argument in this context, though, is that it runs aground on the prior commitment to statism, for statism itself represents centralization of power in the hands of the state at the expense of the individual. To insist that powerful actors in the world community cannot make decisions on behalf of the community without the consent of individual states seems inconsistent with the willingness to allow states to make decisions on behalf of their individual citizens without their consent. If there is to be a preference for smaller constituent actors over centralizing political tendencies, then this preference should operate at the level of domestic politics as well as at the level of international politics.

The decentralization argument favors a "bottom-up" rather than a "top-down" view of politics; the smaller units in a system retain the right to consent or not to consent to the actions of those at the higher level. But the liberal model of state consent to international hegemony is bottom-up only in part. It is bottom-up when the question is the relative powers of states and the international hegemon, but it is top-down when the question is the relative power of states and their individual citizens. In both cases the result is to privilege the state at the expense of its competitor for power; the hegemon and the international system on the one hand (by favoring smaller units), and the individual on the other (by favoring central authority). It is peculiar, to say the least, to show a greater degree of democratic fastidiousness in the international context than in the domestic context, by requiring the consent of states but not of people.

The claim that international hegemony must be grounded in the *consent* of states is thus undermined by the fact that it is the consent of *states* that is taken to be central. While consent has obvious appeal as a normative first principle, it is hard to square that appeal with the privileging of states as primary actors. To put the problem another way, there is a tension between the statist focus, which favors the larger unit at the expense of the smaller, and consent, which favors the smaller unit at the expense of the larger. The state is an intermediate institution, larger than its citizens but smaller than the community that it inhabits. The very liberal arguments that justify choosing it over the world community point toward moving to a still lower level, the individual. The very community-oriented arguments that justify choosing it over its citizens point toward moving to the larger unit of organization still, the world community. As Andrew Linklater writes, "On these foundations, a critical theory of international relations can argue that the state does not exhaust our moral and political obligations. The obligations that survive the political fragmentation of the human race are not simply the obligations that states acquire as equal members of a society of states. Universal obligations that exist alongside the obligations that individuals possess as members of particular communities require their political representatives to promote higher levels of human solidarity and community."[36]

CONCLUSION

I have argued that there are fundamental problems with a theory of international politics generally, and of international hegemony specifically, that tests legitimacy by whether states have consented. In the first place, states do not exist independently of the international system to which they supposedly consent. In addition, the choice of states as the primary entities entitled to grant or withhold consent is a purely conventional one that cannot be justified in liberal terms. While states, it is true, currently possess the lion's share of power in international politics, there is no particular reason to conclude that this is the way that things ought to or have to be, or to build a normative justification around this current, but contingent, fact of life.

To some degree, these arguments have mirrored claims that critics of liberalism have developed for domestic politics. To that extent, the problems I have outlined are criticisms of liberalism per se. But to perhaps as great a degree, I have focused on difficulties in applying liberal arguments to the relations between states specifically, pointing out their inconsistencies with theories based on state consent but leaving domestic liberalism itself at large to fight another day. For a substantial part of the problem is that principles of individual consent cannot simply be translated into international relations without a risk of serious distortion. The critical attacks on liberal premises find an easier target in international, as opposed to domestic, liberalism.

In part this is because domestic critical attacks must rely so heavily on cognitive, as opposed to behavioral, accounts of how social influences shape individual identity. In the international setting, the impact of socialization on state decisions is mechanistic and easily observable. External pressures influence the choice of regime and the choice of which states exist, systematically favoring (as by a process of natural selection) those actors that are sympathetic to existing practices and to the leading powers in the world community. Autonomy is compromised in a methodologically straightforward way. No one doubts that puppet governments exist.

Socialization of individuals in the domestic setting, however, acts primarily through cognitive processes that are not directly observable and to which liberals attach independent normative importance. While it is clear that socialization can be effective (witness the variation of preferences and beliefs among different cultures), it operates in methodologically more mysterious ways and is shielded by the respect that liberals wish to accord to individual decision processes—a respect not granted to state decision processes, especially those of nondemocratic states. When individuals make decisions, their free will seems to be implicated, even when they respond to outside pressures, because in some sense they decide to ratify the outside point of view.

If it is easier to make the critical argument in the international setting, it is also harder to make the liberal defense. The claim that decentralized decision is preferable, that decisions must for normative reasons be made with the consent of constituent actors, is already compromised at the outset by the fact that power is vested at an intermediate level—the state—rather than at the lowest level possible—the individual. Statism is an unstable convention, because it is a compromise between centralizing and decentralizing tendencies. Compromises are notoriously hard to defend on principle; why should the line be drawn at one particular point rather than at some other? State consent is difficult to defend because it must be defended on two sides simultaneously, and the arguments needed for defense on one side seem inconsistent with the arguments needed for defense on the other.

Yet, there is no denying that state consent has been and continues to be a central intuition in popular assessments of the legitimacy of international norms and of the actions of powerful states. The previous chapters have documented the emphasis commonly placed on obtaining state agreement to international institutions. This emphasis may be nothing more than an unreflective borrowing of norms that have a legitimate place in domestic political relations, without accommodation to the peculiar circumstances of a setting in which states rather than individuals are the relevant actors. It is also possible that more needs to be said on behalf of state consent than the arguments uncovered here. If so, we will have to wait for their development by others.

At a minimum, however, it seems fair to conclude that state consent cannot simply be taken at face value, as if it set to rest all doubts about international legitimacy. Real consent must rest on something more than the fact that state leaders have added their signatures to international agreements. The question remains whether the leader is expressing indigenous values and preferences or accommodating international pressures from powerful outside interests that help to keep the local elites in power. Enforcement of agreements of the latter sort may conceivably rest on justification of some other kind, but not on liberal premises of state consent.

CONCLUSION

My object in the pages above has been to explore the possibility that liberalism might provide a somewhat adequate account of American hegemony. We have sought to test consistency between American domestic political values and American foreign policy. One would expect to find a certain degree of consistency, if not complete agreement.[1]

The consistency that does exist is probably attributable to the natural inclination to understand the different parts of one's world as fitting into a coherent whole. If we find some particular American policy to be legitimate, it is natural that we will try to explain that perception of legitimacy in terms consistent with our own domestic values. A liberal, then, will turn naturally to the most familiar tools of justification: consent theory of various sorts and substantive moral rights. As the explanations that we tend to give come to focus increasingly on liberal values, liberal values may also come to influence what we should do in future cases. It is striking the extent to which international law and international normative argument already incorporate intuitions quite familiar to domestic political philosophy. It is also striking how far one can go toward building a coherent picture of American foreign policy by reference to such concepts.

But the lack of complete agreement is undeniable. This should not be surprising, given the absence of institutional mechanisms for ensuring respect for international political morality. There can be no doubt that often stronger nations do as they like when what they like and international morality conflict. Often they make no bones about it. This fact of life puts a somewhat more pessimistic cast on the consistency that does exist between hegemonic practice and liberal political morality. Simply by coincidence, one would expect the two to coincide on numerous occasions. Is this all we are seeing when we detail circumstances in which America abides by liberal principles in its foreign policy?

Such pessimistic doubts increase when one acknowledges the issues raised by the last two chapters. To the extent that existing justifications turn on state consent, they run aground on questions of why state consent is normatively meaningful. We have a rough idea why individual consent should matter, even if there is no complete response to critical claims that individual consent is an illusion. But why state consent? Why is the state privileged over the individual, and why is it privileged over the international community? Liberalism has no ready answers.

There are two important final issues to address. The first is how to use the arguments above in recommending what an ideal foreign policy would be. The second is how to design institutions that increase the chance that such ideal solutions are adopted. Each calls for more extended treatment than is possible below, but some things can be said in summary.

IDEAL POLICY DESIGN

Having rejected the claim that anarchy makes political morality irrelevant in international affairs, my goal obviously is to promote a moral foreign policy. National self-interest must act within the bounds of political responsibility, of the responsibilities we owe to other (most specifically, weaker) states. What responsibilities do we have? Some things follow fairly naturally from the arguments that we have explored.

There is an obligation, first, to promote individual universal human rights. This is the sort of claim, admittedly, that makes certain realists cringe; but saying more of what we mean by it should make the claim appear a bit more "realistic." Promotion of human rights must be pursued pragmatically, with the closest possible attention to the consequences of contemplated policies around the globe. If in fact it is true that pressuring other nations to conform to human rights is in certain circumstances counterproductive, then this is something that must be taken into account in fashioning human rights policy. In addition, the commitment to furthering human rights is not boundless. It arises because America itself uses human rights as a justification for intervention. Doing so imposes duties to behave consistently. If the obligation to provide support for human rights is too onerous, a legitimate response would be withdrawal.

Second, other explanations for hegemony rest more or less directly on consent of states. Regardless of the type of consent at issue, the basic point is protection of weaker states from imposition by the stronger. While no one theory of consent is adequate in and of itself, the theories lean on one another, providing the whole with a certain measure of philosophical credibility. This logic puts a premium on multilateralism, on working through existing international political institutions, and on working to achieve consensus. It is permissible to bribe other states, at least so long as what is offered is genuinely the stronger state's to give. It is permissible to hold states to their earlier agreements, at least to the extent the earlier agreement contemplated hegemonic enforcement. And it is acceptable to pressure states to contribute to what can genuinely be characterized as public goods, at least if the distribution of those goods is truly fair and the "good" in question is not simply a priority of the hegemon.

Now what of the critical claim that state autonomy should not be central? A liberal is not about to accept the argument that autonomy per se is normatively irrelevant, despite the critics' arguments. But a liberal must be prepared to make some concession to the claims that state autonomy specifically is problematic. It clearly comes in conflict with the central liberal goal of protecting individuals, and there is no way liberalism can avoid that fact. If the world were full of democracies (or other states organized in such a way that we had confidence that state leaders represented the wishes of their people), the problem would dissolve, for we could argue that state consent was both responsive to individuals and not overly determined by the world community. State autonomy would then make sense. But of course much of the world is not democratic, and even those democracies that do exist are far from perfect in these two regards.

At first this problem seems to deal a fatal blow to the theories founded on consent of states. And in a sense it does, for it means that we are not entitled to treat as conclusive the agreements that states have actually made. This conclusion seems harsh, given that in many cases it is not our fault that states lack democratic structures and that we seem left without any legitimate mechanism for reaching political accommodations with much of the world. Is there nothing that we can do that would be right? The problem on closer look is more theoretical than practical. The reason is that nothing prevents a stronger power from itself trying to take the interests of citizens of other countries into account.

There is of course no perfect mechanism for determining the interests that citizens of other countries think they have. We are not authorized to make that decision for them; that is what their own political processes should do. We are not, for this reason, entitled to treat as conclusive our decisions about their interests (as we would be if they had reached the same conclusion democratically). This does not mean, however, that speculation on their wants is out of order. We knew or had reason to know during the Vietnam War that the government of South Vietnam was not representative of its citizens' wishes; we had an obligation to look behind its official decisions to try to see what the people of South Vietnam might desire. The same might be said about our relations with Vietnam as a whole twenty years later. The conclusions we might reach this way are only tentative. But in light of the awareness liberals must have about the inadequacies of state consent, no other course would be legitimate.

This means, in practice, that the interests of people in other states (as best we guess them) must be a check on our agreements with their governments. We should not go along with states' agreements that we think their people do not want. This is a necessary, if not a sufficient, condition for international political legitimacy. Agreement with Syria about nuclear nonproliferation stands on a rather different footing than our response to South Vietnamese requests for U.S. military involvement. At the point (if it arrives) that the states in question become democracies, they will have to make their own determinations of how well we guessed what they would want.

ACCOUNTABILITY

These comments deal, however briefly, with what we ought to do; how are we to increase the chances that hegemons do as they should? Some readers who are impatient with normative theory may have already given up on this project; but even those who have so far stayed with it may be ready to turn their attention to more practical concerns. Theories about how world politics ought to be arranged do not necessarily tell us anything about how to close the gap between the actual and the ideal. With all the attention the previous chapters have paid to the standard for what would count as legitimate international hegemony, I have said almost nothing about how to improve the chances that these standards will be met.

The question is how to improve the accountability of the world's strongest powers. In an ideal world the strong would exercise their powers over other nations only when there was an adequate justification for doing so, and not simply to further their own selfish interests at the expense of those who could not fight back. In practice the strong will often be tempted to pursue their own agendas; and nations that believe that they are being treated unjustly will often lack the capacity to resist. I have not so far said anything about how to make strong nations accountable to the weak, so that their conduct can be kept in line either by preventing illegitimate actions before the fact or by providing adequate remedies afterwards.

It might seem that the problem is, almost by definition, hopeless. If the strongest powers in the system set out to bully and oppress the weaker, there is no court of higher authority to which the weak can turn. This follows from the "anarchical" structure of the world system; even if one rejects (as I did in an earlier chapter) the claim that there are no normative standards in an anarchy, there may still be no guarantee that the normative standards that do exist will be obeyed. To call some nation hegemonic is to suggest that there can be little effective remedy for its excesses. How is it possible to make a hegemon accountable to weaker states?

The analogy between international hegemony and domestic governance suggests that the task is difficult but not hopeless. At one time it must have seemed just as hopeless ever to make domestic governments accountable; indeed, in some states even today it is hard to see how government will ever be brought to heel. But virtually every state that is democratic today had earlier periods in which its rule was autocratic. While there are a small number of nations that were founded, originally, as democracies, most democracies developed slowly, as absolute power was steadily reined in and limits placed on what a ruler could do at the expense of his or her people. To find out how England moved toward democracy, or Chile, Poland, or South Africa (in recent times), one must study their political histories. The process is difficult, progress is not irreversible, and outcomes are impossible to predict—as the uncertain futures of Chile, Poland, and South Africa illustrate. But there is certainly no reason to think that powerful rulers are beyond restraint forever.

In the international as well as the domestic arenas, the greatest threat to the absolute power of the strong is the solidarity of the weak. "People power" became a cliché in the late 1980s, and it was clear then (and is even clearer today) that the euphoria of democratization provided no antidote to other entrenched ills, such as economic backwardness or ethnic conflict. Yet the world's continuing problems should not overshadow the remarkable opportunities for progress made available by the fact that in many nations across the world mass action has helped to sweep away autocracies. One of the keys to mass action is mass expectations: widely shared beliefs that the existing structures of governance are illegitimate.

That fact returns us to the question of the relevance of this, normative, project. Part of any long-range effort to impose accountability on the world's strongest nations must be an effort to illuminate the standards by which the world's strongest powers must be judged. Before domestic masses can insist on the right to govern themselves, there must be a shared ideal of democracy. Before the nations of the world can insist on a legitimate world political ordering, they must be more or less agreed about what sort of ordering that would be. Not very long ago, the normative demands of many of the world's weakest nations seem to have converged on Marxist rhetoric as providing the relevant political standards; but Marxism was not widely enough believed, and since then it has become quite clear (even to many of its earlier proponents) that there are good reasons why.

To tame international hegemony, there must first be some agreement on some standards (even if only in theory, and even if only reluctantly) that the stronger and the weaker nations share. It is harder for the United States to fight arguments based on international liberalism than it is for it to resist arguments based on a Marxist foundation that few Americans ever found attractive. The link between normative theory and practice is that normative theory not only attempts to help define the direction in which we should be moving but also provides a psychological wedge to appeal to shared values across the world. If it can both unite the weaker states in their expectations about how international power should be used, and take hostage the principles stronger nations feel committed to, then the long-run prognosis may not be so bad. In particular, recognizing explicitly that hegemony is one form of world governance improves the chances that accountability will be demanded and perhaps provided.

The costs, it should be noted, will be felt on both sides: by states demanding more accountability as well as by states from which it is demanded. The reason is that legitimacy is not only a lot to demand of a hegemon, it is a lot to concede. If standards are developed to evaluate the international political legitimacy of the most powerful state, these standards validate the hegemon when it is acting in accordance with those standards, as well as providing ammunition to criticize the hegemon when it is not. An admission that the United States may sometimes be acting justly even when it exercises disproportionate power may be further than some states will be willing to go. On the other hand, insisting that the United States is behaving illegitimately no matter what it does is not the best strategy for influencing U.S. behavior.

It may not be too optimistic to see signs that changes are occurring in the way that powerful states exercise their prerogatives. One of the noteworthy aspects of the Persian Gulf war, of course, was the fact that the United States acted through the United Nations—even though the Security Council was acting at American instigation, and even though the United Nations exercised virtually no control over how the war was carried out and how it was ended. U.N. approval was also sought before the intervention in Somalia. Conversely, the United States held back from military involvement in the conflict in the Balkans in part because its NATO allies disapproved its contemplated actions.

In all of these examples, it must be admitted, one can find reasons of real-politik that would explain American multilateralism, or at least explain it in part. For one thing, it is often cheaper to do things multilaterally—one's allies will share the costs. Perhaps most important, why shouldn't the United States seek world approval (or NATO approval) if it expects to get authorization when it wants it and if it will be restrained only when its desire to get involved was half-hearted anyway? Conceding this point, it nonetheless remains the case that approval was sought, and that each instance where the United States acted as though multilateral approval was necessary adds to the precedential value of the others. If such instances ever come to reach a critical mass, it will be taken as settled practice that the United States will, and should, consult the United Nations (or regional organizations) before acting. Such norms shape expectations powerfully, not least in the eyes of the American public.

The decision to seek U.N. approval in such instances has been influenced by the awareness that we no longer need to fear the automatic use of the Soviet Union's Security Council veto. Without the changes that took place in the Soviet Union's domestic situation at the end of the last decade, probably none of these efforts to work through the Security Council apparatus would have been possible. This illustrates, quite clearly, a key advantage of hegemony. The anarchy logic suggests that in a world of roughly balanced players where each fears for its own life, none may be able to risk its vital interests by being principled. Situations of international hegemony, however, do not present such a world.

Hegemony provides the strongest power with the opportunity to oppress, but also with the opportunity to be principled. Just as domestic governments sometimes use oppressive methods from a sense of weakness, states in the international system feel that they cannot afford to be principled when their international existence is at stake. The United States no longer faces the sort of challenge that it did when Soviet military power was expanding around the globe, and when the Soviet rhetoric led to a genuine (if not always realistic) fear that U.S. national existence was at issue. The more secure its own position, the better positioned the hegemon is to act in ways that are beneficial to the world community and faithful to its principles. From such a position of strength, the next logical step would naturally seem to follow: consolidating one's material strength with the missing ingredient of legitimacy.

Hegemony creates the need for political morality, for the dominance of one actor in the system violates the cardinal expectation that all actors should be treated equally. Politics is, in large part, about the dominance of centrally located and stronger actors over the weaker; and political morality, in large part, concerns the situations in which such dominance is legitimate. But hegemony also creates the opportunity for political morality. Now on a more secure international footing, the United States can afford the luxury of attending to principle. As the sole remaining superpower, its constituency has expanded to include nations that would earlier have turned to the Soviet Union for help. The conflict between the superpowers generated and helped to keep alive conflicts between and within less powerful nations; conversely, the resolution of superpower conflict has opened the door to resolution of regional conflicts around the world. The opportunities for a more moral international politics are in front of us, if only our luck perseveres and if only we can somehow gather the resolve to take advantage of them.

NOTES

INTRODUCTION

1. Patrick E. Tyler, "U.S. Strategy Plan Calls for Insuring No Rivals Develop," *New York Times*, March 8, 1992: 1.

2. Tyler, "Pentagon Drops Goal of Blocking New Superpowers," ibid., May 24, 1992: 1.

3. Charles Krauthammer, "The Anti-Superpower Fallacy," *Washington Post*, April 10, 1992: 27.

4. Krauthammer, "Unipolar Moment," in Graham Allison and Gregory F. Treverton, eds., *Rethinking America's Security: Beyond Cold War to New World Order* (New York: Norton, 1992), 296–298, 306. Compare Richard M. Nixon's recent contribution to the cause of American exceptionalism, *Seize the Moment: America's Challenge in a One-Superpower World* (New York: Simon and Schuster, 1992).

5. From a telephone poll of 1,000 adult Americans taken for Time/CNN on March 7, 1991 by Yankelovich Clancy Schulman.

6. Paul Kennedy, *The Rise and Fall of the Great Powers: Economic Change and Military Conflict from 1500 to 2000* (New York: Random House, 1987).

7. *U.S. v. Alvarez-Machain*, 119 L.Ed.2d. 441, 112 S.Ct. 2188 (June 15, 1992). For a description of the U.S. indictment of Pablo Escobar and Dandeny Muñoz-Mosquera, see Arnold H. Lubasch, "U.S. Indicts Colombians in '89 Deaths," *New York Times*, Aug. 14, 1992: B3; for a general discussion of the application of American criminal law extraterritorially, see Lea Brilmayer and Charles Norchi, "Federal Extraterritoriality and Fifth Amendment Due Process," 105 *Harv. Law Rev.* 1217 (1992).

8. See, e.g., the editorials "A Learning Time for the Pentagon," *Christian Science Monitor*, Aug. 10, 1990: 20 (Gulf war); "America as Vigilante," *Los Angeles Times*, Metro Section, Jan. 5, 1989: 6 (Libya); "America the Arrogant Trade Cop," *New York Times*, April 17, 1990: 24 (trade); "The World Isn't Dodge City; We're Not Matt Dillon," *Newsday*, March 11, 1992: 52 (criticizing Pentagon draft report).

9. See, e.g., Joseph S. Nye, *Bound to Lead: The Changing Nature of American Power* (New York: Basic Books, 1990); Henry Nau, *The Myth of America's Decline: Leading the World Economy into the 1990s* (New York: Oxford University Press, 1990); Richard N. Rosencrance, *America's Economic Resurgence: A Bold New*

Strategy (New York: Harper & Row, 1990). For two earlier articles disputing the hegemonic decline thesis, see Bruce Russett, "The Mysterious Case of Vanishing Hegemony; or, Is Mark Twain Really Dead?" 39 *Int. Org.* 207 (1985); and Susan Strange, "The Persistent Myth of Lost Hegemony," 41 *Int. Org.* 551 (1987).

A commonly held response to the thesis of decline is that American power has declined relatively but not absolutely, due to the postwar resurgence of Europe. See, e.g., David P. Calleo, *Beyond American Hegemony: The Future of the Western Alliance* (New York: Basic Books, 1987), 10.

10. See, e.g., Charles Kindleberger's classic study *The World in Depression, 1929–1939*, rev. ed. (Berkeley: University of California Press, 1984), which argued that the Great Depression could have been prevented only by a single power taking charge of the world economy. Britain, claims Kindleberger, was unable to carry out this role; the United States was unwilling. See also Robert O. Keohane, *After Hegemony: Cooperation and Discord in the World Political Economy* (Princeton, N.J.: Princeton University Press, 1984), which discusses whether, in the absence of a hegemon, international regimes might carry out some of the same functions. These books, and hegemonic stability theory, are discussed at greater length in chapter 5 below.

11. Kindleberger, "Dominance and Leadership in the International Economy: Exploitation, Public Goods, and Free Rides," 25 *Int. Studies Quarterly* 242 (1981).

12. Robert Gilpin, *War and Change in World Politics* (Cambridge: Cambridge University Press, 1981), 34. Gilpin also lists two other reasons: the hegemon's demonstrated ability to enforce its will, and ideological or religious support from like-minded states.

13. See, e.g., Duncan Snidal, "The Limits of Hegemonic Stability Theory," 39 *Int. Org.* 579 (1985); Isabelle Grunberg, "Exploring the 'Myth' of Hegemonic Stability," 44 *Int. Org.* 431 (1990).

14. The primary examples here are the world systems theorists, such as Immanuel Wallerstein, and the dependency theorists, such as Andre Gunder Frank or Fernando Cardoso. On the double standard that they apply to capitalist and socialist hegemony, see Robert A. Packenham, *The Dependency Movement: Scholarship and Politics in Development Studies* (Cambridge: Harvard University Press, 1992).

15. Keohane, *After Hegemony*, 249. Compare also Hedley Bull, *The Anarchical Society: A Study of Order in World Politics* (New York: Columbia University Press, 1977), 228 (discussing briefly what it would take to make a "great power" system just).

16. Calleo, *Beyond American Hegemony*, 143. Special mention must be made of Bull's brief discussion of the justice of great power dominance (*Anarchical Society*, 227–229). Bull lists four conditions for great powers legitimizing their role: they should not try to formalize their superior position, they should obey the rules themselves, they should meet some of the just demands for change that weaker and poorer states make, and they should cooperate with secondary (regional) powers. See also G. John Ikenberry and Charles A. Kupchan, "The Legitimation of Hegemonic Power," in David Rapkin, ed., *World Leadership and Hegemony* (Boulder, Colo.: Lynne Rienner, 1990). It should be noted that this article focuses on the question of how weaker states come to accept the hegemon's power. My analysis does not treat acceptance as equivalent to hegemony, although certain forms of consent may be relevant to the issue of legitimacy.

17. See n. 16.

CHAPTER 1

1. The status of Germany and the other nations of Europe is unclear at the current time, as it is not possible to guess the likely future of European integration. A unified Europe, obviously, would possess much greater political and military power than the individual nations themselves.

2. See, e.g., Hedley Bull, "Intervention in the Third World," in H. Bull, ed., *Intervention in World Politics* (New York: Oxford University Press, 1984), 135, 154. Political inequalities have been taken

seriously by Marxist and neo-Marxist writers, as we will note at various points in the discussion below. The argument here, however, is that inequalities should be of concern to persons of all political persuasions (and in particular to liberals), not just to Marxists.

3. Stephen D. Krasner, *Structural Conflict: The Third World Against Global Liberalism* (Berkeley: University of California Press, 1985), 3, 27. See also, Robert Tucker, *The Inequality of Nations* (New York: Basic Books, 1977), 106. Tucker and David Hendrickson have noted that the resentment of less powerful nations is increasingly becoming a threat to the more powerful, as the less powerful seek ways to strike back (for instance, through nuclear proliferation). *The Imperial Temptation: The New World Order and America's Purpose* (New York: Council on Foreign Relations Press, 1992), 35.

4. Tucker, *Inequality*, 63; see also 107. As David Baldwin put it, power is "relational." *Economic Statecraft* (Princeton, N.J.: Princeton University Press, 1985), 21; "Interdependence and Power," in *Paradoxes of Power* (New York: Blackwell, 1989). It should be added that Baldwin disputes the claim that power is zero-sum while economics is not (*Economic Statecraft*, 22), but the reason he gives is that power is multidimensional. On a single issue, under this reasoning, power is still nonetheless zero-sum and the gain to one state is a loss to the other.

5. These two types of power discrepancies are not completely disconnected, of course. If the U.S. has greater influence over world affairs than Bhutan, then it shapes the environment in which Bhutan operates. Structurally, Bhutan is subordinated to the U.S. even if the two have no direct interaction. The difference lies in how direct the influence of the stronger power is over the weaker. The more direct the relationship, the more troubling the political subordination.

6. "Hegemony, from the Greek," says Robert Gilpin, "refers to the leadership of one state (the *hegemon*) over other states in the system." *War and Change in World Politics* (Cambridge: Cambridge University Press, 1981), 116. Hegemony, as used here, is different from what Hedley Bull calls either "great powers" or "hegemony." He restricts his own use of "great powers" to states that recognize a special responsibility based on their superior strength, thus explicitly excluding Napoleonic France and Nazi Germany. He also asserts that there must always be more than one great power. *The Anarchical Society: A Study of Order in World Politics* (New York: Columbia University Press, 1977), 200–202.

Bull limits *hegemony* to distinguish it from other forms of preponderance, such as *dominance* and *primacy*. *Anarchical Society*, 214. Primacy, in Bull's terminology, is a form of preponderance that basically respects the contours of international norms. Dominance is at the opposite end of the spectrum; small states are treated as second-class citizens. Hegemony is somewhere in the middle; it is (here Bull quotes Georg Schwarzenberger) "imperialism with good manners." I use the term *hegemony* more broadly than Bull does; all of his forms of preponderance would be included.

7. Robert O. Keohane, *After Hegemony: Cooperation and Discord in the World Political Economy* (Princeton, N.J.: Princeton University Press, 1984), 31 ("the theory of hegemonic stability [holds] that order in world politics is typically created by a single dominant power").

8. Ibid., 32.

9. Ibid., 35, citing Robert O. Keohane and Joseph S. Nye., *Power and Interdependence: World Politics in Transition* (Boston: Little, Brown, 1977), 44.

10. Immanuel Wallerstein, *The Politics of the World-Economy: The States, the Movements, and the Civilizations* (Cambridge: Cambridge University Press, 1984), 38.

11. Joseph S. Nye, *Bound to Lead: The Changing Nature of American Power* (New York: Basic Books, 1990), 39.

12. Robert Bocock, *Hegemony* (London: Tavistock, 1986), 11. See also Pieter Hendrik Kooijmans, *The Doctrine of the Legal Equality of States: An Inquiry into the Foundations of International Law* (Leiden: A. W. Sythoff, 1964), 95–96 (discussing hegemony as depending on consent of the subordinate state); G. John Ikenberry and Charles V. Kupchan, "The Legitimation of Hegemonic Power," in David Rapkin, ed., *World Leadership and Hegemony* (Boulder, Colo.: Lynne Rienner, 1990).

13. Robert W. Cox, "Labor and Hegemony," 31 Int. Org. 385, 387 (1977). See also Cox, *Production, Power, and World Order: Social Forces in the Making of History* (New York: Columbia University Press, 1987), chaps. 6 and 7. Compare Keohane's insistence that hegemony need not involve false consciousness (although he does emphasize the importance of willingness and deference). *After Hegemony*, 45.

14. For assertions that the two important hegemons of the last two hundred years were Great Britain and the United States, see Keohane, *After Hegemony*, 31; Ian Clark, *The Hierarchy of States: Reform and Resistance in the International Order* (Cambridge: Cambridge University Press, 1989), 107; Gilpin, *War and Change*, 145. For criticisms of the analogy, see Nye, *Bound to Lead*, chap. 2. Wallerstein also gives the example of the United Provinces in the mid-seventeenth century. *Politics*, 39.

15. Nye, *Bound to Lead*, 52–63.

16. Raymond Aron, *Peace and War* (New York: Doubleday, 1966), 1.

17. David P. Calleo, *Beyond American Hegemony: The Future of the Western Alliance* (New York: Basic Books, 1987), 13.

18. Compare, in particular, Nye, *Bound to Lead* with Kennedy, *Rise and Fall of the Great Powers*.

19. Bruce Russett, for example, argues that the United States received substantial private benefit from running the international order. "The Mysterious Case of Vanishing Hegemony; or, is Mark Twain Really Dead?, 39 Int. Org. 207 (1985). Compare Mark Boyer, *International Cooperation and Public Goods: Opportunities for the Western Alliance* (Baltimore: Johns Hopkins University Press, 1993).

20. There were, of course, nations in other parts of the world that fell under the influence of the Soviet Union (e.g., Cuba and Afghanistan). I focus on the Warsaw Pact as a particularly interesting example in that the assertion of hegemonic power was relatively institutionalized.

21. See, e.g., Jan Triska, ed., *Dominant Power and Subordinate States: The United States in Latin America and the Soviet Union in Eastern Europe* (Durham, N.C.: Duke University Press, 1986).

22. See, e.g., the discussion in chap. 2 of the normative relevance of security risks from outside the sphere of influence.

23. See generally Ian Clark, *The Hierarchy of States: Reform and Resistance in the International Order* (Cambridge: Cambridge University Press, 1989), chap. 6.

24. Edwin Dewitt Dickinson, *The Equality of States in International Law* (Cambridge: Harvard University Press, 1920), 296.

25. F. Northedge and M. Grieve, *A Hundred Years of International Relations* (London: Duckworth, 1971), 278.

26. Clark, *Hierarchy*, 114. See also Robert A. Klein, *Sovereign Equality Among States: The History of an Idea* (Toronto: University of Toronto Press, 1974), 8.

27. Dickinson, *Equality*, 308. See also K. J. Holsti, "Governance Without Government: Polyarchy in Nineteenth-Century European International Politics," in James Rosenau and Ernst-Otto Czempiel, eds., *Governance Without Government: Order and Change in World Politics* (Cambridge: Cambridge University Press, 1992).

28. Nye, *Bound to Lead*, 39. Compare Wallerstein: "I do not mean to suggest that there is ever any moment when a hegemonic power is omnipotent and capable of doing anything its wants. Omnipotence does not exist within the interstate system." *Politics*, 39.

29. Nye, *Bound to Lead*, 38.

30. Another characteristic is less relevant here; joint consumption. Public goods are not used up when they are enjoyed by one individual. More individuals can enjoy the benefits of the public good without a simultaneous rise in the cost of production. The public goods approach to international hegemony is discussed at greater length in chap. 6.

31. Mancur Olson, Jr., and Richard Zeckhauser, "An Economic Theory of Alliances," 48 *Review of Economics and Statistics* 266 (1966).

32. Gilpin, *War and Change*, 144.

33. For a description of this theory, see Robert Keohane, "The Theory of Hegemonic Stability and Changes in International Economic Regimes, 1967–1977," in O. Holsti, R. Siverson, and A. George, eds., *Change in the International System* (Boulder, Colo.: Westview, 1980).

34. Keohane, *After Hegemony*, 31. Keohane's book, of course, sets out to rebut the claim that order cannot continue past the end of hegemony.

35. See generally Keohane, *After Hegemony* and Stephen Krasner, ed., *International Regimes* (Ithaca, N.Y.: Cornell University Press, 1983).

36. See, e.g., Gilpin, *War and Change*, 34.

37. Compare Duncan Snidal's distinction between benevolent and coercive hegemons. "The Limits of Hegemonic Stability Theory," 39 *Int. Org.* 579 (1985).

38. Keohane, *After Hegemony*, 101, 115–16, 244 (contrasting regimes with "quasi-governmental rule makers"). Hegemons and regimes need not be governmental institutions for Keohane's purposes. Hegemons and regimes may successfully promote international cooperation without having official governmental status, and Keohane's object is to show how institutional arrangements are able to do this, either during the period of active hegemony or after hegemony (when the institutional consequences of hegemony still linger). Keohane does not need to make strong claims that "world government" exists; he demonstrates the cooperation can exist even in the absence of a world government.

39. Gilpin, *War and Change*, 28.

40. Ibid., 29–30.

41. Edward Hallett Carr, *The Twenty Years' Crisis, 1919–1939* (London: MacMillan, 1951), 107.

42. John Westlake, *International Law* (Cambridge: Cambridge University Press, 1904), 309.

43. Thomas Joseph Lawrence, *The Principles of International Law*, 6th ed. (Boston: D. C. Heath, 1915), 275. See generally Kooijmans, *Doctrine*, 104–06.

44. See also James Lorimer, *The Institutes of the Law of Nations*, vol. 1 (Edinburgh: W. Blackwood and Sons, 1883), 168–71.

45. Here one thinks of the writing of John Ruggie, James Rosenau, or Freidrich Kratochwil. We return to these authors briefly in chap. 10.

46. Probably the chief disadvantage of using the term *proto-government* is that it suggests that hegemonic systems are in the process of transforming themselves into true world governments. This inference would be unwarranted. Not all domestic primitive governance systems evolve eventually into states; it all depends upon historical circumstances and fortuity.

47. The analogy between international and primitive societies is, of course, familiar. See, e.g., Bull, *Anarchical Society*, 59; Roger Masters, "World Politics as a Primitive Political System," 16 *World Politics* 595 (1964). Typically, though, the reason for raising the analogy is to show that even anarchies possess order and norms. My comparison is between international relations and early societies that are no longer really anarchies.

48. Henri Claessen and Peter Skalnik, "The Early State: Theories and Hypotheses," in Claessen and Skalnik, eds., *The Early State* (The Hague: Moulton, 1978), 1, 23. See also Robert Nozick's description of hypothetical state formation in *Anarchy, State, and Utopia* (New York: Basic Books, 1974), chap. 2.

49. There are other ways of arguing that governance exists in the international system, ways that do not rely on the presence of a hegemon. "Governance," for example, can be thought to arise out of the rules and institutions that regulate international activity. The focus, then, is not on the existence of an actor that provides governance (as the hegemon does, I am arguing) but on the converging expectations of the "governed." See, e.g., Rosenau and Czempiel, *Governance Without Government*.

50. Kenneth Waltz's commitment to formal equality (and the resulting "anarchic" characterization of the international system) are discussed in chap. 2.

51. Claessen and Skalnik, "Early State," 67.

52. It is in fact not clear that it is fair to ascribe this view to the realists, as I will explain in the next chapter. It has commonly been ascribed to the realists, however, and that is why I mention the association here.

53. Carr, *Twenty Years' Crisis*, 153.

54. Georg Schwarzenberger, *Power Politics: A Study of International Society*, rev. ed. (New York: Praeger, 1951), 218.

55. Compare my *Justifying International Acts* (Ithaca, N.Y.: Cornell University Press, 1989). There I focused solely on the vertical relations between states and citizens of other states. Here I broaden *vertical* to encompass relations between two states, which are formally equal as a matter of international law but as a matter of fact are hierarchically arranged.

56. Later chapters examine the differences between choosing one variant of liberalism rather than another. Four variations on the liberal theme are investigated in chaps. 4–7.

57. This is not to say that there have not been liberals who have addressed issues of international justice; liberals have written many important works of normative international theory. My point is that they have not concerned themselves with international political hierarchy as leftist critics have. Instead, they have addressed other, equally important, normative issues such as wealth distribution, human rights, and humanitarian intervention.

58. Johann Galtung, "A Structural Theory of Imperialism," 8 *Journal of Peace Research* 81, 81 (1971).

59. For other left-oriented accounts of international power asymmetries, see Wallerstein, *Politics* (taking the world systems approach) or Fernando Cardoso and Enzo Faletto, *Dependency and Development in Latin America* (Berkeley: University of California Press, 1978) (taking a dependency theory approach).

60. For one contribution to the debate, see Charles R. Beitz, *Political Theory and International Relations* (Princeton, N.J.: Princeton University Press, 1979).

61. Helen Milner, "The Assumption of Anarchy in International Relations: A Critique," 17 *Review of International Studies* 67, 81 (1990).

CHAPTER 2

1. In the discussion below, I will not explicitly address the issue of whether the anarchy argument is defensible as applied to the relations between lesser powers, arguing only that whatever sense it makes in that context, it does not make sense as applied to the actions of a hegemon. A number of the arguments below, however, cast doubt on the claim that there is no international morality between states of equal power. For example, the comparison to domestic political relations strongly suggests that the jurisprudential version of the anarchy argument is simply wrong (see below). While I do not explicitly develop the implications of these arguments for relations between equals, the present chapter should not be taken as an endorsement of the anarchy argument in that context.

2. See, e.g., Kenneth Oye, ed., *Cooperation Under Anarchy* (Princeton, N.J.: Princeton University Press, 1986).

3. For a standard neorealist analysis, including balance-of-power theory, see Kenneth Waltz, *Theory of International Politics* (New York: Random House, 1979). For game theoretic approaches, see the articles printed in Oye, *Cooperation*. For a discussion of classical realism, see Michael Smith, *Realist Thought from Weber to Kissinger* (Baton Rouge: Louisiana State University Press, 1986).

4. For one description of this debate, see Charles Beitz, *Political Theory and International Relations* (Princeton, N.J.: Princeton University Press, 1979), pt. 1. For an account more sympathetic to the realist tradition, see Steven Forde, "Classical Realism," in T. Nardin and D. Mapel, eds., *Traditions of International Ethics* (Cambridge: Cambridge University Press, 1992).

5. Robert Art and Kenneth Waltz, "Technology, Strategy, and the Uses of Force," in Art and Waltz, eds., *The Use of Force: International Politics and Foreign Policy*, 2d ed. (Lanham, Md.: University Press of America, 1983), 1,6. See also E. H. Carr's description of realism, *The Twenty Years' Crisis, 1919–1939* (London: MacMillan, 1940), 153.

6. On this point, see generally J. Rosenthal, *Righteous Realists: Political Realism, Responsible Power, and American Culture in the Nuclear Age* (Baton Rouge: Louisiana State University Press, 1991). See also Jack Donnelly, "Twentieth-Century Realism," in Nardin and Mapel, *Traditions*, 85, 97 ("most realists hedge the amoral statesmanship that they describe or advocate").

7. On Morgenthau's beliefs, see Greg Russell, *Hans Morgenthau and the Ethics of Statecraft* (Baton Rouge: Louisiana State University Press, 1990).

8. Robert Holmes, *On War and Morality* (Princeton, N.J.: Princeton University Press, 1989), 96. See, for example, Russell Hardin's argument that nuclear deterrence must be analyzed in consequentialist terms. "Deterrence and Moral Theory," in Kenneth Kipnis and Diana Meyers, eds., *Political Realism and International Morality* (Boulder, Colo.: Westview, 1987).

9. Carr, *Twenty Years' Crisis*, 89.

10. See, e.g., Robert O. Keohane, *After Hegemony: Cooperation and Discord in the World Political Economy* (Princeton, N.J.: Princeton University Press, 1984). The proviso that a commitment to anarchy analysis need not result in moral skepticism or a recommendation of blind pursuit of national interests applies with even greater force to such individuals.

11. Thomas Hobbes, *Leviathan*, ed. C. B. Macpherson (New York: Penguin, 1981), 196.

12. The security dilemma argument is sometimes coupled with the observation that states act as agents for their citizens; that while an individual might be entitled to sacrifice his or her own self-interest, a state is not entitled to put the interests of its citizens at risk. It is not clear that the agency notion adds anything to the argument, however. The question would remain why the state should be entitled to do anything on behalf of its citizens that they were not entitled to do on their own account. It would still have to be shown, in other words, that individuals acting on their own account were entitled to ignore moral principles. But if this can be shown, then we need not raise the agency issue because we can simply argue directly that states are entitled to ignore morality in order to protect their self-interest.

13. See, e.g., Art and Waltz, *Use of Force*, 5–7.

14. On the effect of uncertainty about one's opponent's strategy, see generally Robert M. Axelrod, *The Evolution of Cooperation* (New York: Basic Books, 1984).

15. Carr, *Twenty Years' Crisis*, 68.

16. Machiavelli, perhaps, is one of the rare exceptions to this generalization.

17. Compare Michael Doyle, *Empires* (Ithaca, N.Y.: Cornell University Press, 1986), 11: "Imperialism's foundation is not anarchy, but *order*, albeit an order imposed and strained."

18. Helen Milner, "The Assumption of Anarchy in International Relations Theory: A Critique," 17 *Review of International Studies* 67 (1991).

19. Waltz, *Theory*, 13.

20. Michael Taylor, *Community, Anarchy, and Liberty*, (Cambridge: Cambridge University Press, 1982), 4–10.

21. Actually, presence or absence of hierarchy can be either an empirical or a formal matter; for purposes of this section, it is treated as an empirical criterion. We will return to the question of formal hierarchy in the next section.

22. Oran O. Young, "Anarchy and Social Choice: Reflections on the International Polity," 30 *World Politics* 241, 242 (1978).

23. Milner concludes that this is not what international theorists have in mind. It does capture, however, one of the ordinary meanings of the term; for anarchy seems to connote a lack of organi-

zation. See Milner, "Assumption," 69–70. See also Donnelly, *Twentieth-Century Realism*, 85, 87; Young, *Anarchy*, 242.

24. Waltz, *Theory*, 103.

25. Ibid., 104, 105, 77. It should be noted that for Taylor's purposes the fact that domestic societies may be anarchical is not problematic. He has no reason to deny that domestic anarchies exist; indeed, his book is specifically concerned with the phenomenon of domestic anarchy.

26. Milner, "Assumption," 77.

27. Ibid., 75.

28. Robert Gilpin, *War and Change in World Politics* (Cambridge: Cambridge University Press, 1981), 28.

29. See, e.g., ibid. at 29, 33, 232. It should be noted that Gilpin sometimes places governance in shudder quotes.

30. Young, *Theory*, 242.

31. Nicholas Onuf and Frank F. Klink, "Anarchy, Authority, Rule," 33 *Int. Stud. Quarterly* 149, 150 (1989).

32. Milner, "Assumption," 77 (emphasis added).

33. Similarly, one might choose to model domestic politics either in terms of equality or in terms of hierarchy. There are respects, after all, in which all citizens are formally equal—all are entitled to equal civil and political rights, all are required to obey the criminal law, etc.—as well as respects in which political roles (as citizen, soldier, senator, or judge) are differentiated. Neither model is a priori better than the other in all respects; the decision about what formalization to employ is a choice, not an objective response to some reality that is actually "out there."

34. Cf. Barry Buzan, Charles Jones, and Richard Little, *The Logic of Anarchy: Neorealism to Structural Realism* (New York: Columbia University Press, 1993), 194.

35. International law, of course, prescribes formal equality for all states; but realists can hardly afford to rely on international law as the foundation for their models.

36. Or, as Onuf and Klink put it, the presumption of anarchy inhibits our acknowledgment of hierarchy. *Anarchy, Authority, Rule*, 164.

37. Milner, "Assumption," 74.

38. Waltz, *Theory*, 112, 103–104.

39. Ibid., 111, 105.

40. To be really precise, we should not talk about self-help regimes generally, but about regimes that rely on self-help on certain issues. Self-help is issue-specific. In the U.S. we rely on self-help on such issues as continued employment or business success, but not (typically) for retaining possession of personal property of for freedom from physical assault. In international hegemony, likewise, some issues are self-help and others are not. The hegemon is available when its interests are threatened; when its norms are violated, self-help will not be necessary. Self-help is required on other issues, however, when the hegemon has no inclination to become involved. In either domestic or international relations, some issues are self-help and others are not.

41. I would like to thank Andy Moravscik for showing me the relevance of this point.

42. Art and Waltz, *Use of Force*, 6 ("every state . . . has to be prepared to do that which is necessary for its interests as it defines them").

43. Milner, "Assumption," 78–79.

44. Waltz, *Theory*, 103.

45. Ibid., 103–104.

46. Note here that we would call Nazi Germany a self-help system precisely because *legitimate* interests in physical security went unprotected.

47. The key to unraveling this odd logic is to notice, as I will argue immediately below, that "morality" cannot possibly include political morality.

48. It is possible to argue that the notion of legitimacy that Waltz contemplates is not normative but descriptive. Legitimacy might be understood to connote only that the actors in the system think that the hegemon is legitimate. Gilpin, for instance, cites Kissinger's notion of legitimacy, which turns on acceptance by the major powers. *War and Change*, 12. He explicitly distinguishes legitimacy from what he calls the "justice" of a system, as defined by authors such as Charles Beitz (in *Political Theory and International Relations*), Hedley Bull, and Richard Falk.

The chief difficulty with defining legitimacy in terms of acceptance is that it cannot explain the kind of acceptance that the major powers extend. (It is also unclear why we should ask only about the attitudes of the major actors, but that is another matter.) When an actor accepts a system as legitimate, it is making a normative judgment. The system is found to be fair, just, correct, or right. A definition based solely on acceptance cannot explain why such judgments make sense and cannot help the actors to decide whether it makes sense to accept a system as legitimate. Moreover, even if legitimacy does boil down to nothing more than acceptance, this definition still contemplates the making of normative judgments, for the actors themselves must be willing to make normative judgments for the definition to hold.

49. This is not to concede that the argument works well in that context; some of the arguments in the text also undermine its effectiveness there. In particular, even between equals the anarchy argument presumes an ability to differentiate legitimate from illegitimate interests, as argued above. The main point here, however, is that regardless of what one thinks about its persuasiveness between equal states, it is not persuasive in hierarchical relationships.

50. Waltz, *Theory*, 104, 113.

51. This feature may also be important for descriptive purposes, as Helen Milner suggests in a number of the quotations from her article in the discussion above.

52. This argument is developed at greater length in chap. 2 of my *Justifying International Acts* (Ithaca, N.Y.: Cornell University Press, 1989).

53. Compare Hedley Bull's claim that the Hobbesian argument is not relevant where states are not all equally vulnerable. "Society and Anarchy in International Relations," in Herbert Butterfield and Martin Wight, eds., *Diplomatic Investigations: Essays in the Theory of International Politics* (London: Allen and Unwin, 1966), 46.

54. Furthermore, the fact that morality does not apply to actors at the top of the hierarchy threatens the moral obligations of lesser actors. The reason is that if moral evaluation of the top actor is impossible, then the less powerful actors will be in anarchy because there is no legitimate government.

55. Bull, "Society and Anarchy," 35.

56. Perhaps it would be argued that this example is inapposite because there was no real security threat from Japanese-Americans. But what matters is that it was genuinely believed that there was a security threat, for the point in question is how one should deal with what one perceives to be a genuine clash between national security and moral values. The problem with our treatment of the Japanese-Americans in World War II is not simply that American authorities were mistaken about the facts, but that even if they were correct about the facts, they should not have acted that way.

57. Holmes, *On War and Morality*, 106.

CHAPTER 3

1. Compare Hedley Bull's charge that the role of great powers is unjust (although not intolerably so) because they secure special privileges for themselves and have a special stake in the world order. *The Anarchical Society: A Study of Order in World Politics* (New York: Columbia University Press, 1977), 227.

2. There are other understandings of what liberalism means, of course, some of which are employed in international relations theory. Anne Marie Burley lists what she calls "the core assumptions of liberal theory" as the term is used by some international relations theorists: (1) "The fundamental actors in politics are members of domestic society, understood as individuals and privately constituted groups seeking to promote their independent interests. Under specified conditions, individual incentives may promote social order and the progressive improvement of individual welfare." (2) "All governments represent some segment of domestic society, whose interests are reflected in state policy." (3) "The behavior of states—and hence levels of international conflict and cooperation—reflects the nature and configuration of state preferences." "International Law and International Relations Theory: A Dual Agenda," 87 Am. J. Int. L. 205, 227-228 (1993) (citing Andrew Moravcsik, "Liberalism and International Relations Theory," working paper, Center for International Affairs, Harvard University, 1992). It should be clear that this notion of liberalism is very different from the liberalism of normative domestic political theory, which is my focus here.

3. But not all. The International Socialist Organization, for example, posted an invitation to a meeting at Columbia University that was to be held on February 3, 1993, to oppose the intervention in Somalia. The poster, titled "The Two Faces of U.S. Imperialism," read: "Many people expected the murderous bombing of Iraq to end once Clinton took office. But he waited less than 24 hours to continue Bush's policy of bombing Iraq into compliance with United Nations Resolutions. . . . Is the 'humanitarian' invasion of Somalia any different? Are U.S. troops there simply distributing food—or are they trying to create a pro-U.S. government in a strategically important part of Africa? In fact, the United Nations held up the bulk of the food shipments to Somalia for nearly a year before the U.S. invasion, and the famine was ending by the time the troops arrived. And it was Washington's warlords who created the crisis by pouring weapons into Somalia to prop up the now-deposed dictator, Siad Barre."

4. Leftist theory is also critical of American hegemony, of course, but it has been far less critical of Soviet or Chinese dominance. Its main complaint is with capitalist hegemony, not hegemony per se.

CHAPTER 4

1. For a general typology of different sorts of nonviolent sanctions, see Margaret Doxey, "International Sanctions: Ethical and Practical Perspectives," in Moorhead Wright, ed., Rights and Obligations in North-South Relations (New York: St. Martin's, 1986).

2. On the uses of economic power generally, see David A. Baldwin, Economic Statecraft (Princeton, N.J.: Princeton University Press, 1985) and Richard B. Lillich, ed. Economic Coercion and the New International Economic Order (Charlottesville, Va.: Michie Company, 1976).

3. For one participant's description of the U.S. role in the Camp David peace process, see Jimmy Carter, Keeping Faith: Memoirs of a President (New York: Bantam, 1982).

4. The accords originally committed the U.S. to $1.5 billion in annual aid to Egypt. William B. Quandt, Camp David: Peacemaking and Politics (Washington, D.C.: Brookings Institution, 1986), 314. As of 1991, Egypt had received $2.5 billion. James Flanigan, "Post–Cold War Period Full of Hopes for Peace, Prosperity," Los Angeles Times, Oct. 27, 1991: D1.

5. Between 1946 and 1976 the Philippines received about $876 million in military assistance grants as indirect compensation for the bases. A. James Gregor, Crisis in the Philippines: A Threat to U.S. Interests (Washington, D.C.: Ethics and Public Policy Center, 1984), 17. After 1979, however, compensation was directly connected to the bases, at first set at $500 million annually and rising to $900 million in 1983. Ibid. The eruption of Mt. Pinatubo on June 9, 1991, caused approximately $800 million in damage to Clark Air Force Base and contributed to the U.S. hesitation to pledge suf-

ficient funds to maintain control over the bases. Teresa Albor, "Filipinos Vocal in Response to New Base Pact," *Christian Science Monitor*, July 19, 1991: 7.

6. For a description of the fight over Israeli loan guarantees, see M. Graeme Bannerman, "Arabs and Israelis: Slow Walk Toward Peace," 72 *Foreign Affairs* 142 (1993).

7. For a recent round in this debate, see Steven Greenhouse, "Renewal Backed for China Trade," *New York Times*, May 28, 1993: A5.

8. David A. Koplow and Philip G. Schrag, "Carrying a Big Carrot: Linking Multilateral Disarmament and Development Assistance," 91 *Columbia Law Review* 1047 (1991).

9. Ibid., 1047–51.

10. Kenneth E. Boulding, Introduction, in Kenneth E. Boulding and Tapan Mukerjee, eds., *Economic Imperialism: A Book of Readings* (Ann Arbor: University of Michigan Press, 1972), xii.

11. See, e.g., Frank F. Klink, "Rationalizing Core-Periphery Relations: The Analytical Foundations of Structural Inequality in World Politics," 34 *International Studies Quarterly* 183, 186 (1990).

12. See generally Roy Mersky, ed., *Conference on Transnational Economic Boycotts and Coercion* (New York: Oceana, 1978).

13. One might offer Cuba as a possible counterexample, or else the nations that have endeavored to lead the nonaligned movement. In Cuba's case, the latitude for grand policy was to some degree created by Soviet subsidies; in its current financial situation, its diplomacy is more limited. (In addition, some of its actions, such as the interventions in Angola, involved military means.) And the nonaligned movement would undoubtedly have been more successful if its members' resources were not so limited. It is generally the case that consensual methods are more available to the rich and powerful; poorer nations are more likely to resort to forcible methods such as war.

14. See generally William C. Potter, *Nuclear Power and Nonproliferation: An Interdisciplinary Perspective* (Cambridge, Mass.: Oelgeschlager, Gunn, and Hain, 1982), 3. Israel, India, and Pakistan are also believed to have nuclear weapons or the ability to assemble them quickly. Iran, Iraq, Libya, and North Korea currently have nuclear weapons programs. The breakup of the Soviet Union has of course increased the number of nuclear states, because some of the former republics, which are now new nations, inherited nuclear weapons. The Commonwealth of Independent States currently exercises unified command over nuclear weapons in Russia, Ukraine, Kazakhstan, and Belarus. On March 24, 1993, South Africa announced that it had previously built six crude atomic bombs but then destroyed them, ostensibly because they were no longer needed after the end of the Cold War. Bill Keller, "South Africa Says It Built 6 Atom Bombs," *New York Times*, March 25, 1993: 1.

15. The regime is also consensual in another sense; the signatories to the nonproliferation treaties, including current non-nuclear states, agree to support the two-tiered regime. This form of consent will be discussed in the next chapter, for it is an instance of ex ante agreement to legal rules and could involve coercion if the stronger states decide to use force to compel obedience. It is not clear at present whether sanctions will be applied to North Korea for its decision to exit the nonproliferation treaty; but even if such actions qualify as ex ante consent, they do not count as contemporaneous consent. Of course, contemporaneous consent also does not explain certain other sorts of attempts to prevent the spread of nuclear weapons, such as Israel's bombing of the Iraqi nuclear reactor near Baghdad on June 7, 1981.

16. Potter, *Nuclear Power*, 25.

17. But note the Indian application in 1981, which was approved despite U.S. objections. See Kendall W. Stiles, *Negotiating Debt: The IMF Lending Process* (Boulder, Colo.: Westview, 1991), chap. 6. The U.S. eventually abstained in protest. Ibid., 117, 120.

18. Cheryl Payer, *The Debt Trap: The IMF and the Third World* (New York and London: Monthly Review Press, 1974), 217.

19. Ibid., 218. See also Robert S. Browne, "The IMF in Africa: A Case of Inappropriate Technol-

ogy," in Robert Myers, ed., *The Political Morality of the International Monetary Fund* (New York: Transaction Books / Carnegie Council on Ethics and International Affairs, 1987).

20. Koplow and Schrag, "Carrying a Big Carrot," 1042.

21. See, e.g., G.A. Res. 2625, 25 U.N. G.A.O.R, Supp. 28, at 123 Doc. A/8082 (1970): "No State may use or encourage the use of economic, political, or any other type of measures to coerce another State in order to obtain from it the subordination of the exercise of its sovereign rights and to secure from it advantages of any kind."

22. Baldwin, *Economic Statecraft*, 358: "In sum, there are very few clear-cut, legally binding international norms regulating the use of economic statecraft. There is a large body of international opinion, mostly in communist and Third World states, that favors the regulation and perhaps prohibition of such measures. Judged in terms of the criteria suggested here, however, the case for broad legal bans on economic statecraft is not compelling."

23. Richard N. Gardner, "The Hard Road to World Order," 52 *Foreign Affairs* 556, 567 (1974). Conversely, it should be noted, the Western objections to the oil embargo were hardly consistent with the more typical Western position that economic pressure is not prohibited by international law.

24. This does not mean that there might not be other justifications for an action taken by an unrepresentative leader; for an agreement might also be upheld because it is substantively just (see chap. 7) or on the grounds of hypothetical consent (see chap. 6).

25. Payer, *Debt Trap*, 41.

26. Food subsidies, for example, can disadvantage agricultural producers—often the poorest in the country—in order to satisfy the urban classes, who may be considerably better off. In addition, protection of local manufacturing may raise consumer prices while guaranteeing a market and higher prices to local industry, which is likely to be owned by local elites. See generally D. Gale Johnson, "IMF Conditionality and Agriculture in the Developing Countries," in Robert Myers, ed., *The Political Morality of the International Monetary Fund* (New York: Transaction Books / Carnegie Council on Ethics and International Affairs, 1987). Whether particular IMF policies help the poorer or the better off is obviously an empirical question which probably must be addressed on a case-by-case, not a wholesale, basis.

27. Payer, *Debt Trap*, 43.

28. I developed this argument at length in my book *Justifying International Acts* (Ithaca, N.Y.: Cornell University Press, 1989).

29. Payer, *Debt Trap*, 48–49.

30. Nicholas Onuf and Frank Klink, "Anarchy, Authority, Rule," 33 *International Studies Quarterly* 149, 169 (1989).

31. George M. von Furstenberg, "The IMF as Market-Maker for Official Business Between Nations," in Myers, *Political Morality*, 121.

32. See, e.g., Thomas Pogge, *Realizing Rawls* (Ithaca, N.Y.: Cornell University Press, 1989), chaps. 5 and 6; Henry Shue, *Basic Rights: Subsistence, Affluence, and U.S. Foreign Policy* (Princeton, N.J.: Princeton University Press, 1980); Charles Beitz, *Political Theory and International Relations* (Princeton, N.J.: Princeton University Press, 1979), pt. 3.

33. See, e.g., a letter to the editor of the *San Francisco Chronicle*, March 12, 1992: 18: "Certainly the United States government, as the proposed guarantor of the loans, should have the right to indicate the conditions of the guarantee. Israel, as recipient, has the right to accept or reject. Unfortunately, after nearly a half century of extensive and generous aid to Israel, amounting to many billion dollars, that nation and her more zealous supporters seem to regard grants/loans/guarantees as entitlements to which they may set the conditions. . . . It may be time for a fresh review of our policies vis-a-vis Israel."

34. Payer, *Debt Trap*, 48. It should be noted that it is not clear how the fact that forgiveness is not considered (if in fact that is the case) shows that the debts serve a function above and beyond the money that is to be repaid. It may, of course, only show that continued existence of the debts serves to raise the probability that the money will be repaid.

35. John Williamson, "Reforming the IMF: Different or Better?" in Myers, *Political Morality*, 7, 10.

36. Jordan J. Paust and Albert P. Blaustein, "The Arab Oil Weapon—A Threat to International Peace," in Richard Lillich, ed., *Economic Coercion and the New International Economic Order* (Charlottesville, Va.: Michie Co., 1976), 133.

37. On other aspects of the American hypocrisy surrounding the Arab oil boycott, see Andreas Lowenfeld, ". . . Sauce for the Gander": The Arab Boycott and United States Political Trade Controls," in Mersky, *Conference*.

38. J. Dapray Muir, "The Boycott in International Law," in Lillich, *Economic Coercion*, 22, 26, 34

39. Note that if one had a different view of property, one might object to there being a market for such items as well. It would therefore be consistent for a socialist country to take a different view of what should count as inalienable than a capitalist country, and it should therefore not be surprising that some Third World nations would take a broader view than Western nations about what sovereign rights are best treated as inalienable.

40. Tim Golden, "Mexico Says It Won't Accept Drug Aid from U.S.," *New York Times*, July 26, 1992: 14.

41. Steven A. Holmes, "India Cancels Dam Loan from World Bank," *New York Times*, March 31, 1993: 5.

42. China has protested the linkage of MFN status to human rights. See Sheryl Wu Dunn, "China Denounces Terms of Clinton's Trade Deal," *New York Times*, May 30, 1993: 12.

43. In this respect, it is interesting to compare the boycott of South Africa (or the former Yugoslavia) with the U.S. trade sanctions against Cuba. The former sanctions are designed to compel adherence to international law; the latter constitute a U.S. effort to unseat a government that the U.S. finds repellent but is not, by and large, thought to be violating international norms. The U.S. efforts to induce other states to boycott Cuba have been widely condemned by the international community. See Paul Shneyer and Virginia Barta, "The Legality of the U.S. Economic Blockade of Cuba Under International Law," 13 *Case W. Res. J. Int. L.* 451 (1981); Michael Krinsky and David Golove, eds., *United States Economic Measures Against Cuba: Proceedings in the United Nations and International Law Issues* (Northampton, Mass.: Aletheia, 1993). The legitimacy of this embargo should be evaluated in light of the monopoly argument, discussed in the next section, both because the U.S. occupies such an important trading position and because it has employed strong measures to induce other nations to participate.

44. I do not wish to take a position one way or the other on this substantive issue. The matter must be resolved by international norms, which will be discussed in the next chapter. The importance of international norms to this issue, and to questions of consent in general, will be discussed in the final section of this chapter.

45. This, of course, is not terribly easy to ascertain.

46. One might say that there is a difference between a general right to control resources—which cannot be alienated—and the specific right to a particular resource, which can be alienated. The general and inalienable right to control resources is more valuable precisely because the right to a particular resource is alienable.

47. In the 1840s the Western powers negotiated a series of treaty arrangements with China under which China effectively relinquished control over important aspects of its domestic sovereignty, including the right to try cases in Chinese courts. See Jonathan Spence, *The Search for Modern China* (New York and London: Norton, 1990), 158–163.

48. The Soviet Union coerced the Baltic states into signing the Mutual Assistance Treaties in 1939. I. Joseph Vizulis, *Nations Under Duress: The Baltic States* (Port Washington, N.Y.: Associated Faculty Press, 1985), 29–37. Vizulis argues that these treaties were coerced and therefore not valid under international law.

49. Note that the same cannot be true for most of the examples in the preceding paragraph, for the Baltic states, China, and the conquered colonies truly gained little if any advantage from being able to give up the rights in question. The only reason that these states agreed to go along with the proposed "exchanges" was that they were militarily coerced.

50. Or by a single buyer; here I am treating the debtor country as a "consumer" of credit and the lending countries which dominate the IMF, in particular the U.S., as the "seller." But the point is the same when there is a single buyer rather than a single seller. Indeed, this is the basis of complaints that the U.S. keeps prices of raw materials artificially low, to the detriment of Third World nations, which are predominately raw-materials producers.

51. In some circumstances private lenders might provide competition. The problem with relying on them to establish terms for lending is that in practice private lenders rely on the IMF to set conditions for restructuring debtor nation economies. Thus, while there may be some competition for loans, in practice there seems to be little competition in the setting of economic restructuring conditions, once a nation is in sufficient financial trouble to necessitate recourse to IMF credit.

52. Note that the logic is symmetric; if some nation possesses the only possible site for a U.S. military base, then it is in a monopoly situation vis-à-vis the U.S.

53. Klink, "Rationalizing Core-Periphery Relations," 204–206. Klink argues that states in the periphery may be able to improve their bargaining position if there is competition in the core. He notes that where the core states have defined spheres of influence, however, this obviates the beneficial effects of competition. Note, though, that the stability of division of the periphery into spheres of influence depends in part on whether states in the core define their interests in relative or absolute terms. For if they define their interests in absolute terms, the game is positive-sum; both can gain from a stable division of the periphery. If they define their interests in relative terms, however, the game is zero-sum; for the fact that one solidifies its power over the periphery is not advantageous if the stable spheres of influence allow the other to do the same.

54. It should be noted that the passing of the Cold War altered the competitive calculus in another way: some of the services that developing nations successfully marketed during the Cold War are no longer of particular use to the U.S. For example, the value to the U.S. of military bases in foreign countries has diminished.

55. Or whether, in the alternative, a new entity of this sort might enter the market.

56. This argument about the advantage of monopoly power might seem to contradict the claim, in chap. 6, that smaller states are able to exploit the largest by "free-riding." But the free-rider argument about exploitation is addressed only to cases of public goods, where it is not possible for the strong state to prevent the weaker ones from sharing in goods toward which they did not contribute. The goods at issue here (loan money, for example) are, however, distinctly private goods.

CHAPTER 5

1. Japan refers to these islands as the Northern Territories. Russia has occupied the islands since World War II, although Japan has lobbied for their return since 1951. See Ronald Yates, "Japan, Soviets Seek Accord Over Islands: WWII Treaty, $28 Billion at Stake," *Chicago Tribune*, April 14, 1991: 21.

2. For these purposes, the Russian claim need not be entirely valid; it is enough that the claim is colorable and made in good faith. Similarly, in domestic contract law one can legally settle a disputed claim even if the claim would turn out, on litigation, to be ultimately groundless.

3. The importance of contemporaneous or overlapping performance has been well analyzed in the rational choice literature. Where the parties have no effective neutral enforcement mechanism, they may still be able to ensure compliance by breaking their performances down into a series of small steps, so that breach of the agreement by one side allows the other to terminate its own obligation. See, e.g., Thomas C. Schelling, *The Strategy of Conflict* (Cambridge: Harvard University Press, 1960).

4. For an argument that the standard "morality of states" interpretation of international relations is similar to Robert Nozick's libertarianism, see Frank Klink, "Core-Periphery Relations and Social Justice: The Moral Standing of Structural Inequality in the Post-Colonial World" (paper presented to the 1991 Annual Meeting of the Midwest Political Science Association).

5. There may be some difficult issues of terminology at stake here. It is possible that some who identify with anarchism would instead adopt the position that I describe as libertarian. For example, Robert Paul Wolff asserts that an anarchist would find a state legitimate if it limited itself to enforcement of those norms to which everyone had agreed ex ante. See *In Defense of Anarchism* (New York: Harper and Row, 1970), 22.

Robert Nozick, on the other hand, seems to view the difference between anarchists and libertarians much as I have described. He discusses the progression that would occur as society formed itself into states, and assumes that anarchists would wish to stop at the pre-state stage while libertarians would continue on with state formation but limit the powers of the state. *Anarchy, State, and Utopia* (New York: Basic Books, 1974), 4–6. Michael Taylor, likewise, seems to define anarchism as resting primarily on objections to coercive states. *Community, Anarchy, and Liberty* (Cambridge: Cambridge University Press, 1982), 4–10.

Other authors seem to use the terms *anarchist* and *libertarian* virtually interchangeably. See, e.g., David Goodway, Introduction, in Goodway, ed., *For Anarchism: History, Theory, and Practice* (New York: Routledge, 1989). The proper role of the state in enforcing prior promises seems to vary throughout anarchist thought. See Robert Graham, "The Role of Contract in Anarchist Ideology," in Goodway, *For Anarchism*.

6. This, at any rate, is Robert Nozick's argument.

7. I say that it is almost tautologically true because the very fact that A can successfully coerce B shows that, on that issue at least, A is more powerful than B.

8. James L. Brierly, *The Law of Nations*, 6th ed. (New York: Oxford University Press, 1963), 49–51; Hans Kelsen, *Principles of International Law*, 2d ed., ed. Robert W. Tucker, (New York: Holt, Rinehart, and Winston, 1966), 442–443.

9. On natural law, see Joseph Boyle, "Natural Law and International Ethics," in Terry Nardin and David Mapel, *Traditions of International Ethics* (Cambridge: Cambridge University Press, 1992).

10. "The doctrine of positivism . . . teaches that international law is the sum of the rules by which states have consented to be bound, and that nothing can be law to which they have not consented." Brierly, *Law of Nations*, 51.

11. Even a natural lawyer would probably be willing to acknowledge that state agreement might be an *additional* source of international law, at least so long as the agreement was not itself a violation of morality. Thus, a natural lawyer ought to recognize ex ante consent as a sufficient alternative justification for international enforcement in most circumstances. The main difference between positivism and natural law theories is over whether state agreement is a *necessary* condition.

12. Brierly, *Law of Nations*, 54.

13. Ibid., 53. See also Brierly, *The Basis of Obligation in International Law and Other Papers* (Oxford: Oxford University Press, 1958), 12.

14. Many international lawyers have observed that the significance of consent itself must be established by antecedent norms. See Brierly, *Basis*, 10; Brierly, *Law of Nations*, 53; Kelsen, *Principles*, 446.

15. L. Oppenheim, *International Law: A Treatise*, 4th ed., ed. Arnold McNair (New York: Longmans, Green, 1928), 24. Article 38 of the Statute of the International Court of Justice actually lists four sources of international law: (a) international conventions, whether general or particular, establishing rules expressly recognized by the contesting states; (b) international custom, as evidence of a general practice accepted as law; (c) the general principles of law recognized by civilized nations; (d) subject to the provisions of article 59 [stating that Court decisions are binding only between the parties], judicial decisions and the teachings of the most highly qualified publicists of the various nations, as subsidiary means for the determination of rules of law. The first three sources are clearly influenced by state agreement. The last is as well, given that judicial decisions are themselves supposed to reflect other sources of law and that the writings of scholars will often concern themselves with treaties or state practice. It has been observed, however, that the statute does not limit the court exclusively to positive law sources. Brierly, *Basis*, 17.

16. The U.N. Charter refers to General Assembly decisions as "recommendations." See, e.g., chap. IV, art. 10. We will discuss in later chapters how international law is in fact sometimes binding on states that have not agreed.

17. There are limited exceptions, of course. For example, the victim of a crime will have certain rights of self-defense, and in some circumstances a bystander will have rights either to assist the victim or to apprehend the perpetrator. The point here is that matters of remedy are the subject of norms, just as the definitions of substantive right are.

18. There would be hierarchy if this solution were chosen, of course, but it would involve placing the U.N. above its member states, not placing one sovereign state above another.

19. The Charter does, however, authorize the U.N. to assemble a military force from troops supplied by member nations; see arts. 43 and 45. The fact that there is no standing U.N. military force, obviously, makes it dependent upon its member states to obtain these troops.

There is another theoretical possibility: that all states might join in to protect the victimized state. Under this "collective security" approach, the weaker states joining together would not need the assistance of a strong state and would even be able to retaliate against strong states that violated international norms. Furthermore, this solution would avoid placing any particular state (and in particular the strongest state) in a favored position, because the coalition would shift depending on which state violated the rules. The primary difficulty with this solution, which seems extremely attractive in theory, lies in the practical difficulties in organizing and coordinating effective response by a large number of states on an ad hoc basis. Under the League of Nations system, all states were supposed to have an obligation to respond to violations by a state aggressor, although obviously this failed to happen in the Italian invasion of Ethiopia.

20. I will discuss the role of the great-powers veto immediately below.

21. It could be claimed that agreement to hegemonic enforcement, in general, is not the same as agreement to *American* hegemony; that it would be agreed by weaker states that hegemony is desirable but they would not want the U.S. to occupy that role. But once there is agreement to the general notion of hegemony, it will be appreciated that this role inevitably will be filled by the strongest power in the system (unless institutional checks and balances can somehow be created to prevent this). Thus, consent to hegemony forseeably entails consent to occupation of that role by whatever state is strongest.

22. This argument is also a possible justification for American enforcement of norms of substantive morality, to which we will return in chap. 6.

23. Whether international law requires that there actually be a request by the victim is a matter of dispute. See Oscar Schachter, "United Nations Law in the Gulf Conflict," 85 *Am. J. Int. Law* 452, 457 (1991), noting that the Security Council did not seem to indicate the necessity in its reactions to the invasion of Kuwait, but that the International Court of Justice had so indicated in its 1986 Nic-

aragua decision *Military and Paramilitary Activities in and Against Nicaragua* (Nicar. v. U.S.) 1986 I.C.J. Rep. 14, 105, para. 199 (Judgment of June 27).

24. Ex ante consent might also be involved here, if the victim had a treaty with the U.S. either permitting or requiring the U.S. to intervene on the victim's behalf.

25. See generally chap. VII of the U.N. Charter, entitled "Action with Respect to Threats to the Peace, Breaches of the Peace, and Acts of Aggression."

26. Art. 51. Note, however, that the inherent right of individual or collective self-defense is guaranteed only until the Security Council has acted.

27. For example, as a condition of granting a cease-fire after the end of the Gulf war, the Security Council imposed terms on Iraq that Kuwait and its allies would probably not have been entitled to impose on their own; see the discussion below.

28. See, e.g., the response of South Korea and its allies to the invasion by North Korea, an act of aggression that also provoked a Security Council response. See Security Council res. 82 of June 25, 1950; res. 83 of June 27, 1950; res.84 of July 7, 1950. It should be noted that the converse may not be true; during the Cold War, either the U.S. or the Soviet Union could be counted on to veto enforcement action proposals, even in cases where self-defense would be appropriate.

29. Res. 660 of Aug. 2, 1990. U.N. Charter art. 27(3) permits enforcement measures whenever the Security Council finds "any threat to the peace, breach of the peace, or act of aggression . . . ."

30. Res. 661 of Aug. 6, 1990.

31. Schachter, "United Nations Law," 452, 457–462.

32. Res. 687 of April 3, 1991.

33. Res. 688 of April 5, 1991.

34. Schachter, "United Nations Law," 453.

35. Action requires unanimity among the permanent members, and nine votes overall.

36. See Ruth Russell and Jeannette Muther, *A History of the United Nations Charter: The Role of the United States, 1940–1945* (Washington, D.C.: Brookings Institution, 1958), chap. 28, "The Problem of the Great-Power Veto." For an excellent general discussion of the Security Council and of the great-power veto, see David Caron, "The Legitimacy of the Collective Authority of the Security Council," 87 *Am. J. Int. L.* 552 (1993).

37. Arthur H. Vandenberg, Jr., ed., *The Private Papers of Senator Vandenberg* (Boston: Houghton Mifflin, 1952), 200.

38. Indeed, one might count as a key advantage that states agreeing to a general norm cannot anticipate whether they will gain or lose. The states, in other words, might be said to agree to the norm behind a "veil of ignorance." This hypothetical contract explanation will be investigated in the following chapter.

39. In this respect, one might keep in mind the amnesty arranged for human rights violators in the El Salvadoran civil war or the eleventh-hour amnesty that George Bush granted important members of his party just before leaving office. See Carl P. Lubsdorf, "Bush Pardons 6 in Iran-Contra Case," *Dallas Morning News*, Dec. 25, 1992: 1; William Branigin, "Salvadoran, Nicaraguan Amnesties to Be in Place Under Pact: Assembly Passes Controversial Duarte Bill," *Washington Post*, Oct. 29, 1987: 35.

40. Agreement to the hierarchical voting rules of the Security Council should not be read as consent to a pattern of selective enforcement, given art. 24(2), which states: "In discharging these duties the Security Council shall act in accordance with the Purposes and Principles of the United Nations."

41. The decision to intervene in Somalia may be the rare counterexample.

42. See, for example, Dimitri K. Simes, "There's No Oil in Bosnia," *New York Times*, March 10, 1993: 19.

43. Brierly notes: "The evidence of custom may obviously be very voluminous and also very diverse. There are multifarious occasions on which persons who act or speak in the name of a state do

acts or make declarations which either express or imply some view on a matter of international law. Any such act or declaration may, so far as it goes, be some evidence that a custom, and therefore that a rule of international law, does or does not exist; but, of course, its value as evidence will be altogether determined by the occasion and the circumstances. States, like individuals, often put forward contentions for the purpose of supporting a particular case which do not necessarily represent their settled or impartial opinion; and it is that opinion which has to be ascertained with as much certainty as the nature of the case allows." *Law of Nations*, 60.

44. "Custom in its legal sense means something more than mere habit or usage; it is a usage felt by those who follow it to be an obligatory one. . . . Evidence that a custom in this sense exists in the international sphere can be found only by examining the practice of states; that is to say, we must look at what states do in their relations with one another and attempt to understand why they do it, and in particular whether they recognize an obligation to adopt a certain course." Ibid., 59–60.

45. As Hans Kelsen put it, "Given the circumstances that all too frequently attend state action, the distinction between action undertaken for reasons of expediency or convenience and actions undertaken because it is felt to be obligatory or right may prove very difficult to make." *Principles*, 450.

46. Ibid., 444.

47. See Ted L. Stein, "The Approach of the Different Drummer: The Principle of the Persistent Objector in International Law," 26 *Harv. Int. L. J.* 457 (1985).

48. Oppenheim, *International Law*, 17–18.

49. For an example of this sort of argument, see John Locke, *Second Treatise of Government*, sec. 119. For critical discussions of tacit consent, see A. John Simmons, *Moral Principles and Political Obligations* (Princeton, N.J.: Princeton University Press, 1979), chap. 4; Hanna Pitkin, "Obligation and Consent," parts 1 and 2, 59 and 60 *American Political Science Review* (1965 and 1966).

50. Brierly, *Basis*, 16.

51. Kelsen, *Principles*, 448.

CHAPTER 6

1. For a general discussion of the fact that international law can not be explained in terms of consent, and suggesting an explanation based on public goods and free-riders, see Jonathon Charney, "Universal International Law," 87 *Am. J. Int. L.* 529 (1993).

2. One author adduces evidence of the practice in prehistoric times, although tracing the modern principles of diplomatic immunity to the Renaissance. Grant V. McClanahan, *Diplomatic Immunity: Principles, Practices, Problems* (New York: St. Martin's, 1989), 18–27.

3. This concern—substantive desirability—will also be relevant to the following chapter. Substantive desirability matters both in a hypothetical consent context (where it is used to prove that the parties would have agreed) and where the justification rests on morality directly.

4. There have also, of course, been critical accounts; many of these will be discussed later in this chapter.

5. Charles Kindleberger, "Hierarchy Versus Inertial Cooperation," 40 *Int. Org.* 841, 841 (1986).

6. Kindleberger, "Dominance and Leadership in the International Economy: Exploitation, Public Goods, and Free Rides," 25 *Int. Studies Q.* 242, 253 (1981).

7. David Lake, "The Logic of Grand Strategy" (unpublished paper, quoted with author's permission).

8. See generally Mancur Olson, Jr., *The Logic of Collective Action; Public Goods and the Theory of Groups* (Cambridge: Harvard University Press, 1965). With Richard Zeckhauser, Olsen extended this line of reasoning into the international context in "An Economic Theory of Alliances," 48 *Review of Economics and Statistics* 266 (1966).

9. On the problem of whether lighthouses actually fit into this category, however, see Ronald Coase, "The Lighthouse in Economics," 17 *Journal of Law and Economics* 357 (1974).

10. It is clear, and has often been noted, that whether something is considered a public good depends on the level of technology in the society and the amount of money that the society is willing to invest; thus some society might devise a way to prevent those who do not contribute from reaping the advantages (for instance, by putting up costly toll booths on public streets). It should also be noted that there may be differences of opinion on whether some of these things are even "goods"; some people may think that certain pieces of art are public "bads," or that we should get rid of all the snail darters as soon as possible.

11. Various factors influence the extent to which public goods will be underproduced, such as the size of the group. For a discussion of these additional complications, see Olson, *Logic.*

12. Ibid., 35.

13. This assumes that there are no other ways of promoting cooperation, an assumption that may very well turn out to be false. For example, the five biggest companies acting jointly may be able to contribute to the production, knowing that otherwise it will not be produced. They cannot compel the remainder to contribute, but in this respect they are in no worse shape that the single large company.

14. Robert Keohane, *After Hegemony: Cooperation and Discord in the World Political Economy* (Princeton, N.J.: Princeton University Press, 1984), 31.

15. Compare Robert Gilpin's argument that hegemony is legitimate because the hegemon provides public goods, in *War and Change in World Politics* (Cambridge: Cambridge University Press, 1981), 34.

16. Kindleberger, "Dominance and Leadership," 252.

17. Charles Kindleberger, *The World in Depression, 1929–1939,* rev. ed. (Berkeley: University of California Press, 1986).

18. Elaine Sciolino, "Despite Heat, Christopher Has 'the Time of My Life,' " *New York Times,* June 1, 1993: A3.

19. Flora Lewis, "It Isn't 'Yankee, Go Home' Anymore," *New York Times,* Feb. 13, 1993: A21.

20. Michael Doyle similarly suggests that all the city-states around Athens benefited from its hegemony, which provided a relatively stable peace and prosperous trading system. "The second factor that sustained, at the same time as it threatened, the stability of the Athenian empire was the mixture of popularity and unpopularity which Athenian democratic imperialism evoked among subordinate citizens. . . . The reverence and respect stemmed from an awareness that economic exploitation also conferred benefits, among them integration into the Athenian market, Athens' suppression of piracy, and other imperially provided, international 'collective goods.' " Michael W. Doyle, *Empires* (Ithaca, N.Y.: Cornell University Press, 1986), 57.

21. David Calleo, *Beyond American Hegemony: The Future of the Western Alliance* (New York: Basic Books, 1987), 14.

22. Kindleberger, "Dominance and Leadership," 253.

23. This, of course, is a main point in Keohane's *After Hegemony.*

24. It is not clear that strategic behavior should be counted as a transaction cost. We will return below to the issue of how strategic behavior should be viewed.

25. Although some of the transaction costs, it must be admitted, would be lower; for there are fewer international actors and therefore it would be easier to arrange negotiations.

26. Kindleberger, *World in Depression,* 845–846.

27. Compare Duncan Snidal's observation that states will go along with hegemony only where there is a net benefit to them. Snidal, "The Limits of Hegemonic Stability Theory," 39 *Int. Org.* 593 (1985).

28. We will examine in a moment the possibility that hegemony might only be Kaldor-Hicks–

efficient, meaning that the gains obtained by the winners would in theory be enough to compensate the losers. If hegemony is Kaldor-Hicks–efficient, then it will necessarily also be Pareto-superior so long as the winners actually buy off the losers. The problem in the present context, and the reason that Kaldor-Hicks will not typically be enough for present purposes, is that we are assuming a world in which transaction costs are high; that is the basis for not insisting on actual (as opposed to hypothetical) consent. If transaction costs are that high, then it will not be possible to actually compensate the losers, and the losers would not agree to such a scheme.

29. Indeed, given that the conflict may at that point be a zero-sum game, it is virtually unavoidable that one or the other will reject it.

30. It would not be an adequate explanation to say that decisions made earlier are likely to take the long-term view, while decisions made in the midst of a dispute are likely to be influenced by the short term. For even if a decision is made in the middle of a dispute, there is no reason not to take the long-term view. Each decision maker will balance the immediate gain from rejecting the norm against the advantages of the norm in the long run. Besides, a long-term assessment made in the past should include the fact that the rule in question will work out rather badly in the particular dispute in which the parties now find themselves enmeshed.

31. Not all decisions need be impartial, though. Ronald Dworkin gives this example: "Suppose I did not know the value of my painting on Monday; if you had offered me $100 for it then I would have accepted. On Tuesday I discovered it was valuable. You cannot argue that it would be fair for the courts to make me sell it to you for $100 on Wednesday. It may be my good fortune that you did not ask me on Monday, but that does not justify coercion against me later." *Taking Rights Seriously* (Cambridge: Harvard University Press, 1977), 152.

32. James Buchanan and Gordon Tullock, *The Calculus of Consent* (Ann Arbor: University of Michigan Press, 1962), 78–80, 96.

33. Admittedly, Buchanan and Tullock are addressing the issue of constitutional arrangements, which are both more general and also adopted further in the past. For this reason, the problem may be somewhat less acute for them. But it is not for this reason impossible to determine how a constitution will affect one's own interests. Slaves, Native Americans, and women, for instance, would have had little trouble determining which parts of the U.S. Constitution were favorable to their interests. Slaveowners, conversely, could anticipate which portions of the document would further theirs.

34. This is a different question from whether it is *rational* to be partial; for it could be argued that it is always "rational" to behave in a self-interested manner. My point is that even if it is rational to be partial, partiality is contrary to ethical *reason*.

35. John Rawls, *A Theory of Justice* (Cambridge: Harvard University Press, 1971).

36. See, e.g., John Harsanyi, "Cardinal Utility in Welfare Economics and in the Theory of Risk-Taking," 61 *Journal of Political Economy* 434 (1953); "Cardinal Welfare, Individualistic Ethics, and Interpersonal Comparisons of Utility," 63 ibid. 309 (1955).

37. Harsanyi makes a similar argument, promoting expected utility maximization as a decision rule, instead of Rawls's maximin decision rule. Harsanyi, "Can the Maximin Principle Serve as a Basis for Morality? A Critique of John Rawls' Theory," 69 *Am. Pol. Sci. Rev.* 594 (1975).

38. I am assuming here that the total population of society remains constant; the total utility formulation and average utility formulation will diverge if it is possible to change the number of people involved. For example, it would be possible to double the total utility of society without changing the average level of utility if we simply doubled the size of the population.

39. The calculation of expected advantage would be more complicated for states, of course, since they are of different sizes and populations; the average, for this reason, would have to be some sort of weighted average.

40. The argument that hypothetical contract leads to maximizing overall benefit, and thus ex-

pected value is not entirely independent of the transaction-cost argument; the tests of Kaldor-Hicks efficiency and Pareto superiority are contingently linked. The reason is that economists predict that in a world without transaction costs, the parties would bargain their way to the arrangement that maximized overall gain. See generally Ronald Coase, "The Problem of Social Cost," 3 *Journal of Law and Economics* 1 (1960). If one party would stand to gain an amount more than the amount that another would lose by changing to a different arrangement, the first could offer the second a "side-payment" or bribe to go along with the move. Such utility-enhancing moves are not possible, however, where transaction costs are substantial; the costs involved in negotiating side-payments would eat up the entire utility gains that would be achieved from moving to the arrangement in the first place. For this reason, in situations where the transaction-cost approach to hypothetical contract is convincing, the two theories are unlikely to lead to the same results. They are likely to diverge because high transaction costs may make it impossible to achieve the most Kaldor-Hicks–efficient outcome through Pareto-superior moves.

41. This sort of distributional sensitivity does not promote any particular sort of pattern, such as equality; it is protective of whatever happens to be the status quo.

42. Rawls, *Theory of Justice*, 27.

43. For arguments that Rawls's theory can be extended, see Charles Beitz, *Political Theory and International Relations* (Princeton, N.J.: Princeton University Press, 1979); Thomas Pogge, *Realizing Rawls* (Ithaca, N.Y.: Cornell University Press, 1989). Rawls's brief discussion of the principles of international morality is contained in pages 377–379 of *A Theory of Justice*.

44. Rawls, "The Law of Peoples," in Stephen Shute and Susan Hurly, eds., *On Human Rights: The Oxford Amnesty Lectures, 1993* (New York: Basic Books, 1993).

45. There is a question, for all three of these formulations, of what the appropriate baseline for comparison should be. When the test is Pareto superiority, it is clear that the basis of comparison is the status quo; does it make every party better off than it is under the current state of affairs? Both expected value and maximin seem to require a comparison against all possible states of affairs, not just the status quo. This is the comparison that we will make here.

It is arguable, though, that the status quo ought also to figure into the baseline for both of these other two. Under the maximin formulation, perhaps we ought to be asking what state of affairs that we can get to from the status quo does the best for the worst off, once we take into account the cost of moving from the status quo to the new position. Under the expected-utility formulation, we ought perhaps to ask what is the best state of affairs that can be attained from a starting point of the status quo, taking into account the costs of transition. (There are other possible ways of defining a baseline, as well.)

46. Snidal, "Limits," 579, 579 (emphasis in original); see also p. 580, n. 1: "Thus hegemonic stability theory provides a strong normative justification for maintaining that American decline is unfortunate from the perspective of *all* members of the international system."

47. Isabelle Grunberg, "Exploring the 'Myth' of Hegemonic Stability," 44 *Int. Org.* 431, 440 (1990).

48. Snidal, "Limits," 582.

49. Ibid., 581. The phrase "casual empiricism" to describe the support for hegemonic stability theory is taken from Joanne Gowa, "Rational Hegemons, Excludable Goods, and Small Groups: An Epitaph for Hegemonic Stability Theory?" 41 *World Politics* 307 (1989).

50. Robert Jackson and Carl Rosberg, "Why Africa's Weak States Persist: The Empirical and the Juridical in Statehood," 35 *World Politics* 1 (1982); see also Robert H. Jackson, *Quasi-States: Sovereignty, International Relations, and the Third World* (Cambridge: Cambridge University Press, 1990), ix ("The genesis of this book was the realization in earlier work that many Third World states are to an exceptions degree creatures and beneficiaries of international morality and international law").

51. For a discussion of these declinist positions and their connections to the burdens of hegemony, see Bruce Russett, "The Mysterious Case of Vanishing Hegemony; or, Is Mark Twain Really Dead?" 30 *Int. Org.* 223 (1985).

52. Most of the literature on hegemonic stability theory is more concerned with its descriptive accuracy than with its normative implications. Two excellent exceptions are Grunberg, "Exploring" and Snidal, "Limits"; while many of the points made below have already been made by those two authors, they do not frame the normative issues explicitly in hypothetical contract terms. See also Keohane, *After Hegemony*, 252, which analyzes regimes in normative terms, including some references to Rawlsian hypothetical contract theory.

53. Snidal, "Limits," 593–94.

54. Ibid., 612.

55. Ted L. Stein, "The Approach of the Different Drummer: The Principle of the Persistent Objector in International Law," 26 *Harv. Int. L. J.* 367 (1985); John Conybeare, "Public Goods, Prisoners' Dilemmas, and the International Political Economy," 28 *Int. Studies Q.* 5 (1984). For a partial response to some of these objections, see Gowa, "Rational Hegemons," 307.

56. Russett, "Mysterious Case," 216.

57. Grunberg, "Exploring," 440. See also Snidal, "Limits," 612: "It is not surprising, therefore, that adherents of the theory have expressed concern about the decline in American hegemony and the decrease in global order. But some of that disorder reflects dissenting views as to the virtues of American leadership and of the order associated with Pax Americana. In particular, some Third and Fourth World states have viewed American leadership more as a private club than as a public good."

58. The two strategies are not, of course, completely identical, because a liberal would recognize a valid difference between expressed preferences—the fact that a state claims that it does not like some institutional arrangement—and real preferences—what it secretly believes about the institutional arrangement. The liberal, therefore, can dismiss expressed preferences as merely strategic without totally violating the autonomy of the actor, because he or she need not claim better knowledge than the actor itself about what its true preferences are.

Despite this difference between the strategic-preferences and false-consciousness argument, however, there is an important similarity. Both allow the theorist to wish away all disconfirming evidence. To avoid this difficulty, the liberal needs some objective method for ascertaining whether a preference is "merely strategic," because otherwise the category is so elastic that it cannot be empirically disconfirmed.

59. Gilpin, *War and Change*, 145.

60. Snidal, "Limits," 588.

61. For a thorough and critical dissection of exactly this "fairness" argument, see Robert Nozick, *Anarchy, State, and Utopia* (New York: Basic Books, 1974), 90–96. Nozick attributes this notion of fairness to Hart and offers his well-known example about whether one can be compelled to contribute to public radio broadcasts (a classic "public good"). Nozick, of course, does not consider it unfair to refuse to contribute.

62. Compare Russett, "Mysterious Case," 207, 223: "The assessment of inequality in burden sharing . . . should alert us to the normative implications of the prior assumption that the principal goods provided are truly collective. If the goods largely benefit the hegemon, it is hardly fair to berate smaller states for an unwillingness to pay an equal share of the costs."

63. Snidal, "Limits," 583.

64. Stephen Krasner, "State Power and the Structure of International Trade," 28 *World Politics* 317 (1976).

65. Grunberg, "Exploring," 437; Susan Strange, "The Persistent Myth of Lost Hegemony," 41 *Int. Org.* 559 (1987).

66. Strange, "Persistent Myth," 443.

67. Keohane, *After Hegemony*, 45, n. 8. See also his evaluation of cooperation and regimes at p. 252; he concludes that they are not, per se, either good or bad; it all depends on what uses they are put to. As Bruce Russet observes, "The balance sheet of costs and benefits to all parties, coupled with a rigorous application of the criteria for collective good, casts a good deal of doubt on the proposition that the United States provided disproportionate benefits to others. . . . The burdens were not grossly unfair to the United States relative either to the gains to the United States or to the burdens borne by many other noncommunist countries." "Mysterious Case," 227. For an analysis of the contributions some of our allies have made, see Mark Boyer, *International Cooperation and Public Goods: Opportunities for the Western Alliance* (Baltimore and London: Johns Hopkins University Press, 1993).

68. Snidal, "Limits," 614.

69. As chap. 2 illustrated, we should be wary of relying on generalizations about how domestic governance systems differ from international ones. Some domestic systems may fail to protect the weak from imposition; some international systems, conversely, may provide that protection. The contrast relied on here is between an international system in which the hegemon is unconstrained and a domestic system with adequate safeguards against coercion. This is the model that collective action theorists must implicitly have in mind when they assert the ability of the weak to exploit the strong.

70. Kindleberger, "Systems of International Economic Organization," in David Calleo, ed., *Money and the Coming World Order* (New York: New York University Press, 1976), 34.

71. Rawls, "Law of Peoples." 62–65. A well-ordered society is either a liberal society or, if it is "hierarchical" rather than liberal, it must satisfy three conditions: (1) It must "be peaceful and gain its legitimate aims through diplomacy and trade, and other ways of peace. It follows that its religious doctrine, assumed to be comprehensive and influential in government policy, is not expansionist in the sense that it fully respects the civic order and integrity of other societies." (2) "A hierarchical society's system of law [must] be such as to impose moral duties and obligations on all persons within its territory. . . . It is not the case that the interests of some are arbitrarily privileged, while the interests of others go for naught." (3) "Its conception of the common good of justice [must] secure for all persons at least certain minimum rights to means of subsistence and security (the right to life), to liberty (freedom from slavery, serfdom and forced occupations) and (personal) property, as well as to formal equality as expressed by the rules of natural justice (for example, that similar cases be treated similarly). This shows that a well-ordered hierarchical society also meets a third requirement: it respects basic human rights."

72. Michael J. Sandel, *Liberalism and the Limits of Justice* (Cambridge: Cambridge University Press, 1982), esp. 49–50.

73. There are, of course, arguments that even "reasonable Christians" would not set up a Christian state, because (for example) Christians would recognize the importance of liberal values such as the separation of church and state. If so, then one would only need to change the example to another example, so that the religion itself would not lead to this result.

74. Dworkin gives the following example: "Suppose that you and I are playing poker and we find, in the middle of a hand, that the deck is one card short. You suggest that we throw the hand in, but I refuse because I know I am going to win and I want the money in the pot. You might say that I would certainly have agreed to that procedure had the possibility of the deck being short been raised in advance. But your point is not that I am somehow committed to throwing the hand in by an agreement I never made. Rather you use the device of a hypothetical agreement to make a point that might have been made without that device, which is that the solution recommended is so obviously fair and sensible that only someone with an immediate contrary interest could disagree. Your main argument is that your solution is fair and sensible, and the fact that I would have chosen it myself

adds nothing of substance to that argument. If I am able to meet the main argument nothing remains, rising out of your claim that I would have agreed, to be answered or excused." *Taking Rights Seriously*, 151.

CHAPTER 7

1. See Michael R. Gordon, "12 in State Department Ask Military Move Against the Serbs," *New York Times*, April 23, 1993: 1.

2. See Diana Jean Schemo, "Debt to Holocaust Dead Is Warning to the Future," ibid.: 24; see also, Zbigniew Brzezinski, " 'Never Again'—Except for Bosnia," ibid., April 22, 1993: 25.

3. For a chillingly documented description both of what the Allies knew about the Holocaust while it was going on and of the measures that were unsuccessfully urged upon them, see Martin Gilbert, *Auschwitz and the Allies* (New York: Holt, Rinehart and Winston, 1981).

4. This chapter is concerned primarily with coercive methods, as opposed to the promise of benefits. The reason is that where the stronger state induces others not to violate human rights through the promise of benefits, the intervention can be justified under a theory of contemporaneous consent, so that reliance on substantive morality is not necessary. It should be acknowledged, however, that the promise of benefits is one of the primary means used by stronger states to induce respect for human rights.

5. The question is sometimes phrased in terms of the permissibility of intervention in the internal affairs of other states. The reason for choosing this more limited formulation is that the chief objection to intervention is sometimes seen to be state sovereignty, which permits states to regulate their own internal affairs without intervention. I have chosen, however, to include intervention in the state's external affairs as part of the definition of the problem, so that (for instance) substantive morality might form the basis for stepping in to prevent genocide in a war between two nations. The reason is that there is also a need for a justification of hegemony in such circumstances. The violation of state sovereignty is not the only basis for complaint; it is also a grounds for complaint that the hegemon is acting "imperialistically." The hegemon can be accused of overstepping its legitimate authority by telling states what to do, even in their foreign relations.

6. Portions of the Nuremberg prosecutions were securely grounded in international law that Germany had consented to. Count 3 charged war crimes and was based on existing laws and customs of war; it therefore posed no problems. Count 4, however, charged crimes against humanity, which were not cognizable as war crimes; and count 2 charged crimes against peace. Since waging aggressive war was not at that point considered a violation of international law, there were objections that this charge was unjustly ex post facto. George Finch, "The Nuremberg Trial and International Law," 41 *Am. J. Int. L.* 20, 28, 34 (1947). Count 1 alleged a common plan, or conspiracy.

7. For a discussion of a proposed war crimes tribunal, see Theodor Meron, "The Case for War Crimes Trials in Yugoslavia," 72 *Foreign Affairs* 122 (Summer 1993).

8. See chap. 4 above. To the extent that some states might be going along with the embargo only under pressure from the U.N., this pressure could be justified not by contemporaneous but by ex ante consent, for these nations all agreed to the U.N. procedures that resulted in the embargo.

9. John Rawls, "The Law of Peoples," in Stephen Shute and Susan Hurley, eds., *On Human Rights: The Oxford Amnesty Lectures, 1993* (New York: Basic Books, 1993).

10. The same is true if one asks about the legitimacy of forcibly stopping human rights abuses by any of the other parties; the consent of the Bosnian Muslims and the Croatians should not be required before action is taken against them.

11. Thomas Franck speaks of the "emerging" right to democracy but stops short of claiming

that this right has already been adopted definitively into international law. "The Emerging Right to Democratic Governance," 86 *Am. J. Int. L.* 46 (1992).

12. Article 2(7) of the U.N. Charter, for example, states that "[n]othing contained in the present Charter shall authorize the United Nations to intervene in matters which are essentially within the domestic jurisdiction of any state or shall require the Members to submit such matters to settlement under the present Charter; but this principle shall not prejudice the application of enforcement measures under Chapter VII [dealing with Security Council actions in response to threats to international peace and security]." Of course, it is possible to respond to this protective position on state sovereignty that human rights violations are *ultra vires* and not within the states' "domestic jurisdiction."

13. See, for instance, art. 53 of the Vienna Convention on the Law of Treaties (May 23, 1969): "A treaty is void if, at the time of its conclusion, it conflicts with a peremptory norm of general international law. For the purposes of this convention, a peremptory norm of general international law is a norm accepted and recognized by the international community of states as a whole as a norm from which no derogation is permitted and which can be modified only by a subsequent norm of general international law having the same character." Repr. in 63 *Am. J. Int. L.* 875 (1969).

See also "Restatement (Third) of the Foreign Relations Law of the United States," sec. 102, comment k (1987): "Peremptory norms of international law (jus cogens): Some rules of international law are recognized by the international community of states as peremptory, permitting no derogation. These rules prevail over and invalidate international agreements and other rules of international law in conflict with them. Such a peremptory norm is subject to modification only by a subsequent norm of international law having the same character."

The wording of the Vienna Convention seems to suggest that states must accept a norm as jus cogens for it to have that effect. Yet it has been remarked that jus cogens functions as something of a natural law concept. See, e.g., Mark Janis, *An Introduction to International Law* (Boston: Little, Brown, 1988), 30–31, 53; Karen Parker and Lyn Beth Neylon, "Jus Cogens: Compelling the Law of Human Rights," 12 *Hastings International and Comparative Law Review* 411, 414 (1989).

14. This "relative normativity" is recognized and criticized in Prosper Weil, "Towards Relative Normativity in International Law?" 77 *Am. J. Int. L.* 413 (1983).

15. U.N. Conference on the Law of Treaties, 1st and 2d sess., Vienna, March 26–May 24, 1968, statement of Mr. Suarez at 294; cited in Parker and Neylon, "Jus Cogens," 415.

16. It might be easier to argue that they are a product of natural law if they bind all states equally rather than privileging states that already have nuclear weapons.

17. There is a hybrid possibility, as well; the standard of conduct might be justified by state consent, with the right to enforce the standard grounded in substantive morality. Cf. the discussion of ex ante consent in chap. 5 above.

18. On the continuing debate between Western nations and the countries of Asia, Africa, and Latin America, see Paul Lewis, "Splits May Dampen Rights Conference: Some Standards Don't Apply to Third World, It Says," *New York Times*, June 6, 1993: A1. For a general discussion of human rights and cultural relativism, see Jack Donnelly, *Universal Human Rights in Theory and Practice* (Ithaca, N.Y.: Cornell University Press, 1989), chaps. 6–8.

19. Compare Oscar Schachter, "International Law Implications of U.S. Human Rights Policies," 24 *N.Y.L. Sch. L. Rev.* 63, 73 (1978). "Some of the states which object to a general right to censure have themselves engaged in criticism of other states relating to the specific conduct of those states toward their own people. The criticism of Chile, Israel, South Africa and the Soviet Union, for example, has been extensive despite the fact that none of these states has adhered to treaty provisions concerning complaints. Governments, within and outside of the United Nations, have felt free to call attention to the alleged violations of human rights by the governments of these countries."

20. Walzer, "The Moral Standing of States: A Response to Four Critics," 9 *Philosophy and Public Affairs* 209, 225 (1980).

21. There are obvious differences between the examples, of course; in Walzer's hypothetical, most obviously, military force is not employed. But this difference is not as important as it might seem, given that the military occupation was not undertaken with the goal of imposing democracy; it was a consequence of having won the Second World War. The American military was already there and because of this unusual circumstance was able to restructure Japanese society without the usual bloodshed accompanying an invasion. Neither the Walzer hypothetical nor the Japanese example raises the difficult question of whether promoting democracy justifies military invasion; this is the sense in which the cases are similar. At any rate, even if this difference is important, it seems to argue the opposite way. If the Japanese occupation and restructuring was legitimate, a fortiori so would be a cultural restructuring that did not require military intervention. For a discussion of this and the somewhat similar examples of Germany and Austria, see Joshua Muravchik, *Exporting Democracy: Fulfilling America's Destiny* (Washington, D.C.: American Enterprise Institute, 1991), chap. 8 ("Imposing Democracy through Military Occupation").

22. Cf. Anthony D'Amato, "The Primacy of Individual Freedom," in Anthony D'Amato, ed., *International Law Anthology* (Anderson, 1994). D'Amato asks, with characteristic candor, whether there are not some cultures that do not deserve to be preserved.

23. Walzer sets out what he calls "rules of disregard" to define those situations in which it is appropriate to intervene; these include both cases of massacre and enslavement and cases where the state itself is composed of more than one national group. He summarizes these in "The Moral Standing of States," 216; they were originally developed in *Just and Unjust Wars: A Moral Argument with Historical Illustrations* (New York: Basic Books, 1977), 89–108.

24. Walzer does indeed seem to find outsider status crucial. See, e.g., "Moral Standing," 212: "Foreigners are in no position to deny the reality of that union [between the state and its people], or rather, they are in no position to attempt anything more than speculative denials." Or 214: "[Citizens] are as free not to fight [to protect their state from invasion] as they are free to rebel. But that freedom does not easily transfer to foreign states or armies and become a right of invasion or intervention: above all, it does not transfer at the initiative of foreigners."

25. Charles Beitz offers an interesting example in response to Walzer's. He asks us to imagine that the mayor of New York has a magic potion that will destroy the desire to spray-paint graffiti on subways. "Nonintervention and Communal Integrity," 9 *Philosophy and Public Affairs* 385, 389 (1980). His claim is that the potion should not be administered, but that the real reason is that it would violate the *individual* integrity of those whose lives were changed by it. Thus, he agrees with Walzer's conclusion about the Algerian hypothetical but would explain it on other, individualistic grounds. Walzer is concerned about a change to a culture imposed from without; Beitz responds that the real problem is a change to an individual, even if it stems from a domestic source. My concern is with a change to a culture, whether from a domestic or a foreign source.

26. In keeping with the claim that outsider status is a red herring, international law recognizes a class of cases in which all states (and not just individual victim-states) can respond to violations of international law. Just as the international legal concept of *jus cogens* reflects an awareness that natural law may be an appropriate guide to standards of conduct, the notion of rights *erga omnes* recognizes that some especially serious violations are violations against the international community at large. See Barcelona Traction, Light and Power Company, Limited, Judgment, I.C.J. *Reports* 1970, 3; see Oscar Schachter, "International Law Implications of U.S. Human Rights Policies," 24 N.Y.L. *Sch. L. Rev.* 63, 71 (1978) ("obligations derived 'from principles and rules concerning the basic rights of the human person' are obligations owed by all states to the international community as a whole;

[and] . . . all states have a legal interest in the protection of the rights involved since they represent obligations erga omnes").

27. Walzer, "Moral Standing," 212.

28. Walzer also relies on an argument that he attributes to John Stuart Mill, to the effect that it is better that rebellions be won from within than with the assistance of outsiders. He even goes so far as to claim that if there really is strong social support for a rebellion, then it will ultimately be successful even without outside intervention. "Moral Standing," 220. This claim seems less than convincing as an empirical matter, as Richard Wasserstrom has pointed out. Book review, 92 *Harv. L. Rev.* 536, 542 (1978). In particular, the examples of Saddam Hussein's Iraq or of post-coup Haiti apparently refute the generalization.

In addition, the generalization is hard to square with Walzer's argument (p. 217) that counterintervention is permissible when another country has intervened already. Presumably the reason that intervention is permissible then is that it is no longer the case that the side with the most social support should be expected to win. But it cannot be assumed that a government with support from the outside will have more resources at its disposal than a government with no such support but with great wealth (oil wealth, for example). If the socially deserving side always wins, even against a wealthy government, it seems that it should also be able to win even against a foreign power.

29. Or, to put it another way, they support at most a rebuttable presumption against intervention; and Walzer would have to recognize another "rule of disregard" for rebutting the presumption, namely, accurate information about the cultural conditions within the country. A similar point is made by David Luban, "The Romance of the Nation-State," 9 *Philosophy and Public Affairs* 392, 395 (1980).

30. Many would put the U.S. invasions of Panama or Grenada into this category. We will return later in this chapter to the problem of selective enforcement.

31. I have developed this argument in *Justifying International Acts* (Ithaca, N.Y.: Cornell University Press, 1989), chap. 7.

32. Beitz, "Nonintervention and Communal Integrity," 9 *Philosophy and Public Affairs* 389 (1980).

33. Walzer gives the example of the Sandinistas, who chose to face defeat in the fall of 1978 rather than ask for outside assistance. "Moral Standing," 220.

34. There may at first seem to be an inconsistency between the argument that it is irrational to differentiate between resistance from insiders and intervention from outsiders and the claim that the victim's desire to make exactly this distinction should be respected. There is no inconsistency, however. The victim need not have a rational reason for waiving his or her rights; it is enough that he or she chooses to relinquish them. In this respect, liberalism would treat preferences about whether to relinquish rights with the same "hands-off" attitude as any other preferences that people have.

35. In addition to the sources already cited, see Alan H. Goldman, "Foreign Intervention," in Steve Luper-Foy, ed., *Problems of International Justice* (Boulder, Colo.: Westview, 1988); Jefferson McMahan, "The Ethics of International Intervention," in Kenneth Kipnis and Diana Meyers, eds., *Political Realism and International Morality* (Boulder, Colo.: Westview, 1987).

36. In 1979 Tanzanian troops invaded Uganda and overthrew the regime of President Idi Amin, one of the world's most formidable violators of human rights. The invasion was in part in response to an earlier Ugandan incursion into Tanzania. For a critical account of the Tanzanian action, see Farooq Hassan, "Realpolitik in International Law: After Tanzanian-Ugandan Conflict 'Humanitarian Intervention' Reexamined," 17 *Willamette L. Rev.* 859 (1981). A force composed of soldiers from West African nations (mainly Nigerians) entered Liberia in 1990 in response to the Liberian civil war; it is still in place. See Timothy Weaver, "Liberia: Deadly Dreams of Power," 1 *Crosslines* 7 (September 1993).

37. Walzer, "Moral Standing," 224.

38. It should be recognized, however, that the ability to make a binding commitment can in practice increase a state's control over its own destiny, by enabling it to engage in contractual behavior and in this way to influence other states. The method for doing so, though, is by accepting a limitation on its own action.

39. U.N. Charter, art. 2(7). On the ambiguities inherent in the phrase, and some of the hard cases the Security Council has faced, see Thomas Franck and Faiza Patel, "U.N. Police Action in Lieu of War: 'The Old Order Changeth,' " 87 *Am. J. Int. L.* 63 (1991).

40. Williams, *Moral Luck* (Cambridge: Cambridge University Press, 1981), chap. 2.

41. Of course, we do not yet know about the results in the true long run; only fifty years have passed since the restructuring occurred. As well as we can tell so far, however, the experiment seems to have succeeded.

42. We have intervened, militarily or otherwise, in numerous cases where the ostensible goal was to secure democracy: Vietnam, Grenada, Panama, the Philippines, and Angola, to name just a few. On the general success of American efforts to promote democracy through reformist intervention, see Douglas Macdonald, *Adventures in Chaos: American Intervention for Reform in the Third World* (Cambridge: Harvard University Press, 1992).

43. B. Drummond Ayres, Jr., "In American Voices: A Sense of Concern Over Bosnia Role," *New York Times*, May 2, 1993: 1.

44. See, e.g., Peter Singer, "Famine, Affluence, and Morality," in Charles Beitz et al., eds., *International Morality* (Princeton, N.J.: Princeton University Press, 1983).

45. There are at least two different ways that involvement might be selective. The first is that a norm might be enforced in some cases but not in others. The second is that some norms might be enforced but not the rest. The arguments against selective intervention deal with both situations; the problem is with a state using selectively the claim that it is justified in acting to enforce norms.

46. This reasoning suggests that selectivity with regard to the distribution of benefits is a different case from selectivity in the enforcement of norms. Because no coercion is involved, no further justification need be given for the distribution of benefits; the mere fact that the distribution is noncoercive is enough. (Note, however, that the same cannot be said regarding distribution of benefits domestically; government resources are the result of taxes, which are coercive. Thus they cannot be distributed in a discriminatory fashion.)

47. Just prior to the May 1993 referendum in Russia, the U.S. held off pressuring Yeltsin to support stronger actions against the Serbs, hoping to increase his chances to win the popular vote. See "Two Cheers for Demokratiya," *U.S. News and World Report*, April 5, 1993: 42.

48. Analogously, when the basis for intervention is norms of positive international law, these would be the priorities embedded in positive norms.

49. On President Jean-Bertrand Aristide's request for assistance, see "Ousted Haiti Leader Urges OAS Intervention," *Chicago Tribune*, Oct. 3, 1991: 6. The U.S. cooperated with a number of economic measures directed against the military regime. As of this writing, the Clinton administration is reported to be considering further economic measures. "U.S. Reported to Plan Move Against Haiti Rulers' Assets," *New York Times*, May 27, 1993: 11 (threats to freeze assets and revoke visas of the officials and supporters of Haiti's military-backed government). The measures have been criticized as insufficient. Howard French, "Clinton Faulted on Haiti Sanctions: Critics Complain That Steps on Assets and Travel Are Weak and Not New," ibid., June 6, 1993: A7.

CHAPTER 8

1. Address Before a Joint Session of the Congress on the Cessation of the Persian Gulf Conflict, March 6, 1991. *Weekly Compilation of Presidential Documents* 27 (January–March 1991): 259.

2. As Secretary of State James Baker put it during the attempted coup in Moscow, "Legitimacy in 1991 flows not from the barrel of a gun but from the will of the people." Adam Clymer, "After the Coup: Bush Looks Ahead to Accelerated Soviet Reforms and Greater Stature for Yeltsin," *New York Times*, Aug. 22, 1991: A15.

3. Address Before a Joint Session of the Congress on the State of the Union, Jan. 29, 1991. *Weekly Compilation of Presidential Documents* 27 (January–March 1991): 91, 95.

4. Address Before a Joint Session of the Congress on the Persian Gulf Conflict and the Federal Budget Deficit, Sept. 11, 1990. Ibid. 26 (July–September 1990): 1359–1360.

5. Ibid.

6. Challenged to defend the buildup of forces in the Gulf, Baker said, "And to bring it down to the average American citizen, let me say that means jobs. If you want to sum it up in one word, it's jobs. Because an economic recession worldwide, caused by the control of one nation, one dictator if you will, of the West's economic lifeline will result in the loss of jobs on the part of American citizens." David Hoffman, "Baker Calls Iraq Threat to 'Economic Lifeline,' " *Washington Post*, Nov. 14, 1990: A25.

7. State Department briefing with Margaret Tutwiler, May 12, 1992. See also Steven Holmes, "Backing Away Again, Christopher Says Bosnia Is Not a Vital Interest," *New York Times*, June 4, 1993: A12.

8. Address of Sept. 11, 1991. Bush continued, "America and the world must support the rule of law."

9. As Robert Tucker and David Hendrickson put it, "The refusal in principle to discriminate among aggressions on grounds of power, interest, and circumstance of course reflects the domestic analogy on which the idea of collective security rests. An international society is assumed, a society that bears a meaningful resemblance to domestic society. The state-members of this greater society have rights and duties much as the individuals that form domestic society have rights and duties. . . . In either, the attempt to distinguish acts of aggression on the basis of the circumstances attending each act must prove ruinous to the peace of the community, for such attempts must risk giving to the strong what is denied to the weak. . . . The great difficulty with this conception of international order is that it rests on a misunderstanding of the nature of the peace that exists within domestic society. Domestic peace is not . . . maintained by the impartial application of objective criteria to individuals but by reconciling the aims and aspirations of groups, a process that cannot be undertaken on the basis of the impartial application of objective criteria. . . . The rigid legalism that informs the idea of collective security is at odds with the outlook that characterizes the political process." *The Imperial Temptation: The New World Order and America's Purpose* (New York: Council on Foreign Relations, 1992), 50–51.

CHAPTER 9

1. In the discussion that follows, we will refer to this theory (or collection of theories) as "the liberal theory of international hegemony" for convenience sake. It is clear, though, that there might be liberal theories of international hegemony different from the one set out in chapters 4–7; by referring to the development in the last section of this book as "the" liberal theory, I do not mean to exclude that possibility.

2. Michael Sandel, *Liberalism and the Limits of Justice* (New York: Cambridge University Press, 1982).

3. This characteristic is not unique to the theory developed in the preceding chapters; the same could be said of realism.

4. There are, of course, other ways to envision international politics; it is possible, for example, to take a purely cosmopolitan approach. The approach that we have been developing in earlier chapters, however, treats states as key actors (although not as the only actors).

5. An interesting philosophical account of sovereignty (which is somewhat related to statism) is contained in Charles Beitz, *Sovereignty and Morality in International Relations*, in David Held, ed., *Political Theory Today* (Stanford, Calif.: Stanford University Press, 1991). Authors dealing more directly with the conflict between individual rights and the rights of states are discussed below.

A related problem that has received a fair amount of philosophical attention is the extent to which moral obligations between individuals should depend on whether the individuals hail from the same national community. See, e.g., Richard Dagger, "Rights, Boundaries, and the Bonds of Community: A Qualified Defense of Moral Parochialism," 79 *American Political Science Review* 436 (1985); David Miller, "The Ethical Significance of Nationality," Henry Shue, "Mediating Duties," and Robert E. Goodin, "What Is So Special About Our Fellow Countrymen?" in "Symposium on Duties Beyond Borders," 98 *Ethics* 647 (1988).

6. It must be acknowledged, of course, that a state need not be a community. Some states are so heterogeneous that they are, at most, a collection of separate communities. This point does not undercut the general argument here, however, for statism is on even shakier grounds if it cannot be justified in communitarian terms. For a criticism of liberalism on the grounds that it is incompatible with the rights of groups and cannot adequately explain the concept of the state, see Vernon Van Dyke, "The Individual, the State, and Ethnic Communities in Political Theory," 29 *World Politics* 343 (1977).

7. For a similar use of the term *opacity*, see Anne-Marie Slaughter Burley, "International Law and International Relations Theory: A Dual Agenda," 87 *Am. J. Int. L.* 205, 226 (1993).

8. For a historical and critical account of this analogy, see Edwin DeWitt Dickinson, "The Analogy Between Natural Persons and International Persons in the Law of Nations," 26 *Yale L. J.* 564 (1917).

9. Michael Walzer is another example of a philosopher who combines liberal domestic inclinations with an essentially statist view of international relations. See his "The Rights of Political Communities," in Charles Beitz et al., eds., *International Ethics* (Princeton, N.J.: Princeton University Press, 1985), a collection of excerpts and a synthesis of positions taken in his *Just and Unjust Wars* (New York: Basic Books, 1977). Walzer responds to critics of his position in "The Moral Standing of States: A Response to Four Critics," 9 *Philosophy and Public Affairs* 209 (1980).

10. Rawls's brief discussion of international justice in *A Theory of Justice* (Cambridge: Harvard University Press, 1971) is found at pp. 377–379, in a section on conscientious objection. More recently he has returned to the issue in "The Law of Peoples," in Stephen Shute and Susan Hurley, eds., *On Human Rights: The Oxford Amnesty Lectures, 1993* (New York: Basic Books, 1993). This does not, however, alter the basic outlines of the discussion below.

11. On p. 457 of *A Theory of Justice*, for example, he writes that "the boundaries of these [cooperative] schemes are given by the notion of a self-contained national community." This assumption is discussed helpfully and at length in Charles Beitz, *Political Theory and International Relations* (Princeton, N.J.: Princeton University Press, 1979), 129–136.

12. For example, where he argues that we do not own our attributes or the benefits that follow from them but must share them with other members of the community according to the difference principle. No similar claim is made about international sharing. Here, again, Charles Beitz's argument is helpful; see *Political Theory*, 136–143.

13. Ibid., 143–153.

14. Thomas Pogge, "Rawls and Global Justice," 18 *Canadian Journal of Philosophy* 227 (1988) and *Realizing Rawls* (Ithaca, N.Y.: Cornell University Press, 1989), chaps. 5 and 6. See also Peter Danielson, "Theories, Intuitions and the Problem of World-Wide Distributive Justice," 3 *Phil. Soc. Sci.* 331 (1973).

15. Beitz's argument is set out in *Political Theory*, 71–83. On p. 81 he writes: "Assuming that it is

part of the justice of institutions that they treat their members in some sense as autonomous persons, then the claim that unjust states should not be accorded the respect demanded by the principle of state autonomy follows from the claim that it is only considerations of personal autonomy, appropriately interpreted, that constitute the moral personality of the state. This is not so implausible, after all, if one keeps in mind that states, unlike persons, lack the unity of consciousness and the rational will that constitute the identity of persons. If states are not simply voluntary associations, neither are they organic wholes with the unity and integrity that attaches to persons qua persons." It should be emphasized that Beitz is considering only the question of the legitimacy of one state's intervening in another's affairs to put an end to unjust practices and human rights abuses. He does not address the question that is of primary concern here: whether an unrepresentative state is entitled to bind its citizens by undertaking international treaty commitments.

16. To say that a nondemocratic regime may effectively bind the state's people is not to say anything about the right of state citizens to fight to change their government. As Michael Walzer puts it, "The international standing of governments derives only directly from their standing with their own citizens." "Moral Standing," 220.

17. Van Dyke, "Individual," 345.

18. Albert O. Hirschman, *Exit, Voice, and Loyalty: Responses to Decline in Firms, Organizations, and States* (Cambridge: Harvard University Press, 1970).

19. Beitz, *Political Theory*, 121. See also David Luban, "Just War and Human Rights," 9 *Philosophy and Public Affairs* 160 (1980); Richard Wasserstrom, review of *Just and Unjust Wars* by Beitz, 92 *Harv. L. Rev.* 536 (1978); Gerald Doppelt, "Walzer's Theory of Morality in International Relations," 8 *Philosophy and Public Affairs* 3 (1978).

20. Compare the well-known claim that liberal states don't wage war against one another. See Michael Doyle, "Kant, Liberal Legacies, and Foreign Affairs," pts. 1 and 2, 12 *Philosophy and Public Affairs* 205, 323 (1983).

21. The fact that the argument merely restates the importance of state autonomy is shown by its parallels with autonomy claims made on behalf of individuals. One way to phrase respect for individuals is that regardless of whether the decisions that they make are foolish or wise, and regardless of whether their processes of deliberation are rational or not, once they have reached their decisions, these must be respected. In the case of individuals, this argument is based upon strong intuitions that human beings are morally worthy of such protection because they are capable of reflection and free choice; such claims are far less plausible in the case of states. We will return to this point below.

22. Walzer, "Moral Standing," 213. Other objections to this argument are discussed in chap. 6 above.

23. Walzer is interested in outside military intervention at the point that he makes this argument; he is not concerned with the enforceability of treaty commitments made by dictators.

24. If this argument were accepted, one might also want to accept the argument that it is in the interests of the people of the state that the dictator have dictatorial internal powers, for a strong government is better able to deal with problems of crime, subversion, the economy, etc. Yet liberal democrats do not generally consider such advantages to justify dictatorship.

25. If the cost in innocent lives and civilian property was justified, it is because the war was the only way to reverse Iraq's territorial aggression and to come to the aid of innocent Kuwaitis. This argument has little if anything to do with the consent or approval of the Iraqi people.

26. This, fortunately, is not as true as it once was, although access to some institutions (such as the World Court) is still limited to states. See generally Lea Brilmayer, "International Law in American Courts: A Modest Proposal," 100 *Yale L. J.* 2277, 2292–2293 (1991).

27. This is the basis of Peter Schuck's and Rogers Smith's attack on birthright citizenship in *Citizenship Without Consent: Illegal Aliens in the American Polity* (New Haven: Yale University Press, 1985). Their

own solution, it should be noted—giving the child the citizenship rights of the parent—is equally ascriptive and illiberal.

28. For a longer discussion of this point, see my *Justifying International Acts* (Ithaca, N.Y.: Cornell University Press, 1989), chap. 4. The focus there is on how this fact affects domestic political obligations; for the state to which one is obligated as a domestic matter is the same as the state that sets one's international obligations.

CHAPTER 10

1. Keohane, "International Institutions: Two Approaches," 32 *International Studies Quarterly* 379, 380 (1988). Although he is not a member of the critical school, the importance he attaches to it is underscored by the fact that this article was an edited version of his presidential address at the annual convention of the International Studies Association. A particularly clear and concise development of the position Keohane describes can be found in the writings of Alexander Wendt; see, e.g., his "Anarchy Is What States Make of It: The Social Construction of Power Politics," 46 *Int. Org.* 391 (1992). Wendt prefers the term *constructivist* to Keohane's *reflectivist*.

Keohane's generally sympathetic treatment of the reflectivist school has not been enthusiastically appreciated by some of the writers he describes. See, e.g., R. B. J. Walker, "History and Structure in the Theory of International Relations," 18 *Millennium* 163 (1989).

2. These "constructivists" or "reflectivists" are not the only international relations scholars, it should be noted, that pay attention to the role of community norms in the international arena. Neoliberal institutionalists (such as Keohane himself) are also interested in the role of norms. The chief difference, though, is the critical scholars' focus on the construction of state identity and interest, as opposed merely to the influence of norms on state behavior.

3. This is the term that Wendt and Nicholas Onuf, for example, prefer. Wendt, "Anarchy," 391, 397; Onuf, *World of Our Making* (Columbia: University of South Carolina Press, 1989).

4. The extent of interaction in the world community has of course altered over time. "A system in which interaction capacity is relatively low, as during the ancient period of human civilization, is quite different from one in which it is relatively high, as in the late twentieth century. Whether or not interaction capacity is sufficiently developed to allow remote units to trade and fight with each other on a large scale, as in modern Europe, or whether it is only sufficient to allow the carriage of a few ideas, technologies, and individuals between remote cultures, as between classical Rome and Han China, makes an enormous difference to both the nature of international relations and the impact of anarchic structure." Barry Buzan, "From International System to International Society: Structural Realism and Regime Theory Meet the English School," 47 *Int. Org.* 327, 331 (1993). Buzan is distinguishing between cases where states are sufficiently interactive to form a "society," in the sense that Hedley Bull intended, and cases where states merely form a "system," as American neorealism would have it.

5. The state has leaders, of course, but one cannot simply identify their will with the will of the state. Doing so would require a very powerful equation of the state with its leadership that few observers would be likely to subscribe to.

6. A good discussion of the different autonomy interests of states and people can be found in Charles Beitz, *Political Theory and International Relations* (Princeton, N.J.: Princeton University Press, 1979), part 2.

7. One does not want to claim that it is impossible to imagine such occurrences; but counterexamples would have to be unusual and improbable. There might be cases of split personality, for example, or of brainwashing. Note that we might take a rather different view of individual autonomy if we believed (for example) that people held the preferences they do because of "thought

control" beamed in from the White House. If that were the case, there would be a much weaker claim for respecting their individual choices.

8. "U.S. Is No Longer the Biodiversity Bad Guy. Sort of," *Newsday* (Suffolk County ed.), June 17, 1993: 56.

9. Although in Panama, at least, there was a claim that Endara was a rightfully elected leader who had been denied the presidency by a military dictator.

10. Peter Gourevitch, "The Second Image Reversed: The International Sources of Domestic Politics," 32 *Int. Org.* 881, 883 (1978).

11. For general treatments of the dependency perspective, see Fernando Henrique Cardoso and Enzo Faletto, *Dependency and Development in Latin America* (Berkeley: University of California Press, 1979); Andre Gunder Frank, *Capitalism and Underdevelopment in Latin America: Historical Studies of Chile and Brazil* (New York: Monthly Review Press, 1967). There is substantial debate over what precisely should count as a dependency approach; for a discussion of this debate and a more critical account, see Robert Packenham, *The Dependency Movement: Scholarship and Politics in Development Studies* (Cambridge: Harvard University Press, 1992).

12. G. John Ikenberry and Charles A. Kupchan, "Socialization and Hegemonic Power," 44 *Int. Org.* 283 (1990.) See also the claim that choice of how to structure one's military capabilities is influenced by perceptions of how a "modern" and therefore superior military is organized, in Alexander Wendt and Michael Barnett, "Dependent State Formation and Third World Militarization," 19 *Rev. Int. Studies* 321–347 (1993).

13. This is true regardless of whether one thinks that states are defined primarily by their territories or by their populations. Although I discuss below how the world community establishes and secures territorial borders, the community also is involved in determining which individuals belong in which states. For one thing, as territorial borders shift, population often shifts as well, for the state's population may be defined as all individuals living on its territories. In addition, international norms shape a state's population more directly, as where they require states to take in refugees or prohibit depriving individuals of citizenship, thereby leaving them stateless.

On the role of international norms in state identity formation, see the brief discussion in Anthony D'Amato, "Is International Law Really 'Law'?" 79 *Northwestern Law Review* 1293, 1306 (1985).

14. See generally Marc Weller, "Current Developments: The International Response to the Dissolution of the Socialist Federal Republic of Yugoslavia," 86 *American Journal of International Law* 569 (1992); Macedonia is discussed at pp. 593–594.

15. The four states were Transkei (granted "independent" status by South Africa in 1976), Bophuthatswana (1978), Venda (1979), and Ciskei (1981). The U.N. condemned the establishment of these Bantustans in several General Assembly resolutions. See generally J. D. van der Vyer, "Statehood in International Law," 5 *Emory International Law Review* 9, 39 (1991).

16. Robert Graham, "Dogged by Double Standards," *Financial Times*, Feb. 2, 1991: 8; van der Vyer, "Statehood," 44; Thomas Franck, "Of Gnats and Camels: Is There a Double Standard at the United Nations?" 78 *American Journal of International Law* 811, 816–817 (1984).

17. Strang, "Anomaly and Commonplace in European Political Expansion: Realist and Institutional Accounts," 45 *Int. Org.* 143, 149 (1991). See also Robert Jackson and Carl Rosberg, "Why Africa's Weak States Persist: The Empirical and the Juridical in Statehood," 35 *World Politics* 1 (1982).

18. For a general discussion of theories of recognition, see James Crawford, *The Creation of States in International Law* (Oxford: Oxford University Press, 1979), chap. 1.

19. L. F. L. Oppenheim, *International Law*, 8th ed. (New York: Longmans, Green, 1955), 125; cited in Strang, "Anomaly and Commonplace," 143, 150.

20. Strang, "Anomaly and Commonplace," 148.

21. Ibid., 2 ("Among writers the declaratory doctrine, with differences in emphasis, is now predominant"), 4.

22. Art. 1 of the Montevideo Convention of 1933 asserts: "The State as a person of international law should possess the following qualifications: (a) a permanent population; (b) a defined territory; (c) government; and (d) capacity to enter into relations with other States."

23. Hence the importance to PLO recognition that it be accompanied by power over a particular piece of territory; and the importance to its status within a particular piece of territory that it be recognized by other international actors.

24. On the struggle by indigenous groups to attain greater international recognition, see Catherine Iorns, "Indigenous Peoples and Self-Determination: Challenging State Sovereignty," 24 *Case Western Reserve Journal of International Law* 199 (1992).

25. A survey of theories about the relationship between the two is contained in Crawford, *Creation of States*, 154–160.

26. Marian Nash Leich, "Contemporary Practice of the United States Relating to International Law," 78 *American Journal of International Law* 427 (1984).

27. There is no way to cite even a representative sample of this literature, but two names that come immediately to mind are R. B. J. Walker (see, e.g., his "The Territorial State and the Theme of Gulliver," 39 *Int. Journal* 529 [1984] and a volume coedited with Saul Mendlovitz, *Contending Sovereignties: Redefining Political Communities* [Boulder, Colo.: Lynne Rienner, 1990]) and John Ruggie (see, e.g., his "Continuity and Transformation in the World Polity: Toward a Neorealist Synthesis," in Robert Keohane, ed., *Neorealism and Its Critics* [New York: Columbia University Press, 1986] and "Territoriality and Beyond: Problematizing Modernity in International Relations," 47 *Int. Org.* 139 [1993]).

28. Keohane, "International Institutions," 379, 391.

29. See, e.g., Wendt, "Collective Identity Formation and the International State," unpublished manuscript, August 1993.

30. Even then, of course, it must obtain the approval of the world community, as I acknowledged in the previous section.

31. The commitment to ending colonialism does not by itself, of course, necessarily require approval of the means that India used. It is arguable, for example, that India ought to have proceeded peacefully or that it should have held a referendum once Goa was liberated to allow the people of Goa to determine their own fate. My point is simply that the world community's reaction to the Indian annexation was supported by a norm that is, in general, widely shared and defensible.

32. On the importance of norms generally, see Friedrich V. Kratochwil, *Rules, Norms, and Decisions: On the Conditions of Practical and Legal Reasoning in International Relations and Domestic Affairs* (Cambridge: Cambridge University Press, 1989). See also John Ruggie, "International Regimes, Transactions, and Change: Embedded Liberalism in the Postwar Economic Order," 36 *Int. Org.* 379 (1982).

33. In the same way, liberals would probably not try to argue that the rule that norms must be founded on state consent must itself be founded on state consent. See above.

34. A liberal cannot simply respond that many sorts of entities that are purely social creations, like corporations, are bearers of autonomy. True, corporations (which are created by the state) possess much autonomy, such as the right to make contracts or prosecute lawsuits. However, the autonomy that they possess is bestowed upon them by the state when they are created, and only to the degree that the state wishes. The claim of autonomy at issue here is a stronger one; it is the right to resist the state's efforts to impinge on one's autonomy. The autonomy claims made on behalf of individuals are thought to predate the state, and to be morally prior to it.

35. While it is tempting simply to say that the Saudi Arabian woman's freedom resides not in her choice whether to wear the veil but in her second-order capacity for reflection (regardless of what

she chooses), this answer is not complete. The very fact that women in Saudi Arabia exercise their capacity for reflection to different effect than those in Sweden suggests that socialization is at work at this second-order level as well. Neither set chooses to adopt the practices of the other; perhaps the explanation is that socialization prevents all of us from exercising our faculties of independent choice. If our capacities for reflection and independent choice remained intact, we would not see the statistical patterns of choice that we do.

36. Linklater, "The Problem of Community in International Relations," 15 *Alternatives* 135, 143 (1990).

CONCLUSION

1. Compare in this regard David Lumsdaine's argument that foreign aid policies reflect a country's attitudes toward domestic social welfare problems. *Moral Vision in International Politics: The Foreign Aid Regime, 1949–1989* (Princeton, N.J.: Princeton University Press, 1993).

INDEX